958.1044 Girardet, Edward.
GIR
        Afghanistan

860220

DATE			

WITHDRAWN

AFGHANISTAN: The Soviet War

Afghanistan

THE SOVIET WAR

EDWARD GIRARDET

ST. MARTIN'S PRESS
New York

Library of Congress Cataloging in Publication Data

Girardet, Edward.
    Afghanistan: the soviet war.

    Includes index.
    1. Afghanistan—History—Soviet occupation,
1979–   I. Title.
DS371.2.G57   1985   958'.1044   85-17960

ISBN 0-312-00923-2

Printed in the U.S.A.

CONTENTS

To those for whom freedom is worth fighting

ACKNOWLEDGEMENTS

I am indebted to all my Afghan friends who have assisted me while reporting the war and during the research for this book. I am deeply indebted to those members of the resistance who have gone out of their way, often at the risk of their lives, to help me during my travels to the interior. In particular, Agha Gul, Mohammed Shuaib, and Mohammed Es-Haq.

Special thanks to the French volunteer doctors and nurses, notably Laurence Laumonier, Capucine de Bretagne and Frederique Hincelin of Aide Medicale Internationale, whose courage and dedicated efforts to provide humanitarian relief to this war-ravaged country have helped to alleviate some of the suffering and to furnish the outside world with detailed testimony on conditions under the Soviet occupation. My gratitude, too, to members of other international relief organisations active in the interior, including AFRANE, Amis de l'Afghanistan and Afghan Aid for their valuable observations on the situation. Also to Richard Smith of Dignity of Man Foundation who sadly died at the beginning of this year and who gave so much of himself to the Afghan people. My thanks to the United Nations High Commissioner for Refugees (UNHCR) and the International Committee of the Red Cross (ICRC) in Geneva for constant assistance since the start of the conflict.

Furthermore, I would like to express my gratitude to numerous friends, fellow journalists and observers for their views, suggestions and help. William Dowell, Peter Jouvenal, Mike Barry, John and Romy Fullerton, S. Enders Wimbush, Jean-Jose Puig, Louis and Nancy Dupree, Alain Guillo, Christophe de Ponfilly, Olivier Roy, Wayne Merry, Aernout van Linden, Pierre Issot-Sergent, Dominique Vergos, Julian Gearing and fellow hiker-cum-alpinist Douglas Archard, former US Consul in Peshawar. Also to Professor Sayed B. Madjruh, director of the Afghan Information Centre in Peshawar, whose comments, poetry and monthly news bulletin have been more than appreciated.

Without the backing and encouragement of David Anable, Foreign Editor of *The Christian Science Monitor* in Boston, much of my reporting simply would not have been possible. Carolyn Wells of the International Institute for Strategic Studies in London and Rachel Lubbock, formerly of ABC News, Paris, both provided a regular flow of research material, while French painter Jean-Pierre Blanche kindly lent me the quiet seclusion of his home outside Aix-en-Provence to write the initial draft.

E.G.
Paris

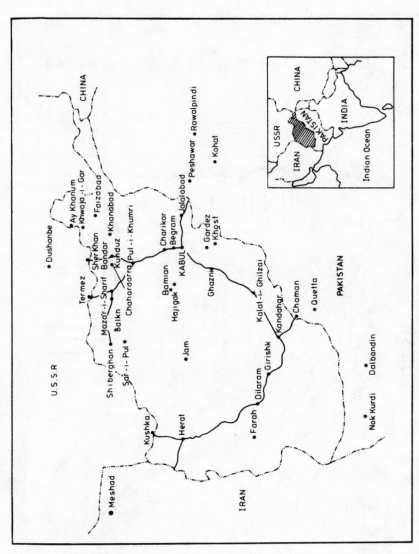

Reproduced by permission of André Deutsch Ltd.

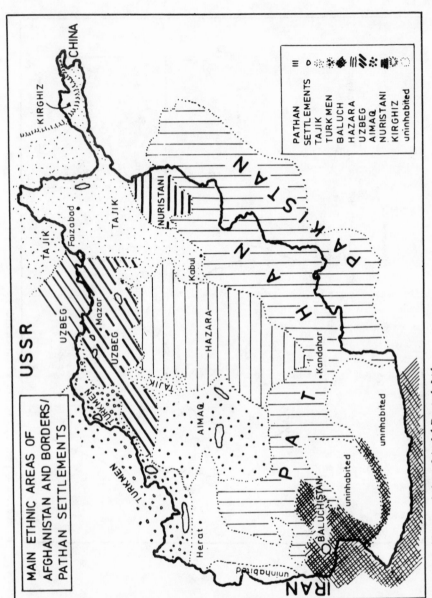

MAIN ETHNIC AREAS OF
AFGHANISTAN AND BORDERS/
PATHAN SETTLEMENTS

PATHAN
SETTLEMENTS
TAJIK
TURKMEN
BALUCH
HAZARA
UZBEG
AIMAQ
NURISTANI
KIRGHIZ
uninhabited

USSR

CHINA

KIRGHIZ

TAJIK

TAJIK

Faizabad

NURISTANI

UZBEG

Mazar

Kabul

TURKMEN

UZBEG

TAJIK

PAKISTAN

HAZARA

PATHAN

Herat

AIMAQ

Kandahar

uninhabited

BALUCHISTAN

uninhabited

IRAN

uninhabited

INTRODUCTION: Caravans to the Interior

'Que la victoire soit avec ceux qui ont fait la guerre sans l'aimer.'
(That victory be with those who have made war without loving it. —
André Malraux)

The desert moon has just risen from behind the mighty Hindu Kush.
Like a steady flow of quicksilver, the first ghostly shadows emerge from
the huddled village in the northern Pakistani region of Chitral. The
guerrillas, their spartan belongings — a cup, flour for bread, tea, sugar
and perhaps an extra shirt — trussed up in woollen 'patou' blankets tied
like rucksacks across their shoulders, trudge along the rutted highland
track towards the Afghan frontier. Behind them, hooves crunching into
the stony ground, come the horses, fifty of them, heavily laden with
weapons, crates of ammunition, medicines and food. Apart from the
dull thud of feet and the occasional low muffled cry or whistle to egg
on the animals, the men make little sound as they move through the
Asian night.

It is late summer in 1981, eighteen months after the Russian
invasion of Afghanistan. For the past week, throngs of mujahideen, or
holy warriors, have gathered at the mountain village, waiting for the
caravan to leave, one of dozens along this clandestine route during the
snow-free summer months. Crates of ammunition, rifles and the dis-
assembled parts of a Russian ZPU-2 anti-aircraft gun litter the ground,
while young men, woollen 'kola' caps perched on the backs of their
heads, crouch on their haunches sewing the supplies into coarse hemp
sacks. Over by the trampled sports pitch of a local school, the Afghan
drivers move along the pack animals, testing saddles or hammering on
new horse shoes. The Pakistani authorities remain discreetly at their
checkpoints further down the road.

The caravan finally ready to leave, the men have prayed down by the
river and then returned to their tents for a final dinner of rice, meat and
nan (bread) washed down by heavily sugared green tea, or 'kowa.'
Shortly before midnight, the caravan commander whispers the order to
leave. 'Boro, boro. Let's go!' Grateful to be moving at last, the
guerrillas, some seventy men in all, surge forward in small groups, with
the animals, straining under their burdens, plodding behind. Rushes of
cool, moist air from the thundering torrent that tears its way through
the defiles of the valley dispel the dry heat of the night and the clouds

1

of powdery dust thrown up by feet and hooves. Only later will the biting chill of the night set in.

Following brief stays in Pakistan where they had purchased or otherwise procured badly needed supplies, the guerrillas are returning to their home regions — the Panjshair, Badakashan and Takhar. There they will rejoin local resistance units to fight the 'Jihad,' the Holy War, against the 'infidel' intruders from the north. Clutching World War II vintage Soviet Simonov rifles, now only used for ceremonial purposes in the USSR, the men walk in loosely-knit formations. All are dressed in pyjama suits, a jacket if they are lucky, plimsols or plastic shoes — paltry attire indeed for a trek that will take them over several hundred of the world's most rugged miles. They are young, most of them, in their late teens and early twenties, walking at a stiff, determined pace with the innocent self-importance of school boys eagerly spilling out on to the football field for the big match of the year.

During the British Raj in India, it was whimsically known as 'the Great Game' — decades of frontier skirmishing with Afghan tribesmen, who, as Kipling deftly wrote, ' . . . being blessed with perfect sight, pick off our messmates left and right.' Nevertheless, as the inscriptions of faded and now sadly desecrated tombstones in the overgrown Empire cemeteries in Peshawar and other Northwest Frontier towns testify, romanticism and hot-blooded British verve remained a prerogative of newspaper dispatches and Victorian poetry. Curiously, tribesmen on both sides of the 1893 Durand Line, the arbitrary boundary drawn by British colonial administrator Sir Mortimer Durand which divides Afghanistan and present-day Pakistan, today still harbour a sense of fond esteem for the Englishman. 'Fighting him was good "shikar" (sport)', remembered a venerable Afridi partriarch in a tribal hamlet only miles from the Khyber Pass. 'We respected each other. We could look one another in the eye. We had certain rules.' But the war with the Soviets has no rules. The 'Great Game', if it ever truly displayed a sense of fair play, has become a gruesome, pitiless contest of strength, endurance and basic survival, for the greater part ignored and forgotten by the rest of the world.

In the diffused moonlight, one can distinguish the silhouetted saw-toothed peaks of the mountains, the irrigated wheat fields and the willow and walnut trees which line the narrow track as it tapers into the distance like a long white ribbon. Choruses of howling dogs rise from the apple orchards as the snorting horses, their loads moving rhythmically with the rise and fall of hooves, pass through the last villages to the border, still a solid 20-hour march ahead. Sometimes, the long, straggling caravan grinds to a halt. The men drop to their haunches, their backs propped against the mud-packed walls of irrigation canals. Hands dip into the water to drink a few quenching mouthfuls, or to splash perspiring faces. The horses, their heads down and breathing heavily, wait patiently beneath their burdens. No one speaks. Some try to catch a few winks, others just gaze around them. The unit leaders growl 'Boro, boro' and the caravan pushes on.

At 2 a.m. the Afghans stop to sleep and rest the horses. The track has begun to climb steeply as it weaves through fields of rock riddled with hollow-sounding brooks. The men unload the animals and hang oat bags around their necks, and then curl up on the ground, tightly wrapped in their patous against the now penetrating wind that sweeps down the valley.

It is still dark when the caravan awakes. The false dawn hangs like a dull, glowing mantle over the towering range. The mujahideen, their all-purpose patous drawn over their shoulders, stand in huddled knots around huge fires, warming their hands and boiling water for tea in soot-blackened kettles. While the horses are being loaded, they chew on pieces of nan and goat jerky gulping down cups of hot tea. Then, the horses moving off in threes and fours, they continue along the narrow track to the border.

At the last Pakistani frontier post, a shabby couple of tents nestled in a stunted willow grove at the end of the valley; the caravan leaders go over to chat with the police while the men and horses pass ahead. Few Northwest Frontier Pakistanis hide their sympathies for the Muslim Afghan cause, but some financial persuasion is still required for the supply convoy to be officially registered as an ordinary merchant's caravan and allowed to pass.

Leaving the main valley, the path now cuts straight up to a high pastured plateau cordoned off by precipitous ridges. As the day wears on, the sun beats down with growing intensity. It is rough going for the horses. The Afghans, sweat glistening on their bronzed faces shout and whistle at the animals, sometimes remorselessly whipping them up the mountain. One of the horses, gingerly treading over loose sliding stones, stumbles and falls several hundred yards, strewing ammunition crates and supply bags on all sides. Surprisingly, it is only slightly injured, but two men quickly climb down to remove the remains of its load and distribute it among the other animals.

The caravan climbs steeply for twelve hours, occasionally resting by cascades of snowmelt roaring down from the rearing escarpments above. Thick copses of willow grow along the water's edge, providing the men with shade from the blistering sun as they brew up tea and nibble nuts and dried fruit. Again the cry, 'Boro, boro' and the caravan lumbers forward. The mujahed camp for the night is at the base of the 15,000-foot-high Diwana Baba Kotal, the 'silly old man' pass, leading into Afghanistan. Although not yet dusk, they prefer to tackle the final three-hour ascent at day-break.

The sun has yet to rise over the jagged palisades of the pass as the men prepared to move. With the cold of the morning still numbing their bodies, they edge their way up its near-vertical ramparts. The stark metallic skyline rapidly changes into a deep azure in the growing light. Goading shouts and whistles reverberate across the valley. With the drivers labouring to prevent them from plummeting into the abyss below, the horses strain to surmount each torturous step.

The top of the Diwana Baba pass, a barren, ice-draped corridor, is cloistered by monumental gothic ridges. Huge, sinister ravens croak hoarsely from its craggy parapets, and just overhead, a lone eagle gracefully soars on the rising and plunging air currents. Although the sun's rays beat down with vengeance at this altitude, a ripping wind tears through the mountain portals. On one side, Pakistan; on the other, a sprawling sea of 20,000-foot-high snow-capped peaks and cloud stretching for miles to the West – Afghanistan.

When the Soviet Union invaded Afghanistan on 27 December 1979, overthrowing the increasingly self-willed communist regime of President Mohammad Hafizullah Amin, the Red Army became involved in its first real war on foreign soil since 1945. It also incited the most enduring armed revolt against the Kremlin's authority to date, and one with widespread popular support.

Active opposition to the Marxist-Leninist government in Kabul began to develop within months of the coup d'etat of 27 April 1978 which ousted President Mohammad Daoud. But it took the physical presence of Soviet troops and tanks to provoke most of Afghanistan's 15-17 million Muslims into the time-honoured tradition of grabbing their guns to defend the independence of their homeland – a homeland which, for many, has always resembled a spiritual emotion rather than a nation.

For millennia, this mainly arid, mountainous country, the size of France, Switzerland and the Benelux countries combined, has absorbed a host of foreign cultures. Ranging from the Greeks under Alexander the Great to the Mongol hordes of Genghis Khan and the British in the nineteenth and early twentieth centuries, they have swept and thundered, ridden and caravaned across its rugged but magnificently beautiful lands. A people of vastly conflicting ethnic and tribal cultures, present-day Afghans strongly reflect these outside influences in their physical features, language, religion and, to a degree, xenophobia. While the clannish and often mutually hostile ethnic groups have never really experienced genuine unity, ironically the Soviet occupation itself has begun to foment an emerging sense of national identity and pride for the first time in their long and turbulent history.

Technically, opposition to the Kabul regime stopped being a rebellion or civil war when the Soviets intervened and installed their own puppet, Babrak Karmal, in the seat of power. As with resistance movements fighting against the Nazis in occupied Europe during World War II, Afghans now found themselves opposing a foreign invasion force, unwelcomed by all except a small minority of pro-Soviet collaborators and sympathisers. Resistance grew quickly, assuming the characteristics of a nationalist, anti-communist and primarily Muslim-inspired 'jihad' against the 'Shouravi' (Soviets). Within months, all of Afghanistan's 28 provinces were caught up in the fighting. Even members of the communist People's Democratic Party of Afghanistan (PDPA), notably of the Khalq (Masses) faction, protested against Russian meddling in their affairs, but, on the whole, for different reasons; the Soviets heavily favoured Karmal's minority Parcham (Banner) wing rather than their own.

Now well into its sixth year of occupation, the USSR has still failed to bring the Afghan resistance to heel, despite the massive political and military resources at its disposal. Although the Soviets are in no danger of being thrown out by the mujahideen, they certainly cannot be pleased by the way the war has been progressing. To all intents and purposes, it has come to a complete military impasse: the communists occupying the towns, the mujahideen the countryside.

Since the invasion, the Soviets have progressively introduced tactical modifications into their anti-insurgency strategy. While continuing with aerial bombardments against civilians and selective anti-guerrilla 'cordon and thump' operations, they have sought to maintain a limited holding pattern around the main population centres, military installations and highway links that ring the country. Circumstantial evidence also strongly suggests the use of toxins and other chemical agents. At the same time, they have resorted to a subtle and extremely varied combination of psychological pressures, economic inducements, subversion, indoctrination, bribery and manipulation of the various tribal and ethnic groups in the old British 'divide and rule' manner, in their efforts to weaken the resistance and establish a 'progressive' pro-Moscow regime in Kabul with at least a semblance of broad popular backing. As for the guerrillas, the average mujahed has come a long way in his 'jihad'. What started out as a disorganised, untrained rabble of turbaned fighters using old-fashioned methods and weapons has developed in many parts of the country into a formidable resistance force. Compared to the Yugoslav partisans during World War II or the Eritreans in Ethiopia, Afghan guerrilla warfare remains, in many respects, distinctly nineteenth-century. But this has begun to change. A primarily peasant resistance with only a narrow intellectual leadership base it has proved far more obstinate and stalwart than the Russians, or, for that matter, many Western observers, expected. The mujahed's firm belief in Islam has been, and still is, the greatest strength of the resistance — a fervid emotion too easily dismissed by outsiders.

Analysts have often sought to draw parallels with the wars of Vietnam and Algeria. The conflicts remain substantially different, but some familiar patterns have emerged. If anything, conditions in Afghanistan bear greater similarities to those of French Algeria with its shorter logistical lines, mountain and desert guerrilla warfare and Muslim population. Nevertheless, it is certain that the Kremlin has taken the Indochina experiences of both France and the United States into account.

As with the French and the Americans, the Soviets have underestimated the resilience of a resistance force intent on gaining its independence. However, they do not face the same sort of domestic political unrest, which ultimately forced France and the United States to terminate their respective involvements. Unwilling to tolerate dissent, the Kremlin does not have to worry about anti-war demonstrations and an untimely withdrawal of troops before the task is completed. As a result, in contrast to the half million Americans in Vietnam at the height of the war, it can rely on a limited expeditionary military force in Afghanistan (some 115,000 men not including the deployment for special operations of an additional 30,000-40,000 based inside Soviet Central Asia) and pursue a long-term policy designed to wear down the resistance eventually. Whether this will succeed is another matter.

The brutality and ugliness of the war are aptly illustrated by the way it is being prosecuted by both sides. Estimates of the number of civilians killed since the 1978 coup d'etat vary from 250,000 to 500,000 and even a million. Communist aerial bombardments and ground operations have partially or wholly devastated countless farms and villages. Vivid tales of atrocities abound; some, products of the rumour mill, others, tragically substantiated. Entire communities have been massacred or ruthlessly ravaged by Soviet and Afghan troops, while tens of thousands of political opponents, including communists, have been, and still are, incarcerated and tortured in government jails, many of them never to emerge alive.

On the communist side, up to 25,000 Soviet soldiers may have died. Some sources even put the number of deaths at over 40,000. Afghan communist casualties are generally considered to be twice if not three times as high. Government officials or sympathisers have been shot in the streets, blown up in restaurants, or captured and then executed according to Islamic law by the resistance. Despite the gradually expanding pools of Soviet prisoners held by the mujahideen, neither side has made a habit of taking its opponents alive. Only captured ordinary Afghan troops, usually conscripts, are released to go home or to join the resistance ranks.

Perhaps most poignant of all is Afghanistan's dramatic refugee exodus, the largest in the world. In what amounts to a calculated policy of migratory genocide, the Soviets have forced between one quarter and one third of the Afghan population to flee abroad. Some five million Afghans are in Pakistan, Iran and other second or third asylum countries. More are leaving. In Afghanistan itself, hordes of families have sought refuge in the cities or mountain hideouts to escape the fighting.

Both the international community and the Islamabad government have demonstrated generous concern for refugees in Pakistan. Practically no such relief has gone to Iran; only in 1984 did the Tehran government permit the United Nations High Commissioner for Refugees (UNHCR) to set up operations in Iran. Several United Nations organisations have continued to function on a limited scale in Kabul, with some, notably UNESCO, grossly susceptible to government manipulation. For various political or logistical reasons, little international assistance has gone to the 6-8 million civilians striving for survival in the areas of Afghanistan not controlled by the government. Compared to the organisational ability and resources of other liberation fronts, the Afghan resistance is still incapable of providing its civilian population with anything other than basic military support. While outside help is growing, the number of international private agencies operating inside the country, notably the French volunteer medical organisations, remains small.

Overall, the real plight of the Afghan people has been quietly abandoned by the wayside. Despite avowed concern on the part of the West, the Arab and the Third World nations, world opinion has brought little effective pressure on the Soviets to leave. Instead, a general acquiescence has emerged in considering Afghanistan part of the Soviet sphere of influence. For the United States, despite some arms assistance to the mujahideen, Afghanistan has become primarily a rhetorical weapon in its confrontation with the Soviet Union. Saudi Arabia, Kuwait and other Gulf nations, too nervous to criticise the Soviet Union openly, have sought to alleviate their consciences by 'buying' Muslim solidarity through the channelling of funds to the refugees and certain guerrilla parties. As for most non-aligned countries, their moral responsibility has stretched only as far as the symbolic condemnation of the Kremlin at General Assemblies of the United Nations.

My own acquaintance with Afghanistan goes back to the spring of 1970 when, as part of a year off between school and university, I hitch-hiked from Istanbul to Delhi. This took me for a relatively short period through the country, staying at cheap dosshouse hotels and travelling everywhere by bus or on foot. I returned again as a journalist in the autumn of 1979, three months prior to the Soviet invasion.

At that time, fighting in the provinces between troops of the Moscow-backed Kabul regime and Afghan rebels had been going on for well over a year. As a result, the main highways leading to the capital from the principal towns of Kandahar, Herat and Mazar-i-Sharif were cut by the guerrillas for days at a time. Trucks, buses and cars would often depart in convoy accompanied by armoured vehicles; but ambushes still occurred. In one case, bullets from hidden riflemen killed a Swiss and a Canadian tourist as their overland bus from Europe to India passed some outcrops of desert rock in the south. In another case, snipers shot up a car carrying four Afghan government officials and friends from Kabul to Jalalabad, killing everyone inside. This occurred in the same region where, 130 years earlier, Pushtun tribesmen had annihilated an entire British expeditionary force of 16,000 men and camp followers.

Outwardly, the Afghan capital appeared quite normal. Only a few weeks before, on 14 September, Hafizullah Amin, then prime minister, had deposed President Nur Mohammad Taraki following a bloody shoot-out at the Presidential Palace. But tanks no longer patrolled the streets as they did in the immediate aftermath of the putsch. They had either returned to their units just outside the city or guarded the access roads to important government buildings; these included Radio Kabul near the half-empty US embassy in the Karte Wali district.

Nevertheless, the tension, the insecurity, the growing hatred for the communists were apparent just beneath the surface. 'Too many people are in jail for us to forget now', a respected Afghan university lecturer told me. With the growth of repression by the Khalq, the faction in power, and the fighting constantly spreading to new fronts in the countryside, it was evident that something would have to break sooner or later; another coup perhaps, an army uprising, or even a rebel take-over of Kabul. Few people expected anything as drastic as the Soviet intervention.

Following the invasion, I returned to Afghanistan in early January, 1980 on special assignment for *The Christian Science Monitor* and ABC Radio News to cover the war. This first took me on an official visa to Afghanistan's second largest city, Kandahar, in the south. I then toured the ever swelling refugee camps that punctuated the Northwest Frontier and Baluchistan regions of Pakistan. Travelling clandestinely, I later crossed back into Afghanistan with a group of mujahideen to visit a series of mainly Afghan-Baluch partisan bases hidden in the arid Chagai Hills of Helmand province.

Since then, I have headed back to Afghanistan, Pakistan and India at regular intervals for the *Monitor* to cover different aspects of both the Soviet occupation and the resistance. This took me on major trips with the mujahideen to the eastern and northern parts of Afghanistan in 1981 and 1982 and the following year to the border areas. In 1984, I travelled back to the Panjshair Valley north of Kabul with a CBS News film crew to report on stepped-up Soviet attacks against Afghan civilians. Despite at least seven official requests to the Kabul govern-ment for permission to report their side of the war, all applications have been either refused or ignored. Only once in early May, 1982 did I again set foot in 'official' Afghaistan when my Ariana Afghan Airways flight transitted in the capital for three hours.

This book primarily examines Afghanistan since the Soviet invasion. It is not meant to be a scholarly thesis. My main purpose is to provide an informed appraisal of what this tragic conflict is all about. Unlike Vietnam, Afghanistan has certainly been one of the hardest wars to cover. It has also become increasingly dangerous, with the Soviet ambassador in Islamabad issuing a well-publicised warning in mid-1984 that any journalists caught 'illegally' inside Afghanistan would be 'elim-inated'.

It is a conflict about which limited amounts of consistent, reliable information have emerged. While some regions, notably in the east, have been fairly well reported, few journalists and other observers have managed to enter the more distant western and northwestern provinces. Furthermore, apart from certain Western or Third World correspondents, the international non-communist press has been prevented from reporting the Soviet side of the war on a regular and unrestricted basis.

Another drawback is that any attempt to gain a credible impression of what is happening in one particular region means an often physically gruelling journey 'inside', lasting at least three or four weeks. Some journalists and travellers have spent two, three and even eight months with the resistance. Fortunately, the presence of French doctors and other foreign aid workers over long periods in various provinces has permitted reliable long-term monitoring of war conditions.

In such a heterogeneous country of deserts, mountains, irrigated plains and forested hills, circumstances vary from region to region, even valley to valley. Guerrilla fighting techniques, organisation and capabilities differ according to diverse ethnic groups and tribal structures. A bombardment, government infiltration of a resistance group or the death of a commander can transform the situation of a particular zone in a matter of days or weeks. Communications are archaic. To get from one area to another may take two, perhaps three, weeks of solid trekking by foot or horse. Resistance in the Tadjik-inhabited highlands of northern Afghanistan often bears little resemblance to the Pushtun areas of the southeast. And again, the Hazaras, the large Shiite minority of central Afghanistan, face contrasting problems; not only do they look towards Iran for inspiration, but their war experience is totally different from that of the Sunni Tadjiks and Pushtuns.

Under such conditions, it is virtually impossible to gain a first-hand overview of the war. Bearing this in mind, I have tried to put together a picture, one among many, of the Afghan conflict based on my own reporting, the reporting of other journalists, testimony from the French doctors, and interviews with diplomats, relief agency representatives, Afghan government defectors, resistance sources and refugees. I have also made liberal use of thousands of newspaper cuttings and other documents.

As a journalist and fellow human being who has lived, travelled and shared common experiences with the Afghan resistance, it would be dishonest of me to claim that this is a totally impartial appraisal. Victims of what I consider to be a brutal and colonialist form of repression by the Soviets, the Afghan people have all my sympathy. My reporting on Afghanistan for *The Christian Science Monitor* has been criticised occasionally by the Soviet and other East bloc media as 'malicious', 'reactionary' and a 'complete fabrication'. This is not surprising. Until the Kremlin and its communist puppets provide the possibilities (which is unlikely) for journalists, who have witnessed one side, to view their version of the story, coverage of the Afghan conflict will necessarily remain 'one-sided'. Nevertheless, just as I have always endeavoured to write as truthfully and in as balanced a way as possible for *The Monitor* within my own capabilities, so I have done with this book.

1 THE SOVIET INVASION

'The world's attention span has been reckoned at 90 days, which unhappily, is probably right. Afghanistan has all but slipped from sight . . . But still the war goes on. The Russians, incredibly, are no nearer victory than at the start, when experts blandly forecast that their modern army would subdue primitive tribesmen in months. It is bigger news than a bored world realizes.' (*New York Times* editorial, June 1 1982).

The first Soviet Antonov heavy transport planes, carrying 4,000 rapid deployment troops, began rumbling into Kabul international airport on Christmas Eve, 1979. Nearly three days later, a special KGB hit team supported by Soviet airborne commandos assassinated President Hafizullah Amin, thus officially setting in motion the USSR's occupation of Afghanistan. Whereas initial sketches for the invasion of this non-aligned sovereign country had littered Red Army military drawing boards as early as March that year, preparations for its eventual take-over, or at least its total political and economic domination, had been in the making for several years.

Watching the planes dip in through the low cloud cover over the historic Bala Hissar fort, many Kabulis assumed that they were only part of a general airlift bringing in more military advisers and equipment to help combat the rapidly expanding anti-communist insurgency. Unbeknown to them, similar operations were being carried out at Bagram airbase to the north, Jalalabad to the east, Kandahar to the south and Shindand to the southwest. Shortly after Christmas, columns of T-54 and T-64 tanks, heavy artillery, trucks and fuel tankers of Field Marshal Sergei Leonidovich Sokolov's 40th army, which had been massing along the USSR's southern frontier, began crossing the Oxus River (Amu Daraya) on pontoon bridges into Afghanistan.

At the time of the invasion, some 50,000 troops of the defection-ridden Afghan army, many of them half-heartedly engaged in fighting the rebels, were deployed in various parts of the country. A garrison sufficiently capable of wreaking havoc remained in and around the capital. But the Soviets had begun taking precautions already, prior to the airlift. By means of often ingenious ruses and with the aid of reliable Afghan party members and supporters, they rendered helpless virtually all the potentially disruptive forces.

In one case, Soviet advisers told soldiers guarding the strategically vital Kabul radio station with twenty tanks that these were to be replaced by newer models. Unfortunately, they explained, diesel was short. What was already inside the fuel tanks would have to be siphoned off and transferred in order to bring in the new vehicles. Facing little opposition, Soviet airborne troops moved in to take the station, which was unconcernedly broadcasting a radio play. Similarly, both the tank-supported 7th and 8th Afghan army divisions managed never to fire a shot. At one base, the Soviets duped the Afghan commanders into carrying out inventories of 'faulty' ammunition, which meant taking out all the shells, while at Pul-e-Charkhi on the outskirts of Kabul, they instructed tank crews to remove the batteries from 200 vehicles for 'winterisation.' The sabotage operations succeeded almost everywhere. Only a few minor incidents were reported, with sections of at least one Afghan army battalion and two brigades defecting with light weapons to the rebels.

Curiously, as late as 26 December, President Amin showed no indication of recognising what the Soviets were up to. Judging by an interview given to an Arab journalist on the morning before the coup, he may still have believed that the military transports, now landing and taking off at ten-minute intervals on the other side of town, were indeed there to aid his rebel-besieged government. Whether blind to reality or obstinately convinced that the Soviets would never dare take such a step, he continued to insist that Moscow would respect Afghanistan's independence and sovereignty. But he must have had some doubts. Three days prior to the coup, General Victor Seminovitch Paputin, who, as first Deputy Minister of the Interior, had arrived towards the end of November, had tried unsuccessfully to persuade or threaten him into signing a document officially requesting Moscow to intervene militarily. As it later turned out, Paputin was acting as overseer in charge of laying the political groundwork for the invasion forces.

Other incidents also should have warned Amin. In the second half of December, a series of terrorist acts had erupted in the capital, killing certain communist party officials as well as one or two Soviet advisers. Shortly before Christmas, Amin's own nephew and son-in-law, Assadullah, the Afghan security chief, was attacked and severely injured by an Afghan army officer. Apparently not suspecting the beginnings of a Soviet plot, Amin sent him to Moscow for treatment. Three days later, he returned: in a coffin. Whether some of the Kabul attacks were committed with Moscow's blessing, or were the work of rebels, remains unclear. For his own 'protection', however, the Russians advised Amin to move from his city residence to the more fortified Darulaman Palace situated on a 600-foot-high hill not far from the Soviet embassy and five miles from the centre of the capital.

There have been numerous conflicting reports concerning the coup d'etat at Darulaman. According to several sources including Amin's mistress and his nephew, Zalmai, the original plan had been to remove the Afghan dictator quietly to the USSR were he would be kept in political 'cold storage' in case he was needed again. During an elaborately planned banquet, Amin was drugged by his Russian cooks. But the kidnap plan failed when at least one of the presidential bodyguards did not eat the contaminated food and, armed with a Kalashnikov, prevented Soviet advisers in the building from approaching Amin. The Russians, with Paputin in command, then attacked the palace in the late afternoon with an armoured column of several hundred Soviet airborne troops wearing Afghan army uniforms, plus a small contingent of KGB officers.

In a partial stupour, Amin now realised what was happening. While groups of Khalqi faithful put up bitter resistance, the Afghan president desperately tried to reach Radio Kabul as well as the Ministry of the Interior by telephone. But two of the three telephone exchanges in the capital had already been blown up by Soviet demolition teams. The Interior Ministry, a renowned Khalqi bastion, had also been stormed by troops of the 105th Division and taken. During the palace battle, which lasted four hours, Amin's bodyguard fired on Paputin, slicing him in two. At this, the Russian assault troops went wild. Breaking into Amin's quarters, they shot him dead as he stood by the bar drinking, and, in an attempt to leave no witnesses, machine gunned most if not all his family members present, including seven children.

A somewhat different story has emerged from other quarters. If the testimony of Major Vladimir Kuzichkin, an alleged KGB defector, is to be believed the Soviets had no intention of taking the Khalqi president alive. At one point prior to the invasion, they tried to get rid of him by poisoning his food, but as if expecting an attempt on his life, Amin himself switched the adulterated meal at the last moment. According to this account, the assault on Darulaman was led by a certain Colonel Bayerenov, head of the KGB terrorist-training school, rather than Paputin. In a similar effort to leave no witnesses, the KGB officer had instructed his soldiers remaining outside the palace to shoot anyone trying to leave.When Khalqi resistance proved stronger than expected, Bayerenov stepped out of the main entrance to call reinforcements and was instantly killed by his own men.

Whatever the true circumstances, most versions agree that an important senior Soviet officer was killed during the coup. It has been reported that on his return to the USSR Paputin may have committed suicide in disgrace for having bungled his dealings with Amin; a theory reinforced by the absence of Brezhnev's signature to the general's obituary.

In any event, at 9.15 pm local time, the Russians broadcast a prerecorded statement by Babrak Karmal, who was most probably in the Soviet Union at the time, from a transmitter in Tashkent but using a wavelength close to that of Radio Kabul. In it, the Parcham leader declared that he had taken over the government and was appealing for Soviet military assistance. Meanwhile, Radio Kabul continued broadcasting normally, making no mention of the country's change of leadership. Only early next morning did the official Afghan broadcasting network announce Amin's overthrow. Amin, it said, had been tried and found guilty by a 'Revolutionary Tribunal,' and executed for his 'crimes against the people'. The radio also repeated Karmal's earlier statement. Over the next few days, close Khalqi supporters not killed during the coup were thrown into the Pul-e-Charkhi prison, the notorious Afghan detention centre on the outskirts of the capital.

While the 105th secured all strategic positions in the capital — the ministries, the post office, the ammunition depots — the main Red army thrust was coming from Termez, where Sokolov had established his field headquarters. Some 300 tanks and APCs of the 360th Motorised Division, followed by a fleet of supply trucks, moved toward Kabul via the ancient Turkestan city of Mazar-i-Sharif along fast, Soviet-constructed highways. Eighty miles to the east at Nizh Piyanszh, another armoured column, that of the 201st Motorised Division, followed by the 16th Motorised Division, made its way toward Kunduz. Here it split in two, with one part of the force swinging towards Faizabad in Badakshan province, where the guerrillas controlled much of the countryside. The other roared south to Baghlan joining the main Kabul highway. While long convoys of oil tankers provided for much of the invasion force's fuel requirements, Soviet pipe-laying battalions — the only army in the world thus equipped — laid up to 30 kilometres a day of pipe along the Kunduz axis to pump in petrol supplies, a facility such as Rommel could have used to good effect during his North African campaign.

At Kushka to the extreme west, the 66th Motorised Division as well as elements of three other divisions charged southwards toward Herat, Shindand and Farah before swinging east to Kandahar to join up with

Soviet troops being airlifted to the American-built airport some 10 miles outside the city. Providing constant protection from guerrilla attack, the equivalent of two Soviet air divisions, totalling more than 400 aircraft, mainly MIG21, 23 and SU-17 jetfighters and Mi-24 helicopter gunships, thundered back and forth over the main invasion axes. With the airlift still droning overhead, the first columns of vehicles of the 306th began rumbling into the northern suburbs of the capital on the morning of the 26th.

By first light on the 28th, the Soviets had taken all important buildings and installations in the capital. They also controlled the strategic Pul-i-Khumri and Salang passes. Soviet troops, Kalashnikovs slung over their shoulders and flanked by tanks, guarded intersections or openly patrolled the streets. An 11 pm to 4.30 am curfew was imposed. At the airport, a huge tent city milling with soldiers, supplies and vehicles had materialised along the frozen grass verges of the asphalt runways.

By the end of December, some 15,000 uniformed Soviet troops had established their quarters in and around the city. At the Soviet embassy, the invasion force set up its new field headquarters. After months of scheming and intrigue, the mission was finally able openly to adopt its true role.

The Soviet occupation of Afghanistan had begun.

The First Days of the Occupation

During the first ten days, the Soviets methodically consolidated their position. With striking rapidity, they secured the major towns and strategic points; airports, vital communications centres and military posts. Fatigued Soviet soldiers, wearing long overcoats and grey fur caps with the red star insignia, tried to recover from the sleepless rigours of the invasion. In scenes recalling the trenches of the First World War, they huddled around fires or in shelters carved out of the mud and snow. Scores of empty tank carriers parked by the roadsides attested to the enormous firepower that now fanned out across the country, some 300 tanks in Kabul alone, while the rearing silhouettes of long-range artillery pieces dotted the snow-swept fields.

While armoured vehicles and supply trucks poured in day and night, Antonov transports continued to land at Kabul airport. By the end of the first week of January 1980, more than 4,000 flights had been recorded. Within weeks, between 50,000 and 60,000 Red Army troops had been ferried in by land and by air. This did not include the 4,000 civilian technicians and administrative advisers, who had been brought in to help run the new Babrak Karmal administration.

Despite rumours of intense fighting between the Soviets and the mujahideen as well as rebellious Afghan military units, the speed with which the invaders had swept in took most of the population by surprise. In Kabul, people reacted with sullen disbelief and hatred, but, apart from shouts of abuse or stone-throwing, there was little armed resistance. Moscow had chosen an opportune season to make its move. Not only was Western reaction lulled by the festive Christmas and New Year period, but much of the country was covered in snow and ice, making it difficult for the guerrillas to operate in the rugged hinterland where they maintained their bases. In the capital, the Soviets quickly adopted a low profile during daylight hours, but after dusk their tanks groaned and clanked through the streets in a show of force.

By early January, sporadic and sometimes major civil unrest had broken out in Kandahar, Herat and other urban centres. Faced with an alarming rise in Afghan army desertions, the Soviets were obliged to disarm certain disloyal units or, as was the case with the intransigent 26th Afghan Parachute Regiment, suppress them with force. Nevertheless, they still sought to remain discreet and leave the Afghan authorities to deal with local security problems wherever possible.

Kandahar – The Invisible Soviets

Among the first Western reporters to enter Kandahar, French photographer Thierry Boccon-Gibod and I travelled there by bus from the Pakistan border in mid-January. At the sleepy Spin Buldak frontier post, not a Russian was to be seen. In fact, there was no sign whatsoever of the invasion. A paltry group of unshaven Afghan 'Askari' (soldiers) in ill-fitting khaki uniforms lounged by the side of a road barrier resting their assault rifles between their legs. A bored corporal glanced at our passports, both with visas issued by the Afghan embassy in Paris two weeks earlier. Carefully studying mine upsidedown, he made as it to read it, turning the pages from back to front in the Arabic manner. Then he smiled and waved us on.

There was little traffic on the main 80 kilometre-long highway, built by the Americans some years earlier, only a few cars, buses and military trucks carrying groups of unenthusiastic conscripts. Twice we were stopped by Afghan army control points. Searching for weapons, they frisked the passengers in a cursory manner but did not bother with us. Unlike the main road between Kabul and Kandahar, there appeared to be no need to ride in armed convoy. Within twelve months, however, the region had deteriorated into a merciless free-fire zone, with the city and its surroundings suffering some of the worst bombardments and fighting of the war.

We arrived just as twilight was falling. Again, the Russians were mysteriously absent. It had been raining for several days and the normally dusty provincial capital, founded by Alexander the Great, was a quagmire of mud. Motorscooter rickshaws, with coloured plastic tassels attached to their windscreens, zipped through the bazaar barely missing the dirt-caked street urchins selling cigarettes, who pestered passers-by with groping hands and shrill voices. Aggravatingly honking their horns, automobiles jockeyed for the right of way with horse-drawn 'tongas' (dogcarts). Contradicting earlier reports in Pakistan of food shortages, merchants loudly plyed their trade crouched behind abundant stocks of vegetables and spices. A pall of smoke from burning firewood hung in a languid, blue haze over an otherwise peaceful town.

Astonished at the lack of a Soviet presence, we asked about their whereabouts. A young engineering student sitting in a chaikhana (tea-shop) near the Chahr Souq (Four markets) intersection enlightened us: 'They're outside the city. They don't come into town.' As in Jalalabad, Farah and other towns, the Soviets preferred to confine themselves to the airports and other major security points rather than enter the down-town areas. Instead, sulky Askari were left lackadaisically to protect the main post office, the banks, the petrol stations and other essential establishments. Only the occasional government jeep or armoured personnel carrier roared through the streets carrying armed soldiers and officers in Afghan army uniforms. Sometimes, however, they would be accompanied by men with European features in civilian clothes.

By eight o'clock, half an hour before the curfew, the town was empty. We found a relatively modern but empty hotel that had obviously seen better days during the pre-1978 tourist boom which had provided Afghanistan with one of its main sources of hard currency. Over the past few months, only occasional groups of foolhardy, or ignorant, Western travellers still stopped by, the owner explained. He also warned us not to go out into the town again, saying it was too dangerous. Outside, the sonorous wailing of a mobile loudspeaker called on the inhabitants to return to their homes. With a stricter curfew, nocturnal Kandahar was considered far more insecure than Kabul. Urban guerrillas controlled the rooftops and back alleys, while Afghan army patrols cruised along the main avenues shooting at anything that moved. But that night the town remained eerily quiet, with only the muffled sounds from radio and TV sets, the barking of dogs and the grinding engine of a passing military vehicle.

Rumours and Violence

According to foreign residents, Kandahar was subdued by a strange calm on the morning after Amin's overthrow. 'It was a most unusual coup', the Indian consul said. 'There were no observers, no tanks and no excitement.' This persisted for several days. Soviet aircraft had been landing and taking off in slightly larger numbers at the airport since Christmas, but this was nothing unusual. On New Year's Eve, however, the city erupted. Gripped by a general panic, merchants abruptly shuttered their shops at nine in the morning, having only just opened them for the day. Huge crowds gathered in the streets and the main squares. At the central bus terminal, mob violence broke out, with people screaming frenzied insults against the Soviet Union and the new Karmal regime. No one had actually seen the invaders, but fantastic rumours of communist executions, rape, looting and other atrocities had spread.

Armed with sticks and stones but reportedly no guns, the crowds surged through the streets attacking anything and anyone representing the regime. Army vehicles were burned or overturned, office windows and furniture were smashed, and the red Khalqi flag was torn to shreds. Under Taraki, the communists had changed the national flag to one more like that of a Soviet Central Asian republic than of a supposedly independent, non-aligned nation. Government troops quickly appeared on the scene and shooting broke out. Unable to quell the rioting, the authorities called in a dozen MIG-17s of the Afghan airforce. The aircraft strafed buildings and open spaces with cannon fire but seemed to be trying to disperse rather than kill the demonstrators. It was later said that the Afghan pilots had refused to shoot at their own people.

Nevertheless, over a dozen deaths were reported by both sides, among them, three unfortunate Soviet technical advisers from a nearby textile mill. Coming into town to do some New Year's shopping in the bazaar, they were dragged from their jeep and lynched on the spot. Following the incident, Soviet families living in a UN residential complex were immediately evacuated. By late afternoon, large numbers of Afghan troops were patrolling the streets. Jeeps with loudspeakers drove around appealing to the population to remain calm. The crowds began to break up. Throughout the entire affair, the small contingent of Soviet troops already at the airport had wisely remained out of sight leaving the Afghan government to handle its own 'direct relations' with the people.

Shortly after dawn on New Year's Day, the invasion proper of Kandahar began. One transport plane after another droned in from the north, while just outside the airport, tanks, BMD and BMP armoured vehicles of the 66th Motorised Division moved into position. Heavy air traffic, including the arrival of a small fleet of helicopter gunships, continued for two days. For the Soviet airforce, it also meant running sorties almost immediately against guerrilla positions in the nearby mountains northeast of the city.

Before leaving Kandahar, Boccon-Gibod and I managed to slip into the precincts of the airport by telling the Afghan police and soldiers manning the checkpoints that we were trying to catch the daily Bakhtar airlines flight to Kabul. Five camouflaged Antonov transports with red star markings were being unloaded by Soviet troops on the slipways that ran parallel with the main highway. Over a 30-minute period, no fewer than a dozen Mi-8 and Mi-24 helicopter gunships flew in, landed for several minutes without cutting out their engines, probably taking on more ammunition, and then took off again for the northeast. During the same period, a Soviet MIG-23 and an Afghan MIG-17, the latter distinguished by its red, circular insignia, thundered off in the same direction.

Elsewhere in the country, the occupation developed in a similar manner. Reports of stern fighting in the streets of Jalalabad, formerly one of Afghanistan's most important Buddhist sanctuaries before it was ravaged by the Hephtalite Huns at the end of the fifth century, proved false when Western correspondents found the bazaars teeming with merchants, farmers, mountain tribesmen, nomads and travellers. As in Kandahar, the market stalls were full and the streets clogged with buses painted like magic circuses, camels laden wth lumber or firewood and the occasional military vehicle. But as one Pushtun elder told a European journalist: 'Don't be fooled with what you see here. The fighting is still going on.'

In the semi-arid, pine-studded mountains of Surkh Rud further to the west along the main road leading to Kabul, only a few miles beyond the lush orange groves of Jalalabad, rocket explosions and machine-gun fire could be heard. Hindered as they were by winter conditions, guerrillas both here and in other rural parts of northern and eastern Afghanistan had sharply intensified their attacks in the immediate aftermath of the coup. Clashing regularly with loyal units of the 81st Afghan army, scattered mujahed forces launched night-time assaults against government installations or carried out hit-and-run daytime raids in the suburbs of Jalalabad.

Although the estimated 1,000 Soviet troops who had flow in to occupy the airbase characteristically stayed away from the town itself, they immediately assumed control of all anti-insurgency operations in the region. Soviet ground controllers guided Afghan airforce planes to selected targets in the mountains, with pilots of the occupation forces flying some of the missions themselves. Soviet officers, supported by their own combat units, took control of the local infantry and tank forces but left their Afghan commanders nominally in charge. Only Afghan askari carrying Ak-47 Kalashnikovs could be seen on duty at bridges and crossroads, if, as one British reporter noted, that is the correct turn of phrase to describe dozing on a chair in the sun.

Along the main highways to the south, mujahed groups did not hesitate to harass Soviet armoured columns, despite heavy air protection. Nevertheless, because of the harsh winter conditions, resistance was less intense than during the previous summer months. Extravagant claims of devastating Soviet losses by Afghan exile organisations across the border in Peshawar have been generally discounted. Between 200 and 300 invasion troops at the most may have been killed or wounded during the first few weeks, many of them from ordinary deployment accidents rather than partisan bullets.

Some of the Western journalists sent to Kabul travelled as far north as the strategic, tortuously winding Salang Pass. Constructed by the USSR, during the late 1950s as a symbol of mutual co-operation, the 50-mile-long route through the Hindu Kush now served as a conduit for Soviet tanks, armoured personnel carriers, supply trucks and other vehicles. Ironically, it was also pointedly prone to ambush; at different points along the highway, mujahideen periodically fired on the invasion forces from the overlooking heights. According to London *Times* correspondent Robert Fisk, bridges along the way were destroyed and one part of a convoy marooned for almost 24 hours while repairs were carried out. In his dispatch, Fisk wrote that the drivers looked exhausted and each sat next to a Soviet soldier in a steel helmet clutching a rifle. An army truck, its rear section blown to pieces by a mine, lay upturned in a ditch and a fair-haired teenage soldier, who had been shot in the right hand, stood incredulously by the roadside finding it difficult to understand that he was being shot at. Like most Soviet soldiers, he had been told by his commanders that he was being sent to Afghanistan to protect its people from Chinese, American, Pakistani and other 'imperialist' forces.

The First Steps

Preliminary planning for a military intervention is believed to have begun in the spring of 1979. Within weeks of the 1978 coup against President Mohammad Daoud, the new Taraki regime had begun imposing social reforms with a ruthlessness that angered many, including potential reform-minded supporters. Purges, arrests and the assassination of dissidents from all segments of Afghanistan's political and religious spectrum soon followed, resulting in attacks on government officials, the army and the police. By Christmas, 1978, at least a dozen provinces were in revolt.

When Moscow realised that the insurgency was seriously beginning to threaten the Kabul government, it took to dispatching high-level military delegations to gauge the situation. One of these included General Alexei Yepishev, political commissar of the Red Army and a significant figure behind the invasion of Czechoslovakia in 1968, who recommended a substantial increase in military aid and advisers. Another included General Ivan Pavlovsky, Deputy Minister of Defence and Commander-in-Chief of the Soviet Ground Florces. Also a principal perpetrator of the crushing of the Prague Spring Rising, he visited Afghanistan in late summer with at least a dozen generals in tow. Among the remedial suggestions brought back was the possibility of direct Soviet military action. Furthermore, a sign that Moscow was in the process of preparing the legal foundations for such an intervention was a spate of articles in the Eastern bloc press, the first of which appeared in *Pravda* in March 1979, accusing China, Iran, Pakistan and later the United States of instigating trouble in Afghanistan.

Politically and militarily, the Afghan government was in a sorry state, its economy foundering. The communist People's Democratic Party of Afghanistan (PDPA) was torn by bitter and often bloody internecine strife between the two rival factions: Taraki's Khalq and Karmal's Parcham. The two wings had never got on well with each other. Feuding broke out almost from the very beginning of the so-called 1978 'Saur' (April) revolution. After only two months as Taraki's deputy prime minister, Karmal was forced into virtual exile as Afghan ambassador to Czechoslovakia. Other Parchami activisits were similarly sent abroad or later imprisoned, and even liquidated in 'incidents' blamed on the rebels.

Despite repeated Russian warnings to put their house in order, the two factions persisted with their infighting, while callous government repression further alienated the population both in the countryside and in the cities. Although officially headed by Taraki, a 62-year-old fatherly figure described by one Western diplomat as 'the respectable element in the Kabul regime', the Khalqi administration had become steadily more barbarous under the influence of Amin, who took over the premiership in March 1979. A burly former high school teacher of considerable personal charm and warmth, he nevertheless distinguished himself as the leading party inquisitor and bully.

More Advisers

Leadership problems were also gravely affecting the fighting morale of the army, where the situation was going from bad to worse. By the time Moscow intervened, the truncated and demoralised army had shrunk through desertions and defections to the rebels from its original strength of roughly 100,000 to less than half that number. Prior to the toppling of Daoud, the Soviets had only some 350 military advisers stationed in the country, but within the first twelve months of the new Taraki administration, the number had risen to over 1,000. Whereas most had previously been engaged in the training of recruits or the running of the Ministry of Defence, a substantial proportion was now directly involved in efforts to suppress the rebellion. Increasingly, they were found assisting the Afghan Army at the company level or actively flying routine combat missions for the Air Force.

Day by day, the situation was deteriorating. Government buildings, schools, military outposts and highway traffic were falling victim to stepped-up mujahed assaults. Above all, Soviet advisers and their families were being killed. In mid-March 1979, raging mobs in the ancient western city of Herat lynched scores of astonished and panic-stricken Russians with swords, clubs and knives. Later, while soldiers of the 17th Afghan army division refused to put down the revolt, the rebels paraded through the streets with the heads of the decapitated victims impaled on poles.

The Herat uprising dramatically signalled a fresh infusion of Moscow-sponsored military hardware. This included the first batch (a dozen of Soviet-piloted Mi-24 helicopter gunships to arrive in the country, plus 100 T-62 tanks. The helicopters had already proved their worth in Ethiopia against the Eritrean rebels, and Moscow was anxious to put them to use in a terrain not all that different from the Horn of Africa. The Soviet advisory contingent also swelled to some 3,000 men by the end of June 1979. Several weeks later, the first Soviet combat unit, a 400-strong airborne battalion, was flown into Bagram airbase to boost security.

By now, the Afghan army was involved in major offensives against the country's constantly growing opposition movement. Tens of thousands of refugees were fleeing into Pakistan and, to a lesser extent, Iran. Although the Soviets were obviously interested in seeing a secure pro-Moscow regime established, they would have preferred one which commanded a greater degree of popular appeal and credibility. As Amin's behaviour was not likely to achieve this, a drastic political change had become an urgent necessity.

In the hope of finding a Prime Minister somewhat more acceptable to the country's increasingly embittered inhabitants, particularly the more conservative religious elements, steps were being taken backstage in Moscow and Kabul to oust Amin. On 11 September 1979, Taraki stopped off in the Russian capital on his return from the non-aligned summit in Havana to meet President Brezhnev and discuss Amin's replacement. But Amin, who probably had his own informers among Taraki's entourage, decided to strike first. On 16 September he launched a violent putsch, killing Taraki either in battle or shortly afterwards.

The Amin Factor

The Soviets regarded Amin with distasteful suspicion and the new Afghan president knew it. As one senior American diplomat noted: 'Amin, had Brezhnev's build, but with Tito's mind and ambitions'. During the three months that followed his rise to power, he made regular overtures to several Western nations, none of which were taken seriously, and offered to normalise relations with Pakistan. He also refused to accept Soviet offers of troop assistance or to moderate his ruthless policies, which might have calmed at least some of the country's unrest. Even more insulting to the Soviets, he demanded the recall of ambassador A. Puzanov for allegedly conspiring against him, which was probably true.

Such actions, coupled with the danger that the government might fall to the Islamic rebels, only speeded up preparations to get rid of him. Some days after Taraki's overthrow, guerrillas reportedly ambushed and killed 35 members of a senior Soviet military delegation, at least one of whom was a general. Although Islamic rebels were blamed, a shocked Kremlin had strong reasons to believe that Amin was involved.

Mujahed activity was now running strongly in twenty-two provinces and the Soviets could scarcely disguise their contempt for the ineptitude of the Afghan army. Amin's fate was definitely sealed, however, when he refused to grant a Soviet request on 10 November 1979 for exclusive facilities at Shindand, considered one of Central Asia's logistically most important airbases because of its proximity to the Iranian border and the Gulf. Only six days after the taking of the American embassy hostages in Tehran, Moscow was apparently worried that Washington might try to use the base in a military intervention against Iran.

As far as can be determined, the Politburo was in two minds as to how best to deal with the Afghan problem. Brezhnev was apparently in favour of limited intervention only in order to maintain an 'independent' but amenably pro-Soviet Afghanistan, thus keeping the non-aligned nations happy. KGB chief and presidential successor, Yuri Andropov, on the other hand, wanted to turn the country into a Mongolian-style satellite through internal subversion and various political and economic pressures. Just as the Pentagon had clamoured for a free hand in dealing with Hanoi during the Indochina conflict, there were also hawks in the Kremlin demanding a no-holds-barred military solution that would blast the guerrillas back into the Stone Age. When Brezhnev opted for a restrained military commitment, Soviet defence officials later complained that combating the 'bandits,' in Afghanistan was like 'fighting an octopus with one hand'.

The Build-up

US satellite surveillance indicated abnormal Soviet military activity in the Central Asian republics bordering Afghanistan towards the end of November. The Indians and the Pakistanis, too, were aware that elaborate military preparations were in the offing. Relying on first-hand information from their diplomatic missions and consulates in Kabul, Kandahar and Herat as well as from resident nationals, businessmen, travellers and other sources, they warned the Americans that the Soviets were contemplating some form of direct intervention. On 9 December the Russians began trebling their transport flights to Bagram airbase. Bringing in a strike force of up to 2,500 troops supported by armoured vehicles, they informed Amin that these were only reinforcements to help combat growing rebel activity in the northeast; but foreign observers reported Soviet military movements towards the capital shortly afterwards.

Between 11 and 15 December 1979, intelligence sources noted unusual concentrations of heavy transport planes in Moscow, home of the 105th Airborne division, as well as the call-up of reservists, the deployment of motorised divisions and the stockpiling of petrol on the

Soviet side of the Afghan border. Another interesting indicator was the reassignment of key officers and weapons specialists from Eastern Europe to the Central Asian District. Aware that the Soviets were getting serious, the Americans claim to have warned the Kremlin five times not to take any action in Afghanistan but their admonitions were ignored. On 23 December, less than 24 hours before the wheels of the Soviet military machine began turning in earnest, *Pravda* accused the West of fabricating reports of an alleged invasion.

In accordance with Soviet military and political doctrine, Moscow's 'Blitzkrieg' of Afghanistan was swift and decisive: a fait accompli about which the world would howl but, in the end, do nothing. Soviet international standing has never relied on legal niceties, but rather on force and ideology. Nevertheless, as with many totalitarian regimes past and present, it has tried to justify actions such as Hungary (1956) or Czechoslovakia (1968) based on legalistic terms and agreements. Afghanistan is no different.

Officially, the Kremlin claims to have acted according to its treaty obligations with the Kabul regime. On 5 December 1978, the USSR signed a 'Treaty of Friendship, Good-neighbourliness and Co-operation' with Afghanistan. The intervention, the Russians and their Afghan surrogates argue, was therefore a legitimate and moral response to the subversion promoted by 'imperialist external forces'. Since then, the Kremlin has vigorously sought to promote the image of a non-aligned and sovereign state temporarily relying on a limited contingent of Soviet security forces to help stave off alleged 'outside counter-revolutionary interference'. Even after five years of occupation, communist propaganda on all fronts still maintains that the Red Army is involved in a supportive military role only, with the Afghans stoically bearing the brunt of the fighting. Yet, were it not for the invasion, the Afghan army would have collapsed long ago, and with it the Kabul regime.

The Reasons

Western and Third World analysts have put forward numerous hypotheses in their strategic assessments of the Soviet intervention. These range from the historical desire for direct access to the warm waters of the Indian Ocean to the fear of militant Islam spilling over into the USSR. As events have shown, there was probably no single motive behind the action but rather a composite of geopolitical factors considered vital to Moscow's immediate and long-term interests.

Foremost among its most urgent concerns was undoubtedly the need to prevent the communist regime in Kabul from being toppled. The

Soviets had spent more than half a century trying to assert their influence in Afghanistan, both ideologically and economically, and they were not prepared to see their efforts undermined, even destroyed. This meant getting rid of Amin, who was later conveniently labelled 'an agent of American imperialism'. However, in order to bring the situation back to 'normal', this also implied the need for direct intervention to help crush the spreading revolt.

Were the Kabul regime to have fallen, it remains questionable whether a truly non-aligned and independent Islamic republic in Afghanistan could ever have afforded to act inimically towards its giant neighbour in the north. But it is certain that the Russians were reluctant to hazard yet another Khomeini-style Muslim revival on their doorstep. Only ten per cent of the Soviet Union's 45-50 million Muslims are Shiites as in Iran; the rest are Sunni who do not regard Khomeini as a spiritual leader. Nevertheless, the many articles in the Soviet press criticising as 'fantastic gossip' the notion that the intervention was in response to the Muslim threat have only underlined Moscow's concern.

Another probable factor was Afghanistan's strategic position on the periphery of the Middle East. Complete control of Afghanistan would significantly augment Soviet influence in South Asia, Africa and the Gulf, the latter containing 56 per cent of the world's known oil reserves. It would also furnish the USSR with a crucial northern anchor to complement its access to base facilities in Ethiopia and South Yemen. As part of a potential 'strategy of denial' to the West's major energy sources, it would be able to extend itself even further into the Gulf's backyard.

Some analysts argue against the concept of a Soviet masterplan. Yet the intervention represents another convenient stride southwards. Dating back to Peter the Great, it had been a historic Tzarist ambition to expand the Russian empire down to the Indian subcontinent. The annexation of Central Asia by the Bolsheviks in the early 1920s effectively demonstrated that the new Russia had no intention of altering this policy. For a nation which maintains numerically the largest navy in the world, access to a warm-water port such as Gwadar in Pakistan's Baluchistan province would pioneer new frontiers. The USSR has no major open-sea ports which are ice-free throughout the year. Both Murmansk on the Arctic Sea and Vladivostok on the east coast have to be kept clear by icebreakers throughout the winter. In August 1979, four months before the invasion, *Pravda* wrote:

[The Indian Ocean] has a direct bearing on the security of the Soviet Union. The waters of the Indian Ocean, its shores, its insular territories are comparatively near our own country if one applies the radius of action of modern means of strategic attack. Besides, the only year-round sea route linking the European part of the USSR with the Soviet Far East runs through the Indian Ocean.

Most critical of all, in one fell swoop, the Soviets eliminated Afghanistan's traditional buffer role between the USSR and what was once British India. For the West, this severely altered the regional balance of power in Moscow's favour. Unlike the British, the Americans failed to allow for the long-term strategic importance of Afghanistan. Following the partition of India in 1947 and the departure of the British from the region, Washington neglected to fill the resulting power vacuum, despite the recommendations of certain of its foreign service officers that it should show greater interest. Gradually, the Soviets assumed the upper hand.

By occupying Afghanistan, Moscow secured considerable advantages over neighbouring Pakistan and Iran. On the one hand, Pakistan suddenly found itself under pressure on two fronts: Soviet troops to the West, Indians to the East. Through Afghanistan, the Soviets are able to conduct cross-border subversion such as the smuggling of arms to dissidents of the military regime. Initially, they had almost certainly counted on the government in New Delhi to maintain a non-aligned stance with strong pro-Soviet leanings. This, it was felt, would squeeze the Islamabad regime into political compliance. It backfired however, when Prime Minister Indira Gandhi, despite her government's effective condonation of the invasion in the beginning, took deliberate steps to ease her country away from the Soviet embrace. She also demonstrated that it was in India's interest to cultivate a politically stable Pakistan and moved to improve relations with the Islamabad government.

Iran, however, remains the key to the Persian Gulf. It has also begun to assert greater influence among resistance organisations and may play a leading role in the years to come. As suggested by the four to six Soviet divisions reportedly positioned in Western Afghanistan, as well as the 20-24 divisions along the southern Soviet border with Iran, it is against this country that the Soviet focus appears to be directed rather than against Pakistan. Guerrilla activity in Western Afghanistan has at times been intense, with repeated attacks against Shindand and other bases, but it is certainly not enough to warrant such a large Soviet military presence.

Ever since the respective occupations of northern and southern Persia by Soviet and British troops during World War II, Moscow has sought to lay the foundations for pro-Soviet support in Iran by infiltrating the clergy, the miltary and the government and moulding the communist Tudeh party. Although this policy suffered a considerable setback when the Khomeini regime began cracking down on the Tudeh party in 1980 while simultaneously heightening its anti-Soviet rhetoric, the Soviets are in a favourable position to intervene in order to 'protect the borders of the USSR' in the event of civil chaos in post-Khomeini Iran, the spread of the Iran-Iraq conflict, or conceivably even a left-wing backed coup d'etat similar to that of Kabul's 'Saur' revolution.

As regards Afghanistan, however, pure opportunism may have given the Soviets a convenient excuse to invade. US relations with Pakistan were at their lowest following the burning of the American embassy in Islamabad by a hysterical mob in November 1979, while in Iran Washington's hands were tied by the hostage crisis. Fearing some form of US intervention, the Soviets may have wanted to pre-empt the Americans, who were at the time starting to strengthen their presence in the Indian Ocean at Diego Garcia, from establishing a foot-hold in the region. Some analysts have maintained that the Soviet Union was acting only to protect itself against perceived 'encirclement' by the West and China — an argument not all that different from those used by apologists for Hitler's expansionism into Austria and Czechoslovakia in the 1930s.

Lastly, Afghanistan's not inconsiderable natural resources may have contributed towards encouraging a direct takeover. Already in the 1920s, the Russians became aware of its potential, particularly in natural gas, oil, iron ore, copper and uranium. Since the 'Saur' revolution, Moscow's exploitation of Afghanistan's resources has amounted to nothing less than economic pillage; with the invasion, the Soviets secured a completely free hand.

2 THE SOVIET STRATEGY — MIGs, HELICOPTER GUNSHIPS AND KALASHNIKOVS

From dawn to dusk, they doggedly came. First, one heard an ominous distant drone. Then, as the throbbing grew louder, tiny specks appeared on the horizon and swept across the jagged, snow-caped peaks of the Hindu Kush. Like hordes of wasps, the dull grey helicopter gunships came roaring over the towering ridges that ring this fertile valley. Soon the hollow thuds of rockets and bombs resounded like thunder as they pounded the guerrilla positions entrenched among the mountain slopes.

Intermittently, pairs of MIG-23 jetfighters or the new, highly manoeuvrable SU-24 fighter-bombers shrieked across the skies to dislodge their loads over the huddled villagers hiding among the deep ravines and gorges to the sides. As small groups of front-line resistance fighters bitterly fought against specialised Soviet heliborne assault troops, a massive onslaught of tanks, armoured personnel carriers and trucks ground forward along the main valley floor in long dust-billowing columns, determined to crush whatever resistance blocked their path. (Fifth Soviet offensive against the Panjshair Valley, early summer, 1982).

Tactics and Objectives

Most military analysts have considered the execution of the actual invasion as the easiest part; splendidly planned and coordinated, it was the sort of large-scale operation one might expect from a modern army geared for conventional offensive warfare. According to their assessments, it proved that the Soviets were fully capable of rapidly mobilising a major expeditionary force free from logistical breakdown. Nevertheless, only a small proportion of the troops were combat-ready. At the last minute, the Red Army High Command was forced to call up untrained reserves from the Central Asian and Turkestan military districts.

Initially, there was little Afghanistan's poorly armed and badly organised mujahideen could do against such an impressive military machine. But once the Soviets had fully ensconced themselves, it proved to be a heavy, lumbering machine better suited to fighting in the lowlands of Europe than against a basically peasant population in the mountains and deserts of Afghanistan. Soviet military planners had no doubt expected resistance to persist for a number of years, but at a tolerably low level. The ability of the guerrillas not only to survive, but to expand, evinced the Kremlin's poor judgement in gauging the Afghan reaction.

Afghanistan was not to be a mere textbook replay of Czechoslovakia. Bare hands and courage, the Czechs bitterly discovered, were simply not enough to stop tanks. The mujahideen, in contrast, had the terrain, centuries of fighting tradition and Islamic fervour on their side. Nevertheless, whether promoting Marxist-Leninist revolution in the Third World or reasserting its control over insubordinate peoples of satellite nations, the Kemlin has never adopted a short-term approach. Since well before the invasion, it had made it clear that it would never tolerate a Kabul regime hostile to Soviet regional interests. The 'Saur' revolution, it insisted, was 'irreversible'. If brute force was not going to bring the Afghans to their senses, then other, more insidious, tactics would have to be adopted.

Promoting the New Revolution

Among the Soviet Union's first objectives was strengthening the country's foundering and utterly unpopular 20-month-old 'new model revolution'. This meant providing the regime with a fresh and, it was hoped, human face. The more moderate, pro-Soviet Parcham, who had clashed virulently with the Khalq over the ruthless imposition of reforms, wanted above all to disassociate themselves from the previous Taraki-Amin regimes. The new administration was anxious to persuade both the country and the outside world that the Soviets had come as friends. But widespread indignation only accentuated the difficulties the Soviets would confront in trying to whitewash Karmal's blemished image as a surrogate of Moscow. 'No matter what he does', commented a Western diplomat in the Afghan capital, 'Karmal will never be able to erase from people's minds that he was put in by the Soviet army.'

On 9 January 1980, Karmal gave his first press conference at the Chehestoon Palace, a hilltop mansion normally reserved for foreign dignitaries. Protected by Soviet anti-aircraft guns, tanks and troops, the building was being used as Karmal's official residence until the Presidential Palace, badly damaged during the takeover, could be repaired. Over 200 foreign journalists had by now gathered in the capital.

The Afghan authorities had begun issuing official journalists visas only a week after the coup, but some reporters had already slipped into the country as tourists. The press gathering was a stormy affair. Karmal stubbornly sought to justify the Soviet intervention. Denying that his country had now become a client republic of the Kremlin, he declared, to the noticeable embarrassment of his aides, that 'the only thing brighter than sunshine is the honest friendship of the Soviet Union'. The large assembly of Soviet and Eastern bloc journalists, who occupied the front three rows of the medium-sized reception room, were the only ones regularly to break into ripples of applause. When the *Pravda* correspondent solemnly asked Comrade Babrak to express his viewpoint on 'the prospects for friendly relations between the Soviet Union and Afghanistan' he was greeted by howls of raucous laughter and shouts of 'good question!' from the non-communist ranks of reporters. Not to be daunted, the Afghan President stiffly maintained that the number of Soviet troops in Afghanistan had been grossly exaggerated by the 'imperialist Western press'. He added that the troops would leave 'the moment the aggressive policy of the United States, in compliance with the Peking leadership and the provocation of the reactionary circles of Pakistan, Egypt and Saudi Arabia, is eliminated'.

A Red Army War

The occupying force had at least two months in which to prepare for its new war. Once the spring thaw had opened up the mountain passes, allowing the resistance to move with ease, the fighting could be counted on to start in earnest. But even before the snows had melted, villagers, who had previously refrained from taking up arms against the Kabul government, rallied to fight the 'Shouravi', while groups of angry mujahideen from the refugee camps in Pakistan started slipping back across the frontier, their principal weapons British vintage World War I Lee Enfields, Kalashnikovs, shotguns and the occasional home-made ancient flintlock.

Within months, the Soviets had brought in the equivalent of seven motorised rifle divisions plus the 105th Airborne − a total of some 85,000 troops. In general, each ground division consists of three infantry regiments, one tank and one artillery regiment, while the 105th is comprised of six paratroop regiments as well as an artillery one. The Soviets also gradually introduced up to five Air Assault Brigades of specialised heliborne 'rangers' better suited to combat mountain guerrilla warfare, which are deployed in different locations around the country. An additional 30,000 men, some of whom have been used in cross-border operations, were stationed on the Soviet side of the Amu Daraya. Two years later, the Soviet expeditionary force stood at an estimated 105,000-110,000 troops. By early 1985, it had risen to the generally accepted figure of 115,000, with 30,000-40,000 regularly deployed for special operations from bases inside Soviet Central Asia. The Red Army went into action almost on arrival in certain parts of the country, but it still had to show what kind of war it was willing to pursue. An indication of things to come emerged with its first big offensive at the end of February. Directed against the primarily Pushtun (Pathan) Kunar Valley, a 60-mile-long fertile farming district protruding into the Hindu Kush close to the Pakistan border, it involved more than 5,000 Soviet troops supported by heavy armour, helicopter gunships and MIGs. Apart from several government-controlled pockets, most of the region's mud and stone villages, irrigated wheat fields and fruit orchards had fallen into the hands of the insurgents in the summer of 1979. Since then, it had served as a vital corridor for guerrilla supplies into Nuristan, Badakshan and other northern provinces.

For two days, Soviet aircraft and heavy artillery pounded the area. Then, while helicopters dropped troops along the nearby ridges and onto the flat roofs of houses, columns of tanks and BMP infantry combat vehicles swept rapidly northwards, ploughing through whatever was left of the settlements. Kunar refugees in Pakistan later made the first reference to Soviet use of chemicals and toxins in Afghanistan by describing 'gases' which made one cry or laugh hysterically or which painfully irritated the skin. 'It burned the body badly', explained one man at a camp in the Bajaur Tribal Agency just across the frontier. 'It burned so badly that we had to scratch. We dropped our Kalashnikovs . . . Russian guns which we had to buy with our own money', he added, voicing a typical Pushtun preoccupation with weapons.

Fierce street fighting ensued. Shooting from behind wooden doors and dried mud walls, the Afghans vainly tried to defend themselves. 'There were many dead. Russian and our own', recalled Fazi Manan Patch, a 60-year-old tribal chief. 'Women and children too. It was horrible. Terrible . . . Everywhere injured people. Young children and women. Everyone crying.' When their ammunition failed, the villagers attacked the armoured vehicles with sticks and stones before trying to flee into the side valleys or up the snow-covered slopes of the 7,000-foot-high surrounding mountains. Thousands of local inhabitants made their way to Pakistan. Others trekked into Nuristan, eventually ending up in Northwest Frontier refugee camps when the Russians bombed the neighbouring provinces too.

By the end of 1980, most of the valley's 150,000 inhabitants had left. When I last visited the Kunar in September 1984, many settlements in the main valley remained deserted, the bomb-shattered houses were crumbling and the once lush irrigated fields and fruit orchards were little more than dust bowls. However, despite an occasional shelling or helicopter attack, teams of caretaker farmers from across the border had returned in a bid to wrest back their farms from the wasteland that much of this area had become.

The outcome of the offensive, which had resulted in disastrous casualties, was a painful setback for the guerrillas. Still basking in the past glory of having thrown out the communists the year before, they had not expected the Russians to act so quickly in taking advantage of a warm spell which prematurely freed the valley floor. The attack gave the resistance an idea of the magnitude of the Soviet expeditionary force now being deployed in Afghanistan and of the challenge it posed. It was an ominous lesson for the Russians too. Not only had they lost scores, some reports claim several hundreds of men; they also failed to pursue the guerrillas into the mountains. Licking their wounds, it was only a matter of weeks before the mujahideen relaunched their rancorous campaign against the authorities.

The Soviet Counter-insurgency: A Conflict with Parallels?

Western analysts have often sought to draw parallels between Afghanistan and the wars of Vietnam and Algeria. Just as American and French attempts at defeating the liberation movements foundered partly as a result of their underestimation of the resilience of the guerrillas, the Soviets soon found themselves in a similar predicament. The USSR is by no means facing military defeat, but it cannot be pleased by the way the war is dragging on.

As compared with the US experience in Vietnam, the Kremlin has been much more restrained militarily and has only permitted a limited escalation of the war by raising its troop commitment from 85,000 men during the early stages to the present estimates. It recognised that to annihilate the resistance of 180,000-200,000 mujahideen would require an injection of hundreds of thousands of troops, a move it has so far been unwilling to make. During the first three years, it relied primarily on conventional military tactics such as aerial bombardments and combined Soviet-Afghan ground operations in its bid to crush the resistance. The Red Army found itself mimicking the massive but often ineffectual search-and-destroy assaults with which the Americans frittered away so many lives and resources in Indochina. In many respects, the failure of the Spring 1982 offensive in the Panjshair Valley 40 miles north of Kabul, which involved a force of 12,000 Soviet and Afghan government troops and daily sorties of more than 200 MIGs, SU-24s and helicopter gunships, seriously questioned the Kremlin's ability to contain, let alone destroy, a tightly organised and reasonably equipped resistance front.

Furthermore, the Soviets were suffering as many as 10,000 casualties by the end of 1982. Having undisguisedly used the Afghan army as cannon fodder, they found themselves unable to rely on local soldiers as a dependable security force. Afghan soldiers, many of them secret members of the various mujahed parties, often defected within a month of call-up, going over to the resistance with their weapons or simply making their way back home. Increasingly, improved guerrilla weaponry — recoilless rifles, grenade launchers and mines — took its toll of Red Army armoured vehicles. The occupation forces were forced to depend more heavily on overwhelming firepower whenever possible as well as to seek other, more effective means of breaking the resistance.

From Combat to Subversion

If certain reports are to be believed, the KGB was at odds with the Red Army from the very start on how to deal with the insurgency; from late 1981 onwards, the Soviet secret police appeared to be gaining the upper hand. By the time former KGB chief Yuri Adropov replaced the late Leonid Brezhnev as head of state in the autumn of 1982, the Soviet war in Afghanistan was undergoing a subtle, yet dramatic, change.

Selective, and sometimes overwhelming, helicopter-supported ground operations against prominent guerrilla fronts remain a fundamental aspect of Soviet military strategy, together with aerial bombardments against areas suspected of collaboration with the resistance. Deliberate attacks on civilians are similarly part of the Kremlin's policy of 'migratory genocide', designed to rid the countryside of all inhabitants capable of supporting the mujahideen. This was evident in the spring of 1984, when the Soviets launched a series of large-scale offensives against the Panjshair, Kandahar, Herat and several other regions. There is also greater use of well-trained and, according to some guerrillas, extremely brave heliborne troops.

Assaults are regularly carried out in areas where the armed resistance is less assertive, but they are no longer purely reactive as was often the case during the first twelve months of the occupation. These operations, generally small-scale if not sporadic, are principally geared to demoralising civilians. The Soviets retaliate swiftly with draconian reprisals at the slightest indication of guerrilla activity (i.e. the mining of a road or an attack on a convoy), by razing villages to the ground, killing cattle or burning crops. However, the systematic application of KGB-style subversion — the use of psychological and economic pressures, informers, agents-provocateurs, financial pay-offs, imprisonment, threats and privileges — now represents an increasingly effective weapon in the government's efforts to attract or split loyalties among the tribes, ethnic groups, exiled political parties and resistance fronts. This combination of military repression and political division seems likely to continue.

Certainly, the Red Army has made considerable progress in its anti-guerrilla capabilities through modifications of both tactics and equipment. It has made use of Afghanistan as a 'live' testing ground, the results of which (notably helicopter gunship skills) have already made themselves apparent among its forces in Eastern Europe. Motorised riflemen, for example, have become more mobile on the ground, remaining less in their BTR and BMP armoured vehicles which are often sitting targets for the guerrillas. In order to provide a more destructive spread of fire, the slow-firing 73mm cannon on standard BMP vehicles have gradually been replaced with automatic 30mm cannon. Companies also have their own 'anti-sniper' squads and have adopted tactics that permit one section to cover the other as it advances. In the mountains, helicopter gunships now provide the supporting firepower that would normally have come from tanks.

Clearing the Frontier

During the early stages of the occupation, troop deployments in the northern provinces were specifically designed to rid the frontier zones of mujahideen as quickly as possible. Not only was there the constant threat of costly harassment against supply lines leading from north to south, but also the danger of Islamic 'overspill' into the Soviet Muslim republics. Either way, the Kremlin simply could not afford to permit unchecked resistance in these areas. In the east, despite fanciful reports of troops massing along the Pakistan border, the Soviets seemed more concerned with neutralising the mujahideen than with launching an assault against Pakistan. Dropping hints of cross-border 'hot pursuit' operations, they doubtless intended to pressure the Islamabad regime of Zia ul-Haq into curbing resistance activities and other 'outside intervention' among the 400,000 Afghan refugees who had fled to Pakistan by January 1980. Nearly five years later, the communists were still launching regular aerial attacks against frontier towns and camps in an effort to force the Pakistanis to act.

It was no secret that refugee camps in the Northwest Frontier and Baluchistan were not just humanitarian havens for Afghan citizens fleeing from Soviet terror. Many guerrillas used the camps as rest and recreation bases between bouts of fighting, while in Peshawar and Quetta more than a dozen refugee political parties were free to operate, furthering their respective resistance movements through propaganda, lobbying and logistical support for the partisan fronts inside the country.

The Soviets were particularly anxious to put an end to the remorseless trafficking across the 320-odd mountain passes along the 1,400-mile-long Durand Line dividing Pakistan and Afghanistan — some of them, traditional nomad routes, others mere goat paths open only during the snow-free summer months. Almost from the start, the Kremlin showed itself to treat all forms of resistance with the same harsh brutality once used by the European colonial powers against their most obdurate native subjects. Not caring whether they killed or terrorised villagers into leaving, the occupation forces unleashed a deliberate policy of 'rubblisation'aimed at emptying the border regions and turning them into a no-man's land devoid of human habitation except for pro-government enclaves and garrisons.

Through the relentless bombardments of villages and farms as well as the peppering of mountain passes, fields and trails with tens of thousands of anti-personnel mines, they sought to deny the resistance any form of local popular support. By the late spring of 1980, some 80,000 Afghans a month were fleeing from this reign of terror. Pitiful streams of men, women and children, clutching blankets, tea kettles, chickens, carpets and other family belongings, made their way to Pakistan on foot or by truck or camel. By June 1980, the estimated refugee population in the Northwest Frontier and Baluchistan provinces stood at 800,000 — more than double the figure at the start of the invasion. Six months later this wasteland policy of gutted villages, shattered irrigation canals and crater-pocked fields had swelled the refugees to 1.5 million.

Retaliation and Interdiction

During the first three years of occupation, the Soviets found it virtually impossible to halt the movement of supply caravans not only along the border areas, but deep within the country itself. Helicopter patrols regularly overflew certain guerrilla trails, but more often than not failed to take action. Western reporters, French doctors and foreign travellers repeatedly commented on the relative ease with which partisan groups, bolder and more experienced as the fighting continued, were able to travel through most rural areas. Except in open spaces with little cover, the guerrillas did not hesitate to move in broad daylight, often leading horses or camel trains of 50 to 60 animals or more.

Observers familiar with the Indochina war were particularly struck by the general failure of the Soviets to adopt effective interdiction tactics, as well as the poor security arrangements around military installations. Accompanying a horse caravan within a mile or two of Bagram airbase in late summer, 1982, independent American reporter William Dowell, on assignment for *TIME* magazine, and I noticed no Soviet patrols whatsoever in the surrounding rolling plains of Shamali, even in the middle of the morning. As far as we could tell, they made no effort to go beyond the airbase perimeter or to ambush the supply route, one of the most important in the country, that was passing right under their noses. Furthermore, while American bases in Vietnam were normally lit up at night by dozens of parachute flares, only the occasional red or white one would arch up into the sky, glow brightly for twenty seconds and then fizzle out causing a temporary blindness which seemed worse than remaining in total darkness. 'If this had been Vietnam, the Americans would have maintained tight security and constantly patrolled the area', said Dowell, who had spent three years there covering the war.

One possible reason for this reluctance to send out patrols was the likelihood of heavy casualties such as occurred in Indochina. Throughout the war, the Soviets have tended to remain within the confines of their camps, in many cases supplied by helicopter, only to emerge when absolutely necessary. Nevertheless, by mid-1983, the situation had begun to change. Following several highly destructive attacks against Bagram and other major Soviet military installations, the Red Army began instituting active interdiction and patrols in key areas.

In one incident in July, 1983, Soviet troops and tanks succeeded at night in ambushing a major resistance convoy, including a small group of French doctors and Western journalists, in exactly the spot where Dowell and I had passed without difficulty a year earlier. With tanks dug in on two sides and a third flank closing off the rear, they machine-gunned those caught in between, killing or wounding over a hundred mujahideen and drivers. The Europeans, who had been travelling at the head of the caravan, managed to escape when the horses behind took most of the bullets, allowing them to seek refuge in a series of deep, erosion-worn crevices where the armoured vehicles, their headlights full on, could not follow. By 1984, communist ambushes began seriously to threaten guerrilla movements, particularly in the eastern and southeastern provinces.

The Developing Strategy

Despite such anti-insurgent measures, frontier guerrilla operations were not necessarily hindered. During the Amin era, Afghan government forces succeeded in temporarily suppressing the rebels in Paktya, a rugged border province of pine-forested hills and traditional smuggling trails. Bombing villages, destroying farms and killing or arresting hundreds, possibly thousands, they forced some 40,000 people to flee into Pakistan in the late summer of 1979. But the mujahideen soon returned, leaving their families behind in the refugee camps, and immediately stepped up their attacks on government outposts and convoys.

In early June, 1980, the Soviets sought to repeat the operation and moved in to seal off the border. As a large Soviet-Afghan armoured column drove through the Sultani Valley near Urgun, it was ambushed by waiting guerrillas. The besieged column called for more reinforcements, but by then news of the attempted offensive had already spread to the refugee camps of Miramshah in Northern Waziristan, where several thousand tribesmen were mobilising. Flying green Islamic standards, they headed for the 'front' in trucks and vans, picking up their weapons from depots conveniently left across the border, and forced the security troops to withdraw. Four years later, despite further government assaults, several of them extremely vicious, most of Paktya still remained in the hands of the mujahideen.

Other assaults during the first year of occupation were more successful. In July 1980, no fewer than 60 villages were destroyed during a two-week operation south of Kabul. Although many of the district's inhabitants fled, this did not necessarily halt mujahed activities. With varying effectiveness, the Soviets launched numerous major attacks against resistance strongholds throughout the late spring, summer and autumn in Panjshair, Logar, Kandahar, Badakshan and other eastern and northern regions. Reports of major clashes between the occupation forces and the mujahideen in the Herat and Farah regions in the West also emerged.

During this same period, the Soviets sought to strengthen their grip on Kabul and other towns, particularly in the wake of violent spring demonstrations. They also showed no intention of making their stay in Afghanistan a short one. In the government-controlled areas, they were busy expanding the available military infrastructure such as barracks, officers' clubs and supply depots. Work also started on extensive logistical improvements: road building a road-cum-railway bridge across the Oxus and the installation of sophisticated telecommunications systems. The upgrading, notably the lengthening of runways, of six aifields in southern and western Afghanistan, including Shindand and Kandahar, further indicated that the Soviets had ulterior motives other than the suppression of local resistance.

Once the occupation forces were well dug in, the Kremlin decided that much of its heavy 'show of strength' forces and equipment was no longer needed. Seeking to gain political advantage, it announced the pull-out of 5,000-6,000 reservists in June, 1980. This was timed to coincide with the Venice summit conference of Western industrial leaders as well as to quell a rising American-led anti-Soviet mood against the holding of the summer Olympics in Moscow. Amid much publicity, particularly in the West European communist press, plus hints of an eventual full withdrawal, the announcement said that these would include certain tank, missile, anit-aircraft and heavy artillery units. The 'gesture' fell flat, however, when Western defence analysts pointed out not only that most of these specialised units were useless to the Soviets in their anti-guerrilla war but that more experienced replacement soldiers equipped with light armoured vehicles had been ferried in a week earlier. As a result, there was virtually no change in the overall number of occupation troops.

By early 1981, the scale of the fighting had risen dramatically. While numerous mujahed groups persisted with traditional but generally clumsy assaults, others were steadily improving their grasp of modern guerrilla warfare. Through better tactics, organisation and weapons, they were exacting a costly penance from the Russians. Despite the hardships, the population in general showed few signs of diminishing their support and enthusiasm for the resistance.

Adapting the Counter-insurgency

The Soviets had grasped the fact that, without substantially raising their commitment, they would not be in a position to defeat the mujahideen militarily. As this commitment was not going to be forthcoming, at least for the moment, other methods had to be devised. The result was a greater emphasis on the development of a highly calculated anti-insurgency strategy better adapted to local circumstances. Afghanistan was not a homogeneous country which could be controlled by a single, uniform policy. Different peoples, customs and terrains called for different approaches. While still pursuing a predominantly military line, the first signs of KGB-instigated economic, psychological and political warfare could be distinguished.

Without doubt, the Soviets were also learning from their mistakes. As the war progressed, Eastern bloc defence journals regularly published accounts of battle experiences, thinly disguised as 'training exercises' but evidently gleaned from the war in Afghanistan, proposing corrective measures in the art of mountain combat, anti-sniper tactics and heliborne assaults. To facilitate military operations, but, above all, to lessen decision-making by a central authority out of touch with local conditions, the Soviets divided the country into seven tactical and geographical zones. Each had its own Russian military commander as well as Afghan political commissar, responsible for working out more appropriate operational procedures for each region.

Nevertheless, one striking drawback still remains: the inability of officers in the field to use their own initiative in order to modify battle plans if new developments arise. Officers must radio back to the commander-in-charge for permission, an operation which might take hours. Observers have noted helicopter gunships bypassing unexpected targets such as arms caravans without bothering to intervene because they have been instructed to attack elsewhere. Exploited by the more astute guerrilla commanders, these tendencies often give the impression that the Red Army is running a thoroughly bureaucratic, nine-to-five, war.

Unable systematically to root out and destroy guerrilla groups wherever they appeared, the Kremlin concentrated on efforts to isolate resistance fronts both from the local population and from each other. Analysts have used Mao-Ze-Dung's analogy of a 'fish in water' as an appropriate description of the guerrilla's relationship with his surroundings. As far as the Soviets were concerned, they were not out to fish, but to drain the lake. Provoking conditions that would force the population exodus to continue so as to deny local support to the resistance therefore remained an essential element of this policy. Similarly there were more varied underhand tactics such as promises of non-intervention in order to persuade the local inhabitants to co-operate with the government, or at least to remain neutral in the fighting.

One current method is deliberately to lull areas into a false sense of security, and then to attack. In the late autumn of 1980, the Kabul regime announced a series of joint Soviet-Afghan ground and air 'manoeuvres' in several northern provinces. Shortly afterwards, heavy Soviet bombardments followed by massive ground attacks were reported in Baghlan, Kunduz, Takhar and Badakshan provinces. Jean José Puig, a French relief co-ordinator, was one of the first Westerners to witness a major anti-guerrilla operation involving Soviet troops, that of an attack against the Andarab Valley just north of the Panjshair at the beginning of November, 1980. 'The difference between this and previous attacks was that it was quite unprovoked', he recounted. Ever since a Soviet unit had briefly entered the region eight months earlier and destroyed one or two villages, killing several men, it had remained virtually untouched by war. As a result, its inhabitants had not felt the need to organise any guerrilla defence units.

But at dawn, some 300 armoured vehicles rumbled into the valley and surrounded the settlement of Dehe Sallah. Afghan security officials set up loudspeakers in the bazaar and ordered the forced recruitment of all young men into the army. At the same time, a third of the assault contingent entered the side valleys of Ghorisang and Gajghari where tanks and artillery fired indiscriminately in a move to flush out possible resistance fighters. Most able-bodied males had already escaped into the mountains. At midday, helicopter gunships descended into the valley, and the aerial bombardment continued during daylight hours for the next six days.

Helicopter Gunships

The most effective weapon against the resistance is the Mi-24 helicopter gunship. By mid-1982, Soviet helicopter strength (the Mi-6 heavy transport and assault, the Mi-8 medium transport and assault and the heavily armoured Mi-24 Hind gunship) was estimated at roughly 600-700 machines, of which some 200 were thought to be Mi-24 Hinds. Helicopters have given the Soviets a mobility similar to that of the Americans during the Vietnam war, with the US Huey cobra attack helicopter.

Travelling with the guerrillas in Nangrahar province in mid-1980, I found tribesmen panic-stricken by the appearance of gunships on the horizon. For them, 'helicoptr, helicoptr' had become a significant new word in their vocabulary just like 'bombe', roket' and 'Mig'. As the distant chop-chop heralded the machine's approach, they would urge me to hurry as we trekked through badly rocket-scarred villages. Not realising they were practically invisible from the air against a backdrop of rocks, trees and bushes, they would scatter, screaming and moaning, as the helicopter passed overhead. Fortunately, in most cases, the machine would continue on its course unless it had come specifically to bomb the village. Guerrillas travelling in caravan soon learned to leave their animals standing in small groups while they crouched motionless under their brown or grey coloured patous. In more exposed desert areas, camps were pitched at night among nomad tents and herds so that a few extra strings of animals would not stand out in the event of a dawn air patrol.

While less protected Mi-8s were being brought down by guerrilla fire, even sprays of Kalashnikov bullets, the Hinds could fly with relative impunity. Only by the third year of occupation, did one begin to see occasional evidence of Mi-24s being knocked out by the mujahideen. Despite guerrilla claims of shooting down helicopters, a considerable number are known to have crashed or been forced to land for technical reasons. Although considerable numbers of helicopters of all types as well as jetfighters had been shot down by the end of 1984, some of them by anti-air missiles, overall resistance weaponry had still not improved to the point that the Soviets no longer ruled the skies. Nevertheless, mujahed guns were forcing aircraft, including armoured helicopters, to fly high.

As with so much else, the Soviets have rediscovered a great deal of what the British painfully learned during their Afghan campaigns in the nineteenth and early twentieth centuries. The deployment of Air Assault 'rangers' or commandoes relying on Mi-8s as a primary form of transport, while the Mi-24s provide close air cover, has now become part and parcel of Soviet anti-guerrilla warfare. Air Assault rangers have proved particularly effective in establishing forward positions during 'cordon and thump' or 'search and destroy' actions.

Although practised to a lesser degree during the invasion itself, the Red Army makes systematic use of helicopter cover to escort convoys through vulnerable mountainous areas. Flying in pairs, Mi-8s or Mi-24s 'leap-frog' the length of the column, providing vehicles with a constant, albeit not necessarily unassailable, form of protection. Gunships also regularly 'crest the heights' in emulation of the British custom of establishing pickets on mountain tops and ridges in order to control the lower slopes. While the British troops had to climb themselves, the Soviets have preceded ground offensives in highland regions such as the Panjshair or Badakshan by dropping commando units on high points and then picking them up again when the operation is over.

Towards a Stalemate

From 1981 onwards, the resistance became increasingly adventurous in its activities against the government. The airports and even the Soviet embassy compound in Kabul were hit, while the seemingly invincible Mi-24s were obliged to fly extremely high or run the gauntlet of anti-aircraft and heavy machine-gun fire in areas where the guerrillas had established rudimentary but proficient aerial defence systems.

In response, the Soviets stepped up their military operations against both civilians and mujahideen alike. In Kandahar, for example, there were unprecedented clashes between communist troops and the resistance. For well over a year, some twenty different guerrilla fronts had launched intermittent and often highly successful raids against government installations and convoys in and around the provincial capital. Twice, in April and September, 1981, mujahideen temporarily overran the city itself, forcing government officials to flee to the airport, where the Soviets now ran their regional operational headquarters. In retaliation, Soviet planes and artillery mercilessly bombarded the old town, inflicting such heavy losses that the local inhabitants asked the guerrillas to leave, which they did.

In the early spring and summer of 1982, the Soviets carried out huge military operations in western Afghanistan, notably in the provinces of Herat and Farah. During one nasty confrontation not far from Shindand airbase in June, Staale Gundhur, a young Norwegian freelance cameraman, was killed. His notes as well as accounts by resistance sources indicate the sort of problems the occupation forces were facing at the time in trying to control the area.

On 9 June at eight in the morning, a combined Soviet-Afghan armoured column of some fifty vehicles attacked the guerrilla-held village of Rokan, three miles to the south. During the fighting, concealed partisans managed to kill a dozen government soldiers including a Soviet battalion commander. At around midday, Afghan army units tried to penetrate the southern sector of the village, but were forced back suffering further casualties. The Soviets, who normally attempt to take their dead with them (leaving the Afghans behind), then tried to negotiate for the body of the commander, but the talks fell through when the mujahideen insisted on ten Kalashnikovs in return. This led to another communist assault against the village the next day. When the Soviets threatened to take reprisals against civilians from surrounding settlements, the guerrillas eventually agreed to hand the body over. The security forces then proceeded to withdraw to Farah, but were unexpectedly ambushed by another resistance group along the main highway. Following a two-hour bout of firing, the armoured column retreated to the nearby village of Radj, where they were attacked by yet more guerrillas. According to Gundhur's observations, six ammunition trucks were blown up, while two Afghan army defectors brought up a vehicle transporting 'a heavy artillery piece, shells, a mobile army kitchen and three Kalashnikovs . . . ' The next day, the gun was transported to Jabhe Momi Farah, a mujahed base nine miles south of Shindand.

Concerned that the resistance might use the artillery piece against the airport, Soviet and Afghan troops with gunship support encircled and then bombarded the base. In their efforts to break out, the mujahadeen had coordinated simultaneous attacks on the main garrison at Farah by five other guerrilla groups, comprising a total of 600 men. Thus harassed, the security forces suffered considerable losses, 200 dead and wounded according to the Norwegian, while the mujahideen lost six men, among them a principal local commander. Two Afghans, a guerrilla and a farmer, were apparently also captured, beheaded and then burned. The combined government force withdrew on the morning of the 24th, but ran into an ambush of some 1,000 guerrillas positioned on both sides along a one-and-ahalf mile stretch of the main highway. At least one truck loaded with soldiers was blown up by a mine, while guerrillas destroyed half a dozen armoured vehicles using RPG-7 rocket launchers. Almost immediately, the Soviets called in both helicopter gunships and MIGs. It was during this counter-attack that Gundhur was killed together with five other men. Under heavy bombardment, the guerrillas were eventually forced to withdraw.

Unwanted Conquerors

To the disillusionment of many Red Army soldiers, who thought they had come as protectors rather than invaders, the general population despised and rejected them as an ignominious occupation force. Public sentiment, which ranged from barely disguised hatred for the 'godless infidels' to the expressionless cold stare, was hardly improved by the continued efforts of the Kremlin and its Afghan puppets to stifle the resistance. Despite the apparent reduction in fully fledged communist offensives in many areas during 1983, examples of Soviet brutality against the population were in no short supply and hostility toward the Soviets has not lessened.

Bernard Dupaigne, the French ethnologist, who travelled around much of Afghanistan by bus in the late summer of 1980 on an ordinary tourist visa, reported bitter animosity and resentment wherever he went. In one minor but revealing incident, Dupaigne's bus overtook a Russian truck along the Salang Highway. 'The military vehicle accelerated, passed us in turn and then stopped . . . blocking our passage', he recalled. 'A soldier calmly climbed down and then smashed the headlamps of our bus with his Kalashnikov before firing into the engine. Our driver did not move until he left.' Only once did he note a sign of sympathy between native and invader. On his way to Mazar-i-Sharif, he observed one of his fellow passengers, a Mongolian-featured Afghan Turkmen, wave to a Soviet Kirghiz soldier, also Mongolian-featured, in a long, straggling column of tanks. The soldier returned the greeting with a smile.

There were also numerous accounts of Soviet patrols stopping passers by in the streets for body searches and then taking their money and watches. The Red Army Command was apparently aware that such behaviour only produced ill-feeling and by the end of the first year of occupation diplomatic sources reported nearly 200 Soviet soldiers being held at Pul-i-Charkhi prison on the outskirts of Kabul for grave offences, including murder, against Afghan civilians.

Nevertheless, in mid-1982, Afghan truck drivers went on a three-day strike to protest against looting by Red Army troops. According to reports reaching Peshawar, the Soviets were making a practice of stopping vehicles hauling goods between the Pakistan border and Kabul, the route by which most of the country's luxury items such as tape recorders, TV sets, refrigerators and air conditioners were transported. If the drivers protested, they were beaten or dragged off to prison as mujahed suspects. On at least three occasions, drivers were shot dead.

Only among the carpet and souvenir merchants, who rely on foreign customers for their livelihood, is there a sense of openness, although for many it is a matter of hiding their true feelings for the sake of business. During the initial invasion period, shopkeepers used to greet the Russians with glum faces and invective or demonstrative spitting on the ground. Lacking foreign tourists capable of paying in hard dollars or Deutschmarks, except for a small handful of Western diplomats and UN officials, they now have to deal with what is available. Assuming that all customers are Russian, they gesture to their wares calling: 'Tovaritsch, khorosho, khorosho — Comrade, good, good.'

Afghan soldiers and civil servants who deserted from the government ranks have frequently spoken of Russian, as opposed to Central Asian, disrespect and contempt towards them. The Russians, they say, have also adopted brusque, unfriendly and even racist attitudes. Similar complaints have been voiced by Ethiopians, Angolans and Egyptians who, at one time or another, have dealt with Soviet advisers. 'They treat us like dogs rather than comrades', remarked a disenchanted Khalqi army officer who fled in late 1983. Although Soviet conscripts are in general confined to their camps and do not mingle off duty with the Afghans, they maintain a disparaging attitude towards villagers they have come to save not unlike that of many GIs during the Vietnam war. Judging by the feelings expressed by Soviet defectors and prisoners of war held by the mujahideen, much of this certainly has to do with fear as well as with a general loathing for a country they do not know nor wish to sacrifice their lives for.

3 THE GUERRILLA WAR — A PATCHWORK OF RESISTANCE

'Their vices are revenge, envy, rapacity and obstinacy; on the other hand, they are fond of liberty, kind to their dependants, hospitable, brave, frugal, laborious and prudent.' Mountstuart Elphinstone writing about Afghanistan in the nineteenth century.'

It was like a scene from the Mexican revolution. The unshaven guerrilla commander with the handlebar moustache, a burly man of villainous mien, sat regally on a wicker chair under a huge eucalyptus tree and barked orders at his motley band of followers. Scores of rough but proud Pushtun frontier tribesmen milled around, sporting an array of carbines, shotguns, pistols, assault rifles and grenades with colourful leather cartridge belts slung diagonally across their chests. Two bearded mullahs wearing dark Japanese sunglasses, labels still attached, ruminated in their midst. Outside the sprawling compound's mud-caked walls, a turbaned young partisan, hardly seventeen, crouched intently behind a 1938 Czech-made Bren machine gun, surveying the path that led to the village.

The former Afghan army major, a defector to the resistance in Nangrahar province during the early days of communist rule, was evidently one of those high-spirited tribal chieftains who tolerated peace but thrived on war. Owing allegiance to the Hezb-i-Islami (Younis Khales faction), one of the half dozen Peshawar-based resistance organisations, he was in command of 70 men.

Now and again, one of his lieutenants would venture up to him. The chief, his hands planted firmly on his knees, would listen gravely before bellowing forth yet another command. When British photographer Peter Jouvenal and I first arrived at his camp nearly five months after the invasion, he scrutinised us with flinty suspicion for several long minutes while our guide explained who we were. Without breaking his glare, a glare which suggested that his only joy in life would have been to slit our throats, he leaned forward to fire, quite impressively, a globule of 'Naswah', the Afghan equivalent of snuff or chewing tobacco, some fifteen feet across the compound. Another weighty silence, then he suddenly turned aside and shouted: 'Chai! Tea!'

Immediately, his aides placed seats of honour to his right. 'Welcome', he said, nodding appreciatively in our direction. 'It is good to have journalists. You are our guests.' He spoke in a sparse yet understandable English learned while in the army. We shook hands and exchanged traditional courtesies before sitting down. Then he told us about the military situation. Since the Soviet takeover, he explained, the 'Shouravi' had rolled up with their armoured vehicles to the mouths of the forested side valleys of the Safed Koh mountain range that forms the frontier with Pakistan. The guerrillas lacked sufficient weapons and ammunition to stop them, but harassed them as best they could before withdrawing to the hills. Venturing a wry smile, he added: 'But now we have come down to strike hard at the Russians. We shall make them bleed.' His eyes darting across the compound, he paused to shout another instruction in Pashto. Then he glanced back. 'We shall block the road down there', he said gesturing with his head in the direction of Jalalabad some 25 miles to the north. 'And we shall go on hitting them, even if it takes years, even if every last Afghan is killed, until the Soviets leave our soil.'

Five or six mainly Pushtun partisan groups of different political allegiance operated in this part of the country. Although not necessarily always on the best of terms with each other — shoot-outs between rival groups being sometimes as virulent as their attacks against the communists — they took turns in assaulting the government forces in and around Jalalabad. We had already made arrangements to meet another group, so bidding farewell, we headed next morning with our escorts down from the Safed Koh foothills. Crossing a barren, undulating expanse, we reached one of the low-lying irrigated valleys further to the east that stretch like long, green fingers across the plain towards Jalalabad. The occasional plane or helicopter droned lazily across the horizon in the shimmering heat, and only once did two MIGs come roaring in so low that we had to throw ourselves to the ground. They passed twice directly over our heads, but then thundered off to the battle zones of Surkh Rud in the direction of Kabul.

Almost every tree-lined village in the shallow, river-carved valleys had been badly battered by the security forces. Nevertheless, many inhabitants were still choosing to stay rather than seek refuge in Pakistan only two days' trek away. Twelve months later, however, most had gone. Men and women toiled among the chequered wheat, rice and poppyfields, while children swam with the water buffalo in the murky canals. The guerrillas accompanying us stopped twice at pleasantly shaded gardens along the way to eat fruit and drink tea with other mujahed groups. Some had established their local headquarters in houses belonging to communist supporters, who had fled long since to the comparative safety of the towns. Proudly, they showed off their gradually expanding arsenal of weapons; mainly Enfields, but also a few Russian, Chinese and Egyptian Kalashnikovs, Martini Hernys and the odd heavy machine gun.

Just before dusk, we arrived at 'our' guerrilla compound. It was situated amidst a thick growth of mulberry and tangerine groves. Members of Afghan Millat, a now virtually defunct socialist movement in the resistance, the mujahideen numbered some 40 to 50 young men, many of them high school students from Jalalabad and Kabul. In the cool semi-darkness of a bungalow, they sat on carpets spread on the ground or slept with blankets covering them from head to toe. Rifles and boxes of ammunition lay stacked against the walls or the trees just outside the entrance.

In typical Afghan fashion, they immediately offered us cushions and the best positions on the worn but beautifully woven rugs before serving us with tea, sweets and cakes. Being close to the bazaars of Pakistan and Jalalabad, food seemed to be no problem in these parts. Ulfat, a 25-year-old former student teacher from Laghman province explained that it was not their turn to attack that night, but then conferred with his comrades for several minutes. 'It does not matter', he smiled. 'We go tonight.'

The word spread and the men began preparing their weapons, laughing and chatting loudly. One guerrilla affectionately polished a single grenade, carelessly unscrewing the detonator, cleaning it and then putting it back. For many Afghans during the early days of the Soviet occupation, the grenade had become a mujahed status symbol, like a motorcycle or a watch, rather than a weapon for the field. A sign of the times, however, within months the grenade was replaced by the increasingly available AK-47 Kalashnikov assault rifle. The favourite weapon of guerrillas throughout the world, the 'Kala' rapidly developed into a mark of distinction for the ordinary Afghan fighter. As for the commanders and top-notch combatants, the more modern AK-74 Kalakov, battle-tested for the first time by the Soviets in Afghanistan, became the ultimate prestige symbol.

Attacking the Russians was obviously considered a big lark and no one wanted to miss the fun. As unabashedly vain as ever, many a guerrilla carefully combed his hair or trimmed his beard, intently staring into the small metal mirror of his Naswah box. Their weapons ready, the men first gathered at dusk for prayer in the garden before sitting down for dinner, a simple but sufficient spread of nan, rice pilau with mutton and vegetable gormah. They prayed again before leaving, forming units of between 10 and 15 men each. Little boys, sling shots dangling invariably from their hands, watched curiously and full of admiration as ammunition was carefully counted out and the mujahideen shouldered their guns. Each man carried roughly forty rounds with him. One of the elder boys, perhaps fourteen years old, handed round glasses of water. Not yet a mujahed, his facial expression bespoke a deep yearning for the day when he too could go on a raid. With the quarter moon already high, the guerrillas began slipping out of the compound gateway and into the dark shadows of the village.

Moving in single file through the fields and thick foliage of the fruit orchards, other mujahed groups from the neighbouring villages could be heard making their way down to Jalalabad, some three hours march to the north. Through the trees on the other side of the river, now a mere stream toying its way through the stony riverbed, one could trace their progress by their shouts of 'Allah o Akbar' (God is Great) and the relays of barking dogs. Occasionally, the glimmer of a flashlight would pierce the darkness. Accompanied by choruses of frogs, the men walked fast, jumping over the gurgling irrigation ditches and mudwalls without breaking stride. Over Jalalabad, rockets arched into the night sky, while distant explosions rumbled and growled on the far side. It was an unusually magnificent sight to watch this bizarre, pyrotechnic display against the stark Cimmerian outline of the Hindu Kush beyond.

The moon had set and only a few lights marked the perimeter of the Soviet military camp. In the obscurity, it was practically impossible to distinguish more than a few bare shapes. With heavy fighting further north, the guerrillas quietly positioned themselves in the ditches of nearby abandoned wheat fields. Subsequent to the big Soviet sweep into Kunar at the end of February, the region had been reasonably quiet for several months. But once the battered guerrilla forces had regrouped, fighting began anew.

With cries of 'Allah o Akbar' over a megaphone, the mujahideen, by now strung out in a long line across the fields, suddenly opened fire. Tracers streaming like red lace through the night, they fired indiscrimintely into the installation. A Soviet watchtower immediately played a powerful searchlight in our direction, while a single Russian machine gun barked intermittent bursts. There was no counter-assault. The Soviets knew better than to leave the security of their base. Besides, they seemed more concerned by the fighting on the northern side of the town. Barely a few hundred yards ahead, the engine of a heavy tank started up. Abruptly flicking on its headlamps, it outlined the cumbersome shapes of half a dozen other tanks entrenched like squatting toads just outside the wire. The vehicle began rumbling toward the guerrillas, but then veered off to the left and headed for the city where heavier explosions beckoned. The mujahed attack lasted less than half an hour. As an example of modern guerrilla warfare it was not very effective. It seemed doubtful that the Afghans had killed or wounded any Soviets. Nevertheless, their harassment had served a definite psychological purpose. It was this sort of nocturnal action that seemed to contribute towards shattering the nerves of young Soviet conscripts, who were helpless to do anything against the firing and defiant shouts of unseen tribesmen beyond the perimeter rim. It was also important for resistance morale. On the way back, the partisans seemed pleased that once again they had tweaked the noses of their hated occupiers.

While the night belonged to the guerrillas, the day was given over to the frustrations of the Soviets. Shortly after dawn, they emerged from their well-fortified lairs. Firing as they went, six tanks lumbered up the valley toward the resistance positions. Two shells fell within a hundred yards of the compound, but the Afghans, who had no anti-tank guns or rocket launchers to fight back, had already hidden their weapons and ammunition and were walking or running in small groups toward the foothills. The Soviets, who never left the safety of their vehicles, justified their sweep by destroying a few buildings and bulldozing the irrigation canals. By late afternoon, the guerrillas were back in their compounds.

From Untrained Rabble to Formidable Fighting Force

Nationwide resistance did not happen overnight. Essentially, it took both the brute repression of the Taraki and Amin regimes and later the Soviet invasion to move the country's tribesmen, farmers, nomads, shop-keepers, clerics, students and soldiers into opposition. With Islam the binding factor, resistance rapidly assumed the characteristics of a holy war of national liberation, the Jihad.

For the conservative peasantry, the backbone of Afghan society, opposition to the communists was initially a vehement refutation of the ruthless policies practised by a highly insensitive and anti-religious government. The urban elite, on the other hand, regarded it more as a struggle for civil liberties, while the southern Pushtun tribes, among whom the mullahs have only limited influence, responded primarily to infringement of the Pushtunwali, the tribal code of honour. When the communists killed Daoud and members of his family in 1978, many Pushtuns felt that this act of blood could only be answered with blood; the spread of government terror further spurred their duty of revenge. But it was the arrival of Soviet troops on Afghan soil that abruptly transformed the nation's civil conflict into an all-out war against a foreign invader. With national pride and independence at stake, it was no longer a matter of simply opposing a despised government of communist surrogates. It was a question of defending the homeland against a horde of infidels from the north.

During the early stages of this 'people's war', most mujahed groups had yet to come to grips with the true and ruthless nature of the Soviet occupation. Only a smattering of well-led partisan 'fronts' understood the concept of opposing an ideologically inspired adversary with a mighty military and political machine at its disposal. Still fondly recalling the wild exploits of their fathers and grandfathers during 'romantic' frontier skirmishes with the British, they soon came to realise that fighting the Russians was a different form of Shikar. With basic survival at stake, traditional gung-ho tactics no longer found a place against an invader capable of inflicting merciless devastation on Afghan territory.

While the resistance still suffers from considerable, often debilitating, handicaps, it has gone through a major transformation.

The Guerrilla Patchwork

What started out as a disorganised untrained rabble of turbaned fighters using old-fasioned methods and weapons has developed in places into a formidable partisan force. The mujahideen are certainly better armed today than during the first few years and are now applying tactics more consistent with modern guerrilla warfare. To be sure, they have far to go before they can hope to attain the organisational and combat dexterity of the Viet Cong. The Vietnamese had more than 40 years to improve on such skills. Similarly, the Afghans could learn a great deal from the experiences of the National Liberation Front during the Algerian war of independence. Nevertheless, for a primarily non-literate peasant resistance with only a narrow intellectual base, it has proved to be a great deal more obstinate, and stalwart, than the Russians, or for that matter the world, expected.

It is impossible to make an accurate estimate of how many full-time regular armed guerrilla fighters are involved in the war. Their number fluctuates from season to season. Figures between 80,000 and

150,000 have been suggested by various observers. These do not include the hundreds of thousands of civilians, many of them refugees in Pakistan and Iran, who often double up as partisans. Lacking a single umbrella orgaisation like the PLO, the Afghan resistance has generally developed into two principal, but complementary formations: the political parties-in-exile and the so-called 'resistance of the interior'.

Basically, the movement consists of a broad patchwork of guerrilla fronts, perhaps as many as 300, of varying effectiveness, operating throughout the 28 provinces. Some of the fronts are directly run by the parties. But the great majority are led by local commanders who maintain pragmatic and extremely flexible ties with the six Sunni, and mainly Pushtun-dominated, parties (plus several smaller factions) in Peshawar. In return for guns, ammunition and other forms of logistical backing as well as international representation, the fronts provide the parties with political allegiance.

A few, such as the Mongolian-featured Hazara Shiites of central Afghanistan, have resented the continuation of Pushtun dominance in the resistance and have consistently refused to throw in their lot with the Peshawar parties. Instead, they have turned to Iran for help and inspiration, or have relied on their own resources. Ethnic or tribal composition tends to dictate the make-up of each local guerrilla front. Slightly under half of the fronts are based on tribal structure, operating out of mainly Pushtun areas; the others are spread among the Tadjik, Hazara, Turkmen, Uzbek and other ethnic groups. Some incorporate cross-sections of Afghan society. Tadjik commander Zabiullah (killed late 1984) from Mazar-i-Sharif includes Uzbeks, Turkmen and Pushtuns in his entourage, while political groups such as Mohammadi's Harakat or Mujadeddi's National Front command a tribally-dominated ethnic mix.

While the Peshawar groups have managed to glean most of the world's limited attention, their influence over what is happening inside Afghanistan has greatly diminished since the end of 1980. To an extent, by virtue of their own physical isolation, some of the politicians have lost touch with their homeland constituencies. More to the point, their constant bickering, their corruption, their inability to form a genuine common front and the fact that they have chosen to pursue their struggle from outside the country have alienated many Afghans.

Although the parties still command extensive sway, particularly among the refugees, and control the purse strings of most fronts, it is the 'resistance of the interior' which has begun to emerge as the new guiding force. Since 1981, rising impatience with the parties' failure properly to represent the interests of the interior has led many Afghans to look elsewhere for leadership. Over the past few years, partisan commanders, many of them in their twenties and thirties and well acquainted with the art of modern guerrilla warfare, have distinguished themselves in their respective regions as the new young bloods of the mujahideen. In close contact with the local populations and enduring the same hardships, they include Ahmad Shah Massoud of the Panjshair Valley, Mohammad Amin Wardak of Wardak, Zabiullah from Mazar-i-Sharif, Ismail Khan of Herat, Abdul Haq from the Kabul area and Sayed 'Djendral' Hussein from Ghazni. Most have established their reputations through merit rather than traditional lineage.

Some are visibly Islamic, thus appealing to the more traditionalist and religious elements in the population. Yet they remain highly politicised and modernist in outlook. Modern technology is not rejected; they reject what they consider to be the negative aspects of Eastern and Western society. While some of the older generation would prefer to see the clock put back, a striking number of 'grey beards' have realised that the present war is a young man's struggle and have been content to let this new and, on the whole, educated generation take charge.

Not surprisingly, these commanders pose a serious threat to the continued dominance of the exiled parties. Although none has so far gained national authority, they have begun laying the foundations for a truly national resistance. By establishing field alliances which do not reflect the intrigues of Peshawar and by gradually adapting their organisations more realistically to present-day conditions, they have been giving the resistance a much-needed sense of direction in a war that promises to drag on for years. It seems quite probable that if a real overall leader is to emerge, he will come from the guerrilla ranks rather than from among the politicians in Peshawar.

The Parties

Since the invasion, the main Peshawar parties have split into two alliances, both calling themselves the 'Islamic Unity of Afghan Mujahideen'. Separately, they are known as the 'fundamentalists' and the 'moderates'. Organised along military and political lines, they have developed more or less around the personalities of their leaders, whose names Afghans often use when referring to the groups. Although all the parties have political platforms, their main differences result from personality clashes. A non-aligned Afghanistan, open to both East and West, is the commonly expressed desire of most Afghans. At present, the fundamentalists and moderates are split over whether a new Afghanistan should be an Islamic republic, a lay democratic republic or a constitutional monarchy. The fundamentalists are themselves at odds as to whether they want a progressive Islamic republic or one as radical as Ayatollah Khomeini's Iran.

The three main fundamentalist groups are all splinter factions of the Jawana-i-Musalman (Militant Muslim Youth) which developed during the 1960s (parallel to the creation of the PDPA). They include the Jamiat-i-Islami (Islamic Society) led by Professor Burhanudin Rabbani, the Hezb-i-Islami (Islamic Party — Younis Khales faction) and the Hezb-i-Islami (Islamic Party — Gulbuddin Hekmatyar faction). A fourth party, led by Abdoul Rasoul Sayaf, has attained a certain influence over the past few years due to his ability to garner funds from Arab countries and bankroll guerrilla groups inside the country rather than through any particular acumen.

The moderates, also three groups, were formed in the wake of the 1978 *coup d'état*. They are the Mahaz-e melli-ye Islami (National Islamic Front) headed by Sayed Ahmad Gaylani, the Jebhe-ye melli-te Najat-e Afghanistan (National Front for the Salvation of Afghanistan) led by Sibghatullah Mujaddedi, and the Harakat-e enquelab-e Islami (Movement for the Islamic Revolution) of Maulawi Mohammed Nabi.

Although a small number of Hazaras have joined the Peshawar parties, the situation among this mainly Shiite ethnic group has developed in a manner almost totally different from the rest of the country. Reputedly descended from Genghis Khan, the Dari-speaking Hazaras have been for centuries the underdogs of Afghan society. In Kabul and other cities, it is normally the Hazara who performs the menial job. Ironically, the communist takeover has allowed them to take their 'historic revenge' by asserting their own ethnic and religious identity. In many respects, the Hazarajat, an incredibly poor region of arid mountains and plains, has become a separate national entity, a state within a state, isolated from both the Kabul government and the Sunni resistance organisations.

At least three main Shiite groups (all based inside Afghanistan but with offices in Iran and Quetta, Pakistan) have emerged. The traditionalist Shura-ye Ettefagh (Council of the Union), for a long time the largest political grouping, consists of both moderate and fundamentalist elements. Dominated by the mullahs and the Sayeds (descendants of the Prophet Mohammad), it was formed in the summer of 1979 and is presided over by Sayed Ali Beheshti, a regional spiritual leader. Although mainly Hazara, the Shura includes a few Uzbek and Tadjik delegates.

Since 1982, however, Khomeinist groups backed by Tehran, such as the radically Islamic Nasr (Victory) party, began to clash militarily with the Shura. With the Khomeinists able to furnish followers with weapons, training and funds, they quickly expanded their influence in the Hazarajat and among the Hazara enclaves in the northern provinces. By 1984, roughly two-thirds of the region was under Khomeinist control.

Although the Nasr still remains a force to be reckoned with, most Iranian backing is now directed towards the more powerful Afghan Islamic Revolutionary party, the Sepah-e-Pasdara. Created in late 1982 and modelled along the lines of Tehran's own Revolutionary Guards (Pasdaran), who directly control the Afghan branch, its followers are trained and armed in Iran before being dispatched to Afghanistan. Much of the Hazarajat's conservative population remains indifferent to the dogmatic and sectarian ideology of the Khomeinists, but foreign observers in the region report that the groups appear to have no trouble in recruiting followers among Hazara migrants in Iran.

The third organisation, the Harakat-e Islami, which commands considerable support in the Kandahar and Mazar-i-Sharif regions and parts of the Hazarajat, acts as an alternative to the Shura and the Khomeinists.

Although it was to the major political parties that most mujahideen turned for support, numerous independent and minor parties, some of them specialising in urban guerrilla warfare, others in relief operations both inside and outside the country, sprang up before and after the invasion. One of them, the Jabha Mobarezin, which was behind the Bala Hissar revolt in 1979, the first attempt of the resistance at a nationwide uprising, was founded nine months before the Soviet intervention and combined six Islamic organisations and one left-wing group. Another, the Jabha Motahed e Melli (National United Front) included several traditionalist groupings as well as the highly effective SAMA (Sazman-e Azadibakch-e Mardom-e Afghanistan — Organisation for the Liberation of the Afghan People), itself an urban resistance movement composed of five different factions. Mjaid Kalakani, its founder, was arrested in Kabul in late February, 1980 and held in the basement of the Soviet embassy, where he was later murdered. So successful had the front become at carrying out partisan operations that the communists feared he would be sprung; the Soviet embassy was felt to be the only secure location in the capital. Several years into the occupation, some of these groups have disappeared, merged with the larger, politically affiliated fronts or, in a few cases, have joined the government.

Resistance Capabilities

Resistance in early 1980 was still broadly scattered and unco-ordinated. Local guerrilla fronts often demonstrated their own peculiar characteristics and performed with varying effectiveness. In part, this was, and still is due to the overwhelming geophysical isolation of many regions, different tribal or ethnic traditions, and poor communications. As a result, conditions and morale vary from province to province, valley to valley and even village to village. With their deeply engrained tribal structures, the southern Pushtuns have appeared generally less flexible in developing new guerrilla tactics than their Tadjik or Hazara brethren. Notwithstanding their legendary fierce courage, they have proved far less adaptable to changing circumstances.

In the face of tanks, helicopter gunships and MIGs, the guerrillas were also pitifully armed. Only one fighter in ten could boast a proper weapon; an Enfield .303 perhaps, or, if he was lucky, an AK-47 automatic assault rifle. All that the rest could rely on was a collector's arsenal of weapons better suited to a museum. When the Sirdar of Ghazni declared Jihad against the Russians on Christmas Day, 1979, for example, his principal means of defence was an 1895 Belgian rifle. And even if they had the weapons, they lacked the ammunition.

Although the mujahideen had been able to augment their weaponry considerably prior to the invasion through Afghan army defectors, captured materiel or purchases from the arms bazaars in Pakistan, this was hardly enough to fight what had now become a fully-fledged war. Guerrilla capability therefore crucially depended on the quality of local leadership. As the war progressed, it was also a matter of adopting new improved fighting techniques, ensuring regular logistical support and cultivating good relations with the local population. Some commanders rapidly turned their men into smoothly organised and combat-effective resistance formations, while others have developed little or have remained, on the whole, incompetent.

Tactics

Since the invasion, the mujahideen have managed to retain their hold over more than 85 per cent of the country despite repeated communist attempts to dislodge them. Nevertheless, they can still do little to halt the security forces from taking temporary control of their villages and valleys. They are also unable to occupy most of the provincial capitals. Only for short periods have they taken over major urban centres such as Kandahar and then usually at the risk of massive Soviet retaliation. As those practising classic guerrilla strategy recognise, the holding of a town can prove a serious liability.

Despite strict government security, foreign observers touring with the guerrillas have been impressed by the comparative ease with which partisan units often manage to penetrate urban areas. Resistance groups now regularly carry out daring daylight raids ranging from kidnappings (including Soviet personnel) to bombings and hit-and-run assassinations. One French photographer visiting northern Afghanistan in late 1982 witnessed the takeover of the main mosque in Mazar-i-Sharif where the mujahideen used the building's loudspeaker system to broadcast to the local population. When the authorities sent in tanks, the mujahideen destroyed one of the vehicles with an RPG-7 grenade launcher, forcing the communists to withdraw to a safe distance while the guerrillas completed their anti-Soviet litany.

Many mujahed fronts have concentrated on ambushes, the mining of roads, assassinations, rocket attacks against government positions, the beleaguring of towns and general harassment. Hiding among the rocks of narrow gorges or operating only at night, they are virtually impossible to detect by Soviet reconnaissance. Afghan party officials have been shot or stabbed in the streets, while houses belonging to communist collaborators in the rural areas have been destroyed or taken over by the resistance.

Increasingly, mujahideen operating in small but well-trained groups are specialising in urban guerrilla warfare as the most effective way of bringing the war home to the occupation forces. Western visitors to Kabul in the summer of 1984 referred to the capital as a 'city under siege' with repeated firing during the day on the outskirts, while the sound of distant mortars or the sight of rockets streaking across the sky were regular features at night.

Government supply trucks can only travel in convoy, sandwiched between armoured vehicles at either end while helicopters patrol incessantly overhead. But even such precautions cannot protect them from attack. Laying ambushes in narrow gorges, the guerrillas hit the first and last vehicle and then knock off the rest at their leisure, or at least until the planes come in. During the spring 1984 Soviet offensives against the Panjshair and other areas, mujahideen blocked the Salang Highway for days on end at different points stretching from Kabul to the Soviet border, by destroying entire convoys and blowing up bridges.

The occupying forces are forced to transport much of their equipment and supplies by air. Already in the early days of the war, they proved incapable of keeping open the main highway from Kunduz to the northern Badakshan city of Faizabad. When the towns of Khost and Urgun in the south came under heavy guerrilla siege throughout much of 1983, Soviet aircraft were obliged to resupply and strengthen the local garrisons, at one point even ferrying in some 4,000 Afghan troops by helicopter. Toward the end of December, the guerrillas closed in on Urgun, capturing the airstrip and taking a number of Afghan and Soviet troops prisoner. In order to prevent both a military and a psychological debacle, the Russians immediately brought in massive reinforcements and through armoured groundsweeps and heavy aerial bombardments succeeded in driving the insurgents away from both towns.

Hit-and-Run Attacks

Lacking a coordinated central command, the resistance has never had a grand anti-Soviet strategy. Nor is it capable of launching any major regional offensives. Swaggering tribal chiefs have often boasted that they would soon march on Kabul, but large-scale anti-Soviet operations would be only an open invitation to suicide, with huge concentrations of mujahideen an easy target for helicopter gunships and MIGs. Only three months before the invasion, one Western intelligence officer in Kabul told me that when large concentrations of rebels and mutinous troops tried to give the government a 'whiff of the old Jihad', they quickly got a bloody taste of cannon fire and napalm from the air.

Armed opposition has therefore consisted primarily of localised actions. Yet there is a gradual trend toward more regional co-ordination in many areas. While groups still react more often than not according to self-interest, the incidents of mujahideen from neighbouring regions rushing in to help besieged guerrilla fronts are increasing. So are joint assaults involving several different fronts at a time. Such co-ordinated strategy enables the mujahideen not only to attack from different flanks, but also to intercept government reinforcements or to sever communication links.

As astute guerrilla commanders are realising, better organisation and field co-operation and more imaginative tactics remain vital if the mujahideen are to succeed in prosecuting a sustained war of liberation. For the moment, small highly mobile hit teams, usually of ten to twenty men, seem the best response to the military occupation. As with any guerrilla war, natural environment such as a partiuclar terrain or a sympathetic indigenous population is a major advantage. This has been exploited with varying effectiveness.

But even the environment can change. Guerrillas can be flushed from hideouts where they were once secure by specialised heliborne troops, protective cover (walls or trees) can be bulldozed along the highways or villages can be destroyed and the inhabitants forced to leave. For the Kremlin, resistance control of rural areas is not necessarily a drawback; as far as it is concerned, all that matters is the security of the towns and highways.

In order to achieve this, the communists have been prepared to sacrifice troops in ploys designed to keep local guerrillas occupied well away from the zones that really count. In certain areas, they have deliberately maintained fortified outposts (manned by Afghan toops or militia, perhaps with one or two Soviet advisers) well away from the towns and in locations of no military importance whatsoever. If the garrison is wiped out or defects, it is replaced by another. This strategy has begun to falter, however, as partisan fronts concentrate their efforts on strategically important targets such as air bases, ammunition depots and urban installations.

Non-aggression Pacts

In what has proved to be a two-edged sword, the guerrillas have effectively neutralised some of these forts by arranging mutual non-aggression pacts with the local government forces. Apart from ordinary conscripts, these are often militiamen sympathetic to the resistance but who pledge allegiance to the authorities in return for high salaries and weapons. In early 1982, I came across no fewer than three Afghan forts with which the mujahideen had come to an understanding. Outside one of the garrisons, manned by 15-20 men, a group of bored conscripts were kicking an empty can about. We met several soldiers hauling water from a nearby desert well. We shook hands and they watched as dozens of guerrillas marched by, leading strings of pack horses loaded with arms, ammunition and other supplies.

The guerrillas have also sought to make deals with local communist administrations in an attempt to thwart Soviet influence. Government representatives are offered safe-conduct passes in return for information or guides through mine-fields protecting military installations.

The growing practice of guerrilla-government co-operation is viewed with unease by certain resistance commanders. In many cases, non-aggression pacts can result in a virtual cessation of hostilities between the two sides, leading local mujahideen to believe that they are now in 'control' of the area. The Soviets are the ones who benefit. The expansion of non-combat areas, particularly around the towns, allows the government to introduce economic projects or to fill the shops with goods in a bid to win over the population, or at least to keep them out of the war.

The better organised mujahed fronts are now trying to discourage such 'understandings'. At the same time, the regime has shown itself unable to protect its supporters who have come under pressure. In August, 1984, commander Abdul Haq issued an ultimatum to one such militia leader with a long-standing relationship with the resistance by demanding that he choose sides. Hassan Khan Karokhel, an extremely influential tribal chief from Sarobi, who was responsible for guarding the hydroelectric pylons supplying the capital in return for money and arms, protested but eventually gave way to guerrilla pressure and left for Pakistan with 300 families in tow. Shortly afterwards, the pylons were destroyed, causing severe blackouts in Kabul.

But even guerrilla leaders critical of accommodation with the government argue that it is justifiable if legitimate resistance interests are served. A highly controversial truce was concluded between the Panjshair's Massoud and the Soviet forces in January, 1983, which, although initially condemned by other mujahed groups as a sell-out, did in fact benefit the northern guerrillas by allowing them to consolidate their forces, re-stock with supplies and provide the local population with a breather to cultivate their fields.

Infiltrating the Government

Of significant advantage to the mujahideen is resistance penetration of the Afghan army and government. Collaborators are normally people genuinely sympathetic to the anti-Soviet cause, but there are others who are simply hedging their bets by playing both sides. Government officials and military officers are often asked not to defect because of their value as informers. Remaining with the government also permits an official to continue receiving his salary, thus relieving the resistance of the cost of having to support the man's family.

Furthermore, resistance taxes levied on government salaries also help foot the cost of the fighting. Some resistance 'moles' are Parchamis or Khalqis, who are manipulating the guerrillas in order to get at political rivals within the communist fold. Party members or militiamen will often help the resistance with weapons and ammunition for the urban guerrilla fronts in the knowledge that their Khalqi or Parcham counterparts will suffer. To the irritation of the occupation forces, resistance fronts are usually informed well in advance of planned anti-insurgent operations, even the most secret ones.

The Russians have grown wise to such leaks. Nevertheless, their efforts to involve Afghan forces, whenever and wherever possible, have ensured continued security lapses. In the northern provinces, they have sought to remedy this by flying in missions from bases inside the USSR. They have withheld details of planned anti-insurgent operations from Afghan officers until the last moment. In some cases, they have deliberately announced military operations and then changed them at the last minute.

The KGB, which became increasingly active in Afghanistan during the third year of the occupation, has often twisted these inside reports to its own advantage as part of its psychological warfare against the population. French photographer and traveller Alain Guillo, who has toured parts of Afghanistan regularly since the invasion, reported that on at least two occasions in the late summer of 1982 the resistance evacuated villages in Balkh province at night after normally reliable intelligence reports warned them of an impending attack. Nothing happened. 'But it was still traumatic', he said. 'One can well imagine the effect when men, women and children have to flee to safety under cover of darkness. When this happens two or three times, it starts to play on one's nerves.'

Resistance commanders, who have relied in the past on government sources for much of their intelligence information expect the situation to change gradually in favour of the Soviets. With the return in 1984 of the first of an initial batch of 10,000 young Afghan men and women sent to the USSR for training and indoctrination, key army and administrative posts will be filled by a new generation of pro-Soviet cadres, making it more difficult for the resistance to recruit sympathisers.

The 'Jihad' Trail

The vast network of infiltration routes, the Ho Chi Minh trails of the mujahideen, connecting Pakistan with the Afghan interior, are crucial to the resistance. Dubbed more appropriately the 'Jihad Trail,' a significant portion of guerrilla supplies, ranging from guns and ammunition to medicines, are brought in by horse, camel and mule trains across the more than 300 traditional caravan routes and goat tracks that lace the mountainous frontier between the two countries. With the rise of modern road traffic during the 1950s and 1960s, many of these caravan routes had fallen into disuse except by tribal nomads and smugglers. In the wake of the communist revolution, they rapidly reverted to their former use, except this time mainly by refugees and mujahideen.

The striking efficiency of this system, which also includes regular bus, jeep and truck services in the southern and western desert regions, is due essentially to the Afghan spirit of free enterprise. Although the mujahideen organise their own supplies, Afghan merchants provide the transport, charging the guerrillas for every pound of materiel carried. At the same time, both ordinary commercial traffic and smuggling continue despite the ravages of war; timber, semi-precious stones, dried fruits, meat and opium from Afghanistan to Pakistan, and clothes, weapons, wheat, farm utensils and radios on the return trip.

With the resurrection of the ancient caravan routes, there arrived another Afghan institution: the chaikhana, or teahouse. Serving as hotels, bazaars and sometimes local party headquarters, these dried mud and wood establishments have come to replace facilities normally provided by villagers whose homes and shops have been progressively destroyed by the government forces. For a small sum, paid to the innkeeper either in Pakistani rupees or Afghanis, the travelling mujahed can drink tea from steaming samovars and eat a meal, usually 'nan' dipped in a greasy meat and vegetable broth, before rolling up in his patou to sleep. In some parts, groups of chaikhaneh have sprung up in the middle of nowhere with individual merchants selling chewing gum, biscuits, sweets, cigarettes (Pakistani and American brands) and even Coca Cola.

Nevertheless, Soviet ambushes and the occupation of certain vital mountain passes have made travelling to the interior far more hazardous than during the early stages of the war, and have forced the Afghans to find new, and often more difficult, routes. This has caused transportation prices to rise dramatically, costing three or four times more in 1984 than in 1981. As a result, it is usually cheaper for local populations to seek their supplies in the bazaars of Kabul and other government controlled towns.

Weaponry and Training

Overall, the resistance remains a highly motivated force and since 1981 its strike capabilities have improved significantly. Although the mujahideen no longer seem to lack small arms, they are still severely hampered by insufficient weapons of quality, poor training and an obvious shortage of basic communication facilities. They are a far cry from enjoying the impressive arsenals habitually used by the PLO or the rebels in Eritrea and Angola. Even the anti-government guerrillas in El Salvador appeared better equipped in 1984 than most Afghans.

Heavy DShK 'dashaka' machine guns, 82mm mortars, grenade launchers, AK-47s and 74s, recoilless rifles and mines have all become standard weapons among the better equipped front-line units. West German-designed G-3s from the arms bazaars of Pakistan or brought in from Iran are also very popular among guerrilla commanders. Some resistance groups have managed to seize the occasional 76mm mountain howitzer and 122 mm field gun, while small numbers of SAM-7 missiles have begun to appear in the field. Nevertheless, the traditional British-style .303 Enfield, a good rifle in itself, remains the staple weapon of the part-time fighter.

Resistance commanders constantly complain that they simply do not possess the necessary weapons, such as the British-made BLOW-PIPE, to protect themselves and the civilian populations from devastating communist air assaults. Few fronts, however, possess the necessary expertise to operate such sophisticated weapons. Although ordinary anti-aircraft guns have helped establish relatively effective barrages to Soviet attack in mountainous areas, guerrillas operating in flat terrain with little or no cover continue to face a serious threat.

Visiting the stony broad plains of Logar province in April, 1982, British journalist John Fullerton reported that the mujahideen were quite unable to repel a Soviet armoured and helicopter assault against Mizgul, a cluster of villages south of Kabul. Taking cover with some 120 mujahideen in a large storm-water drain running beneath the road, he wrote:

In pitch darkness, the guerrillas prayed for survival as the tunnel shook under the impact of rockets from the helicopters and the weight of tank tracks grinding overhead. Machine-gun fire, the flat boom of supporting fire from a T-54 tank and the unmistakable sound — rather like the tear of cloth — of helicopter Gatling guns continued for some three hours.

Although Western observers have noted a marked increase in anti-aircraft weapons, which have obliged the security forces to be more cautious in their anti-insurgency operations, many guerrilla fronts still have only meagre means at their disposal. 'If we could deal with their helicopter gunships, the whole spectrum of war would change', asserted Col. Abdul Rahim Wardak, deputy supreme military commander of the moderate Islamic Unity.

Arms from Abroad

Arms captured from the security forces or brought in by defectors represent a major supply source for the internal fronts. By August, 1980, the Russians had taken away anti-tank and anti-aircraft guns from all but the most reliable Afghan troops because of the abundance of army stock that was falling into the hands of the partisans. The fact, too, that AK-74 Kalakov assault rifles, carried only by Red army soldiers, are increasingly common among the mujahideen demonstrates in part their ability to capture weapons from the Russians themselves.

Outside assistance remains vital, however, if the resistance is to survive. So far, the appropriate weaponry and, equally important, training to maintain a sustained guerrilla war have yet to be forthcoming. Substantial quantities of mainly small arms, mines and ammunition have indeed come in via Pakistan from various outside backers, notably Saudi Arabia, the Gulf countries, China and the United States. some weapons, destined primarily for the Khomeinist Shiite groups, enter Afghanistan from Iran.

While travelling through Paghman province in late May, 1982, I came across veritable traffic jams of weapons' caravans of Uzbeks and Takjiks weaving their way through the Kohistan mountains, only three or four minutes flying time from Bagram airbase, to Kunduz and Takhar provinces to the north. Dispersed among their horses, donkeys and mules were RPG-7 grenade launchers, 82mm recoilless rifles, 82mm mortars three or four ZPU-2 anti-aircraft guns, mines and boxes of ammunition. Again in the summer of 1984, I encountered several weapons caravans passing through Nuristan to the northern areas.

Most of these appeared to be of Chinese origin, although some of the arms, notably M-1 carbines made in the United States and Canada during World War II, could have come from literally anywhere in the world, as more than 3.5 million were produced by 1945 and are still in use in many Third World states. Overall, cross-border seepage of heavy weapons has remained sporadic. Ammunition, too, tends to be in short supply. Guerrilla units, for example, often have only a handful of mortar rounds at their disposal, perhaps seven or eight, hardly enough for a proper attack, considering that it takes at least three to aim properly.

Observers who have travelled to the interior question claims by US officials that the Central Intelligence Agency (CIA) is running a highly effective and 'daring' military assistance programme to the resistance, estimated at $325 million in early 1984. It is widely held that such executive leaks concerning CIA activities were part of a general disinformation effort by the Reagan Administration to conceal lack of impact. There seems little doubt that a considerable portion of the military aid making its way into Afghanistan has been procured by American help, but many of these arms tend to be of poor quality or insufficient quantity. CIA funds have been directed towards purchasing mainly Soviet-type weapons and ammunition, much of it from Egyptian military stocks provided by the Russians during the 1960s, as well as from the Chinese. But the method of distribution remains a faulty one.

In theory, the weapons are passed on to the Pakistanis for distribution to the Afghans. Pakistan's military intelligence keeps close track of arms movements through its vast network of informers and by recording all weapons entering Afghanistan through frontier posts. But the Islamabad government, which is obviously reluctant to stick its neck out without firm guarantees from the United States (which Washington has no intention of giving) has been reluctant to act too openly as an arms conduit, for fear of Soviet retaliation.

Accordingly, the Pakistan government has prevented too many heavy or sophisticated weapons from slipping through. Pakistani officials, with the connivance of certain Afghan 'resistance' circles, have helped themselves to the shipments, allowing brand-new Kalashnikovs to be replaced by old Chinese-made Pakistan army issue rifles. Crates of new combat boots leaving the port of Karachi arrive at their destination in the form of second-hand rejects. Machine guns simply disappear en route to reappear for sale in the weapons bazaars.

Since the assassination of President Anwar Sadat in October, 1981, the moderate parties claim that their arms deliveries from Egypt have virtually dried up. Only the fundamentalist organisations (and even they complain) are still receiving regular supplies from Saudi Arabia, the Gulf countries and Libya. Arms from China, and more recently, North Korea have filtered through in considerable quantities, but, once again, the Pakistanis 'regulate' deliveries.

Even those weapons that eventually find their way to the resistance fronts are not necessarily free. Mujahideen from the interior are often obliged to pay for their weapons in cash either to the political parties on on the open arms market in the Northwest Frontier tribal areas. All this has prompted rising demands for direct aid to the interior rather than its passing through the hands of so many intermediaries. As a result, certain Western interest groups have been investigating ways of avoiding both the Pakistan authorities and the Peshawar groups.

Of course, all this has furnished the Russians with fuel for propaganda. In Kabul, the regime has established a permanent exhibition of arms allegedly captured from the guerrillas to prove that 'imperialist' China and America are responsible for directing the 'counter-revolution.

Although the mujahideen have generally improved their fighting skills, they still lack proper military training. In particular, many lack the ability to employ improved tactics and the expertise to handle sophisticated weapons like anti-aircraft missiles and even ordinary mortars. Well-trained military cadres acquainted with the art of modern guerrilla warfare are a hard commodity to come by. Only a few fronts such as Massoud's Panjshairis or Ismail Khan's Herat movement can offer anything that remotely compares with the rigorous training and strict discipline found among UNITA guerrillas in Angola. Some military analysts believe that proper instruction in modern guerrilla warfare would be more effective than trying to bring in more weapons.

Despite communist claims that Pakistan is running 'hundreds' of mujahed military camps on its side of the border, this is far from the truth. No more than a smattering of party-run instruction centres, operated by former Afghan army officers or sympathetic Pakistanis, have been established in the frontier tribal zones. The quality of instruction, however, is considered inadequate.

The fact that numerous conscripts have defected to the resistance has not necessarily reflected a significant improvement in resistance combat quality. Most have undergone only superficial military training, in view of government efforts to send them to the 'front' as soon as possible. Some conscripts are given no training whatsoever. As for army officers, some guerrilla commanders, particularly those in the tribal areas, have refused to incorporate newcomers with military skills for fear of communist infiltration or losing face in front of their men. Other ethnic groups, such as the Tadjiks and the Hazaras, are prepared to judge newcomers on their merits; anyone bringing along better military skills, and who can be trusted not to be a government informer, is more than welcome.

4 THE RESISTANCE FRONTS

'Do you think you are going to win?'
'Yes, yes of course.'
'What makes you think so? What makes you think you are
going to win?'
'I believe we are going to win. It's evident!'
(Panjshairi commander Ahmad Shah Massoud in an interview
from the French prize-winning documentary film 'Valley
against an Empire' by Jerome Bony and Christophe de
Ponfilly, summer, 1981).

Guerrilla activity in the eastern and southeastern Pushtun areas has
depended on the whole, on two types of fronts: tribal and political.

Unlike the non-tribal Tadjik regions in the north, where the influence of a single commander can extend well beyond traditional bound-
aries, tribal fronts are regulated in size by tradition and clan loyalties.
All social and economic aspects of life, including the notorious blood
feuds that have dragged on for decades, if not centuries, in some parts,
are strictly governed by the unwritten codes of the 'Pushtunwali'. As
one Afghan scholar has observed, this 'regulated anarchy' has been the
weakness and the strength of the Pushtuns. For generations, they have
sought to maintain loose, and if possible, distant ties with the Kabul
central administration. The weaker the government, the better, has been
the general attitude. Even though almost all of Afghanistan's kings (and
later presidents) have been themselves Pushtun, they have always been
regarded as a 'chief among chiefs'.

Clan or village chiefs usually lead the traditional tribal fronts – in
effect, militias originally established to defend local territory. Not
unlike their mass response to the British during the nineteenth-century
Afghan campaigns, tribesmen often get together for Jirghas (assemblies) to coordinate operations. With organisation and discipline inte-
grated within the tribal structure, it is a matter of honour that each
family sends at least one son to fight. In the event of an emergency,
however, the clans can easily mobilise all menfolk able to hold a gun.

To an extent, tribally-organised fronts are in danger of being overtaken by events. More often than not, traditional chiefs have little idea
of modern guerrilla warfare and have shown few signs of learning. For
many, too, it is not only a matter of obtaining better weapons, but also

69

of learning how to use properly the ones they already have. In one incident, Pushtun tribesmen tried to shell a military outpost with mortars. The only problem was that they had forgotten to remove the firing pins. When this was pointed out by an outsider, the commander at first refused to acknowledge that he had made a mistake and continued to fire several more rounds in the same manner. Only then did he finally, and grudgingly, agree to the suggestion.

The politically-led fronts, on the other hand, have emerged as far more effective, with some producing outstanding commanders and fighting units. As with similar (non-Pushtun) politically-run groups, they have greater freedom to operate over large areas. The tribals rarely, if ever, leave their home territories, but they have the advantage of knowing their surroundings well and commanding food sources close at hand, even though many are now operating in 'empty' areas with their families in Pakistan. Since the invasion, the political organisations have adapted themselves with varying success to the tribal system in order to expand their own influence. One of the Pushtun political organisations to have made considerable headway is Younis Khales' Hezb-i-Islami. Apart from being a member of the strong Pushtun Zadran tribe, Khales has succeeded in cultivating a number of skilful and intelligent field commanders. In the autumn of 1982, however, his forces suffered a severe blow when Abdul Halim, a leading 26-year-old commander, was killed in action during an assault on an Afghan military outpost near the capital. With a distinct shortage of commanders who understand the nature of the war they are fighting, it was a loss the resistance could ill afford.

Nevertheless, there are other Pushtun commanders who have achieved national repute. Abdul Haq, a stout bearded Khales commander and former associate of Halim, is one of several. Barely twenty when the Russians invaded, Haq was already politically active against left-wing elements during the Daoud era. After participating in no less than four attempts to overthrow the regime, he was arrested in October, 1977 and sentenced to death, but was released after the Saur revolution when his family bribed the authorities. He immediately made his way to Pakistan, where he joined the Hezb, fighting principally in the Nangrahar and Kabul region.

According to Anglo-Dutch journalist Aernout van Lynden, who accompanied Abdul Haq for eight weeks in the summer of 1981 and witnessed no fewer than five major Soviet-Afghan assaults against resistance positions, the guerrillas, despite being outgunned and outnumbered, were able to inflict relatively heavy casualties through their 'nearly perfect deployment of men and anti-tank weapons'. Yet the guerrillas, who were positioned among the fertile, green hills only a few miles northwest of Kabul faced numerous disadvantages. In particular the terrain offers easy access to the armoured vehicles that spearhead most anti-insurgent operations and the two asphalt roads that cut through the region make surprise attacks feasible.

For such a highly mobile war over mountains and vast stretches of desert, the shortage of radio transmitters is both a drawback and an advantage for the resistance. Some fronts have managed to procure walkie-talkies to monitor government troop movements or to coordinate military operations, but the lack of basic precautions (few seem to change their codes regularly, if they use deception systems at all) raises the risk of being detected by the communists. Without access to modern communications, most fronts still rely on more traditional means of dispatching or receiving information. News usually travels on foot or by horse and may take two, three or even four weeks to reach its destination. In the western provinces, however, the guerrillas have established special motorcycle squads with Japanese-made machines brought in from Iran, while, in the south, they regularly use jeeps and pickup trucks to tear across the wastelands.

The resistance has shown a remarkable ability to exploit whatever materials happen to come its way. Heavy guns from destroyed helicopters, tanks and armoured personnel carriers are immediately dismantled and carried back. They are then repaired and ingeniously fitted out by local mechanics. During the communist blockade of the Panjshair Valley, which was lifted in January, 1983 for sixteen months, local guerrillas, many of whom are mechanics by trade, transported captured Russian jeeps back across the mountains piece by piece before reassembling them on the other side. At one point, the guerrillas hijacked along the Salang Highway a specially-imported Soviet vehicle destined for the Afghan Foreign Minister; they managed to bring over most of its parts, but found the chassis too large to carry by mule.

Helicopter rocket pods have been transformed into rocket launchers, while, in one case, guerrillas stripped down a four-barrel ZPU-4 gun to turn it into four separate weapons. At one hidden mujahed base in the Panjshair, I was shown a rocket pod which normally holds 32 missiles. Although they lacked the proper firing mechanism, the local commander explained, they could easily make do with a set of torch batteries and two connecting wires. As for a badly damaged 30mm Plamya automatic grenade launcher capable of firing up to 30 rounds from a rotating drum, he simply took a hammer and without more ado struck it on its base. A loud bang shattered the mountain silence on the opposite side of the ravine, attesting to the efficiency of this crude firing method. The guerrillas often take mechanics with them when attacking convoys. If an armoured vehicle is knocked out, they rush in and grab what they can before the helicopters come. Similarly, they will siphon out petrol from tankers for their own vehicles or generators.

As a result of such practices, the Russians have gone to extreme lengths to prevent equipment from falling into the hands of the mujahideen. In the wake of each ground operation, Red Army pick-up teams, using large flat-top carriers or even heavy Mi-6 helicopter transports, will try to remove damaged or destroyed equipment. Anything they are unable to take with them, they render useless. Nevertheless, even when equipment has been wrecked beyond recall, there always seems to be something for enterprising Afghans. Scrap merchants will pick a vehicle clean within two or three hours, using the metal either locally or transporting it to Kabul to sell for hard cash.

War in the Cities

'As long as the Russians have Kabul, they can say they have Afghanistan', observed Khalis guerrilla commander, Abdul Haq. 'Even though we control almost all the countryside, we must show them and their followers that they are not secure even in the capital.' At the end of the 1981-82 winter, the resistance had spread with vehemence to the capital and other urban centres. Although Kabul continued to function as the focal point of the communist administration during the day, the guerrillas were taking over the inner suburbs at night. By the summer, even the regime's prerogative of daytime control was eroded as mujahideen dared to appear in broad daylight in certain city districts. One partisan commander glibly explained that 'there is nothing to do in the mountains and villages'.

Selective sabotage and urban guerrilla attacks were beginning seriously to disrupt city life. In the late spring of 1981, the mujahideen scored their first direct rocket hits on the Soviet embassy compound. Security was immediately tightened, but within six months rocket attacks on major government installations such as the Soviet-built Microrayon residential quarter had become regular occurrences. In December alone, there were no fewer than 16 reported guerrilla incidents in Kabul, ranging from a bomb blast in a communist-run cinema to the killing of two Russian soldiers trying to buy hashish in a bazaar on the outskirts of the capital.

By the end of the summer of 1982, guerrilla activities in urban areas had surged dramatically, bringing a distinct psychological advantage to the resistance. The mujahideen were demonstrating to both the Soviet occupation forces and the Afghan population that they were capable of bringing the war from the countryside to the cities. Shoot-outs and rocket assaults, usually against police and militia posts or government buildings such as the Kote Sangi military high school, were now occurring on a daily basis. In late July, mujahideen attacked a major ammunition depot adjacent to the Khawaja Rawash military airport, rocking the city with violent explosions and sending up thick clouds of smoke and gigantic flames.

At the same time, special hit squads regularly assassinated government officials or well-known personalities collaborating with the Russians. The killers would then disappear into the bazaars or side streets on the backs of motorcycles or in stolen yellow taxis. In March, 1982, for example, guerrillas ambushed and killed Abdul Rahman, president of Kabul University. Fake accidents were staged in the streets of Kabul; when the police arrived on the scene, hidden mujahideen raked them with bullets. Afghan communists found themselves living in constant fear of being killed or kidnapped.

'The communists know we can get them if we really want to. The atmosphere in Kabul has become one of nervousness and fear among party members', declared Haji Safert Mir, a former Tourist Office guide now working with the Panjshair resistance. Party members also avoided travelling by bus between cities, preferring to take planes whenever possible, even for journeys as short as from Kabul to Jelalabad, a mere 95 miles by road. One American journalist visiting Kabul on an official visa in the summer of 1984 reported that the local Bakhtar Airlines agency was crammed every day with functionaries, or relatives of functionaries, waving chits assuring anyone interested that they were important and should be given priority. Everyone, it seemed, had priority.

Although vehicles can travel out of convoy, partisans normally stop them once they are out of the cities to check for communist collaborators. Armed resistance supporters also conduct similar operations in the towns, normally in the suburbs. If a communist is found, he is taken off the bus, killed, kidnapped, or, if he is lucky, forced to pay a fine.

By mid-1982, both diplomats and Afghan residents were reporting the sound of gunfire and explosions almost every night. For fear of ambush, the security forces temporarily abandoned nocturnal patrols in many parts of Kabul. One Western journalist travelling with the resistance in the mountains overlooking Kabul described the city at night as a 'constant display of rockets and flares'. This did not mean that it was in a state of siege, as often seemed to be the case less than two years later, but there was enough guerrilla activity to make the authorities realise that no one was truly safe. Generally, Soviet advisers and their wives could shop openly in the centre of Kabul (only important senior advisers or officers were accompanied by armed escorts), but they were forbidden to enter the old bazaar. By seven in the evening, three hours before curfew, the streets were virtually empty save for the militia checkpoints.

Guerrilla raids were also becoming more daring. In the early summer of 1982, mujahideen, acting on information from sympathisers, killed 37 Soviet army officers and advisers after bursting into a meeting they were holding in the fashionable Herat Hotel near the provincial capital's town centre. In another operation several weeks later, another group of guerrillas attacked Kandahar jail, reportedly releasing as many as 150 prisoners. Using explosives, they breached a gap in the back wall of the prison and burst in, killing twelve guards. By the time Rssian armoured vehicles from a nearby base arrived on the scene, the mujahideen, who suffered four dead and ten injured in the action, had already left. Less than two weeks later, guerrillas conducted a repeat assault aided by resistance collaborators inside the jail, killing 30 government security men as well as destroying or damaging four armoured vehicles outside.

While several major fronts affiliated with Khales' Hezb, Jamiat or Mohammadi's Harakat have come to specialise in attacks against Kabul and its surroundings — an estimated 5,000 are said to be working south of the capital alone — a number of small urban resistance organisations have been operating there since the early days of the occupation. One of them, the Group-e Mujadeddin-e-azad (Group of Independent Mujahideen), is a member of the United National Front and consists of several full-time clandestine members, mainly nationalist ex-army officers, but also works with sympathisers still in the military, who provide the guerrillas with intelligence, weapons and other services. According to Salim, a 26-year-old Tadjik former army lieutenant, the group runs two types of operations: military and political. 'Thanks to the information we receive', he said, 'we can find out the most brutal (communist) militiamen or officers. We study their habits, we watch them for at least a month or two. And then when our plan is perfect, meaning no casualties of our own, we attack.'

Because of the tightening of security, however, such urban guerrilla organisations have been finding it more difficult to operate. Soviet and Afghan government patrols are becoming increasingly suspicious and thorough in their street checks. 'An I.D. card is no longer enough', Salim explained. 'They telephone your place of work to make sure who you are.' Operating costs come to roughly $2,500 a month, which covers petrol, accessories such as military uniforms and the rental of two or three 'safe' houses at any one time. In addition, the organisation must find funds to help support the families of activists who have been killed or imprisoned.

Another commander specialising in urban guerrilla warfare is a former magistrate, Haji Mohammad Rafiq, who in mid-1982 was reported to control some 600 men, with another 600 at his disposal. According to one British journalist who accompanied him on an attack on a military barracks near Pul-e-Charkhi, Rafiq was engaged in four different types of guerrilla warfare. Based in the Kabul suburb of Chewakee, he would operate units of 20 to 30 men ambushing the rear of army columns leaving the city, usually acting on information pro-vided by resistance sympathisers with the government. They would also carry out selective assassinations, 600, they claim, in the first two years of the occupation, ranging from armed soldiers, whose Kalashnikovs they take, to Afghan party members and Soviet advisers. Modern housing blocks for government officials, electricity plants and bridges are also targets. Attacks on security installations, however, are part military, part political, with the mujahideen calling on soldiers or militiamen to defect.

Despite government efforts to tighten security, urban guerrilla war-fare appeared to be getting better organised and more selective. There was greater coordination among certain fundamentalist and moderate groups. The general population was also demonstrating more open defiance. Towards, the end of November, 1983, guerrillas launched a night attack on the Kabul Polytechnic, destroying at least one tank and causing several Soviet casualties. Other actions included an assault in early December on a patrol jeep in the old town's Shorbazaar, killing three Afghan security officers. Similarly, on 28 December the mujahideen struck at a Soviet military post at the strongly defended Red Army base at Tajbeg on the outskirts of the capital, reportedly killing six Russians. At the same time, mujahed light artillery hit the Ministry of Defence headquarters at Darulaman Palace.

There was a notable rise in urban guerrilla activities in the capital throughout much of 1984, ranging from a reportedly heavy rocket and mortar assault against the Soviet embassy in the early part of the year to repeated attacks on Kabul airport and the partial razing of the old bazaar in ealry November by mujahed rockets. A massive bomb explosion at the airport in mid-summer killing at least thirty people, many of them relatives bidding farewell to young Parchamis on their way to the Soviet Union for training, may, however, have been the work of rival Khalqis rather than the mujahideen.

If Algiers or Saigon are any indication, the rise in urban attacks not only in Kabul but also in other towns promises the Soviets a new type of war which they may well find more difficult to accommodate.

Profile of a Guerrilla Front

During the first three years of occupation, certainly the most assertive of all the guerrilla fronts to come to the attention of outside observers was the strategic Panjshair Valley. Led by Tadjik guerrilla commander Ahmad Shah Massoud, this beautiful highland region, carved into the base of the Hindu Kush only forty miles north of Kabul, has managed to stave off eight major Soviet offensives since the invasion and has developed into one of the country's most highly organised resistance movements. Not unlike the maquis of the Vercors Plateau in southeastern France during World War II, Massoud and his defiant Panjshairis long ago earned the admiration and respect of many as a leading symbol of the Afghan resistance.

The Panjshair model has spread. Numerous mujahed leaders from other regions have sent their men to the valley for training. At least a score of similarly structured but less publicised fronts, some of them possibly better organised than Massoud's, now exist. Faced with the prospect of a long-drawn-out, and exhausting conflict, 'lasting forty years perhaps', the young Panjshairi commander with the characteristic hawk-nose and wispy beard has ardently pursued regional co-operation with other fronts as the only way to confront the Russians effectively.

As a more or less self-contained entity, the valley offers several protective advantages. Seventy miles long and 7,000 feet high, the Panjshair (circa 90,000 – 100,000 inhabitants in 1980) is a garden valley of mud and stone villages surrounded by terraced wheat fields, vineyards, fruit orchards and thick mulberry groves. With only one main entry point by road to the south, it is flanked on both sides by steep, rocky escarpments and dozens of side valleys leading to isolated mountain hamlets and alpine pastures. With each attack, the guerrillas have simply withdrawn to their highland bases in the neighbouring areas.

The Soviet Union's continued efforts to destroy, or otherwise neutralise, the valley is an indication of its determination to prevent the 'Massoud' trend from developing further. 'It has become a very hard war. Far harder than before', Massoud told me in August, 1984 during the Red Army's seventh offensive against the region. As we sipped tea in his mountain stronghold only a rifle-shot away from the nearest Soviet observation post, he paid little attention to the sullen roar of artillery and mortar shells exploding on the rocky escarpments. He only looked up when a MIG-27 ground attack fighter streaked in low to bomb a guerrilla position and a 'dashaka' heavy machine gun on a nearby ridge fired in response.

Gesturing with constantly restless hands to the large map of northern Afghanistan spread out before him he explained:

> Militarily the Soviets have failed to achieve their objectives. Every time they have come into the valley, they have tried to destroy the mujahideen. But we have always managed to elude them and then hit them from all sides. Their commandos (heliborne troops) have learned a great deal about mountain guerrilla warfare and are fighting much better than before. They have caused us some serious problems, but we have learned to cope with them.

But it was a very different story for the civilian population.

> Unfortunately, we are in danger of losing our people. This is where the Soviets may succeed. Failing to crush us by force, as they have said they would with each offensive, they have turned their wrath on defenceless people, killing old men, women and children, destroying houses, and burning crops. They are doing everything possible to drive our people away.

Often referred to as the Che Guevara, even the Tito of Afghanistan, Massoud — a good-looking, charistmatic and energetic man approaching his mid-thirties — is an exceptional partisan commander. He has understood the necessity of a tightly-knit movement, organised not only along military but also political, social and economic lines. Using the same approach as Marxist-inspired revolutionaries, he has sought to beat the Russians at their own game by creating a grassroots resistance, strongly coloured by Islam yet based on village structures in a manner which would have made Lenin and Mao proud. This permits every inhabitant to help to the best of his or her capabilities. Not everyone, for example, can become a full-time mujahed. All the men are encouraged to undergo training, but the resistance command carefully selects its fighters, leaving enough qualified manpower to run the administration and cultivate the land when conditions permit.

Not to belittle his impressive organising capabilities, Massoud has encountered fewer difficulties in galvanising his people or expanding his influence than most Pushtun commanders because of the Panjshair's non-tribal society and geographical position. Once having proved his mettle and unencumbered by traditional tribal restraints, he was able to persuade not only the Panjshairis but also inhabitants in the surrounding regions to accept his leadership. Despite an evident sense of war fatigue among much of the civilian population (thousands of people had fled into the mountains during the latest offensives), he has remained revered, with his portrait abundantly displayed in the refugee bazaars of Pakistan.

Learning from Mao

The son of a retired senior military officer and a former pupil of the Lycée Istiqlal in Kabul, a French-run establishment that has produced a remarkable number of resistance personalities, Massoud (a nom de guerre) went to the Russian Polytechnique, also in the Afghan capital, where he studied engineering. But he soon dropped out because of anti-regime activities. Fleeing to Pakistan when Daoud took power in 1973, he closely allied himself with Professor Rabbani within the exiled Muslim Youth movement. Like many other Daoud dissidents, he underwent military training in special insurgent camps established by the Pakistani government under Prime Minister Ali Bhutto and participated in an abortive uprising in the Panjshair in 1975. Massoud then returned to a life of exile in Peshawar where he spent much of his time (apart from occasional clandestine visits to Afghanistan) studying the essential texts of modern guerrilla warfare: Mao-Ze-Dung, Guevara, De Gaulle and the North Vietnamese general, Van Nguyen Giap.

In mid-1978, he headed back to the Panjshair with a mere twenty followers. Once there, he and his fellow guerrillas sought to persuade the local inhabitants to take up arms against the Kabul regime. 'We didn't know how they would react, but they were immediately with us and we soon put together a force of 200 men' said Ahmad Zia, Massoud's brother. The rebels took rapid control of two valley districts, forcing the Khaqli deputy governor to flee. Then they set up a front line at the mouth of valley. But the revolt was poorly organised and when a major contingent of government troops and police arrived on the scene, they were forced to flee. Living in rock shelters among the bluffs at the northern end of the valley where the churning Panjshair river carves its way through a deep gorge, Massoud and his men reconsidered their strategy.

The young commander's first attempt had obviously been too rash and unprepared. Apart from his original band of partisans, his force lacked the necessary training and weapons. He decided therefore to build a guerrilla organisation from scratch by taking ninety volunteers — local farmers, truckdrivers, mechanics and students — as his nucleus. Forming them into small units, he soon began to launch attacks against government installations such as police stations, first at Dasht-e-Rawat in the north, and then gradually progressing down the valley, gathering supporters as he went. By January, 1980, the guerrillas controlled the entire Panjshair. From then on, the Soviet-backed Kabul authorities have made at least two major assaults a year in their attempts to get it back. During the offensives of 1982 (numbers five and six) and 1984 (seven and eight), Soviet-Afghan government forces succeeded in occupying the valley, but failed to bring the resistance to heel.

A Mujahed Elite

Directly commanding an estimated 3,000 frontline fighters, plus a pool of several thousand part-time partisans, Massoud has divided the Panjshair region into seven combat zones to facilitate guerrilla defence and operations. He has created two types of mujahideen: moutariks (mobile groups) and sabbets (local defence units) attached to some twenty-five 'Karegars', or field commands; dispersed up and down the valley.

Each moutarik company consists of separate units of 75 men each as well as several small platoons, each of roughly 30 men. All in their teens and twenties, many moutariks, with long hair, remind one of the weathered Cuban guerrillas of old *Life* magazine photographs. As with most northern Afghan frontline fighters, and increasingly the southern mujahideen, they wear woollen Nuristani 'kolas' (caps), olive-coloured army anoraks, trouser fatigues, and black Czech-made leather boots. Armed with AK-47s or the latest AK-74s, the moutarik is a full-time fighter, receiving a subsistence allowance as well as cigarette and 'naswah' rations. Not forced to worry about planting next year's crops or assuming other responsibilities, the moutarik is free to move wherever and for as long as it is necessary to fight the war. The families are cared for by the resistance administration and receive indemnity in case of the fighter's death or incapacity. The Panjshair is reputed to be the first front to have formed permanent fighting units, although they are now commonplace among many groups. Each group has at least one mortar launcher, a ZPU-2 double-barrelled anti-aircraft gun, three RPG-7 grenade launchers and three heavy machine guns. I have also come across occasional SAM-7 surface-to-air missiles, which have the drawback of leaving a trail of white smoke pinpointing the position from which they were fired; they have proved relatively useless other than forcing enemy aircraft to fly high.

Massoud's moutariks have been used not only to conduct harassment actions whenever the valley is under attack, but also to launch operations against the Salang Highway, and communist bases in Kohistan and as far away as Kabul. Booty taken from convoys (Afghan trucks are simply stopped and goods confiscated in return for a receipt) furnishes the Panjshair with a substantial portion of its requirements like tea, sugar, rice and even petroleum. These are then transported by horse or on the backs of porters for sale in the bazaars or peddled among the mujahideen in the mountains.

On 25 April 1982, moutariks from the Panjshair and the Shamali region launched, under Massoud's direction, a daring commando raid, the first of its kind in the war, against Bagram airbase. Using mortars, rockets, assault rifles and grenades, they penetrated the perimeter shortly after midnight and destroyed or damaged 23 helicopters and planes on the ground. They also attacked a military barracks and a hospital, killing or wounding dozens of Soviet soldiers. More recently, Massoud's moutariks have been involved in attacks on the outskirts of Kabul and against the airport.

Sabbet units, on the other hand, are village-based and function as a local militia with a small number of anti-aircraft guns shared out among them for the general defence of the valley. Their size varies, but they usually consist of between 50 and 100 men. As Massoud's influence has expanded in neighbouring regions such as the Andarab Valley to the north of the Panjshair, he has helped create similar mobile and militia defence groups.

Valley against an Empire

The first large-scale Russian attempt to check Massoud's spreading influence, was the Red Army's fifth offensive in May, 1982.

Within easy striking distance of the Salang Tunnel, the Panjshair represented not only a serious danger for Soviet military supply lines, but also a severe embarrassment for the Kabul regime both at home and abroad. The world services of the BBC, the Voice of America and other Western shortwave radio networks frequently reported the inability of the communists to assert their control over the valley. Apart from flurries of newspaper and magazine articles, the Panjshair's defiance had featured in several television documentaries bearing such titles as 'Valley against an Empire' by a French team. Kabul residents, who secretly followed events in the Panjshair with enthusiasm, jokingly referred to the Panjshair as one of the world's three superpowers after the United States and the Soviet Union. An all-out thrashing, the Kremlin felt, was psychologically imperative if the Karmal regime was to save face.

Throwing in an estimated 8,000 Soviet and 4,000 Afghan government troops supported by tanks, MIGs and helicopter gunships, it looked as if sheer Soviet might would bring the Panjshairis to their knees. For a week preceding the offensive, Soviet aircraft, some of them flying sorties from bases inside the USSR, pounded one village after another with bombs and rockets. Then came helicopter landings at different points in the valley including mountain ridges.

After three days, on 17 May the security forces broke through the bottleneck gorge leading from the plains of Shamali into the Panjshair; a second and totally unanticipated pincer attack descended from the north, resulting in the total occupation of the valley floor. Several thousand more troops were reportedly brought in when the Russian commander demanded reinforcements from Kabul to relieve beleagured troops at the northern end of the valley where guerrillas had put up exceptionally fierce opposition. Pitted against this massive onslaught were Massoud's own forces plus several detachments of partisans from neighbouring regions who had rushed in on foot and by horse to help.

The rapid occupation of the Panjshair suggested a well-performed textbook operation. In fact, the Russians were doing nothing more than applying a strategy normally used in their East European theatre war games, whereby one force spearheads a frontal assault and two or three more strike simultaneously at the middle and the rear. But in a typical guerrilla tactic which has frustrated the Russians from the very beginning, Massoud's men melted into the moutains to pre-arranged positions. From there, his moutariks harassed the invaders by constant sniping, mine-laying, mortar assaults and nocturnal hit-and-run raids. Within two weeks, they had forced most of the heliborne commandos to retreat from the heights and had shattered Soviet ground communications in several places. The guerrillas then began moving in.

From re-occupied mujahed observation posts staked out along the jagged ridges, some of them still littered with Soviet cigarettes and empty cans of Bulgarian beans, I had an awesome view of the field offensive. Strings of helicopter gunships clattered overhead to targets further up the Panjshair, while congested columns of armoured vehicles and trucks, headed by tanks equipped with huge rollers to predetonate mines, ground laboriously along the single dirt road that runs the length of the valley. On the opposite mountain side, heavy firing erupted spasmodically as gunships circled in attack on hidden guerrilla positions.

To our left, lay the partially destoyed town of Onawa where the Russians had pitched a triangular base with tents, corrugated iron huts and supply depots. Formal rows of BM-21 rocket launchers, each capable of firing 122mm projectiles in devastating salvos or 'ripples' totalling four and a half tonnes of explosives, had been positioned on the edge of the camp. Next to them, in well-ordered lines, giant self-propelled howitzers pointed menacingly in our direction. And immediately below us, lay Khonis, a sprawling village neatly framed by cratered fields and splintered trees. Using binoculars, one could distinguish troops, well out of rifle range, quietly basking in the sun on red carpets looted from nearby abandoned houses. A group of soldiers with the help of a tank were trying to push a destroyed vehicle out of the way. At the entrance of the side valley to our right, Soviet units with machine guns, rocket launchers and mortars had dug in to block guerrilla movement back into the valley.

Both the speed with which the heliborne troops had landed and the unexpected pincer movement from the rear via the Andarab Valley initially caught Massoud off guard. Nevertheless, he had been informed weeks earlier by Afghan government officials and senior military officers in Kabul secretly collaborating with the resistance that a massive operation was in the offing. Originally, the Russians had planned it to coincide with the elaborate celebrations of the fourth anniversary of the Saur Revolution on 27 April. And in what was seen as an attempt to furnish the government with added diplomatic leverage, it was timed for the eve of the first UN-sponsored talks on Afghanistan in Geneva.

This gave Massoud enough advance notice to prepare his defence strategy carefully, establish hidden food and ammunition caches in the mountains, and move his men into position. Knowing that the attack would be carried out with harsh vengeance, the resistance tried to forestall it long enough to take advantage of the brief spring rains   and snowmelt which promised to swell the Panjshair River into a raging torrent. By destroying the road in places where the valley narrowed, they could prevent heavy armoured vehicles from crawling up the normally shallow river bed, thus halting the communist advance. Massoud's commando attack against Bagram on 25 April apparently succeeded in provoking a temporary postponement, but failed to halt the offensive completely.

The surprise landing of Soviet heliborne rangers in the early hours of 17 May cut off the escape routes of hundreds of civilians to the mountains. While Mi-6 and Mi-8 helicopters, with Mi-24 gunships circling protectively overhead, deposited commandos on the mountain ridges, others were dropped on the valley floor. From there, they sought to work their up to the guerrilla positions, ensconced along the slopes. Unlike ordinary Soviet combat troops, these elite forces were far better trained and had the ability to move quickly. According to Massoud, their courage even won the admiration of the mujahideen, but, he said, they had never faced real war conditions. 'As soon as they came down and took losses, they evacuated.'

Better acquainted with the terrain, the Panjshairis offered much greater resistance than the Soviet military high command apparently expected. At first the Russians only set up tents on the valley floor. Later, when mujahed firing become murderous, they were forced to dig trenches. Helicopter gunships, MIG jet fighters and the highly manoeuvrable Sukhoi 25 ground-attack aircraft supported the Soviet troops with barrages of heavy rocket and bomb attacks. The mujahideen were particularly impressed by the ability of the Sukhois to dive steeply and turn abruptly in and out of the region's narrow side valleys. Although much of the bombing was relatively ineffective (many bombs never exploded), it had become so heavy in areas that the guerrillas were forced to engage the enemy in fierce hand-to-hand combat.

The Red Army decision to deploy frontline troops in such numbers without the security of armoured vehicles represented a major new tactical departure. Only on a few previous occasions had the Russians been prepared to accept higher losses in an attempt to end the stalemate that has characterised the war since the invasion. During the February 1980 Kunar offensive, for example, Soviet troops severely mauled the resistance but suffered heavy casualties of their own through direct confrontation. When columns of tanks and AMVs began to penetrate the Panjshair on 20 May only at the Anjuman Pass at the extreme north of the valley did the security forces hold the heights.

The first to enter the Panjshair were Afghan army troops. As part of their usual battle procedure, the Russians were sending in their surrogates to take the brunt of the main spearhead. However, as the Afghan troops moved in, the guerrillas made no effort to stop them. It was only when the Soviets tried to penetrate the entrance that the mujahideen dynamited the sides of the gorge causing a landslide to block the road. By the time the Red Army troops managed to bulldoze their way through, scores of Afghans had already defected to the resistance with their weapons, including nine tanks which were turned against the invaders.

The Soviets immediately withdrew several Afghan contingents, putting many of the recruits under arrest. The Afghans, however, were not the only ones to defect. An unconfirmed number (several dozen according to some reports) of Soviet Muslim support troops from the Central Asian Republics had also changed sides by the end of the offensive. While the mujahed withdrawal into the mountains had permitted the security forces to occupy the entire valley, it obliged them also to spread themselves thinly. Moving freely among the side valleys and ridges, the guerrillas struck at the Soviets with savage persistence.

A Frugal Air Defence System

At the time of the May 1982 offensive, Massoud's forces possessed fewer than a dozen anti-aircraft guns. These were positioned at strategic spots along upper regions of the rocky and sparsely vegetated escarpments. Limited though they were, the weapons were not without effect; the guns forced the helicopters to fly high and come in low only to attack. Below one gun position, I could see the mangled remains of two helicopters littering the valley floor, but it was impossible to identify their type. 'If we had more guns, bigger guns, we'd be able to shoot them all down', vowed a heavily bearded unit commander.

Roughly half the Soviet Union's 200-strong force of armoured Mi-24 helicopter gunships in Afghanistan had been called in for the Panjshair operation. Over a single one-hour period, I counted no less than 60 helicopters passing overhead, the majority of them Mi-24s and Mi-8 assault craft. A sprinkling of Mi-6 heavy transports, capable of carrying 70 men or two tanks, were ferrying reinforcements to the northern end of the valley where the fighting was fiercest.

There was a certain helplessness in the angry faces of the Panjshairis as they watched the ugly snout-nosed and camouflage-daubed Hind-Ds, the most lethal of the Mi-24 gunships, circle in packs of six over guerrilla strongholds farther up the valley. Equipped with a four-barrel Gatling turret gun and two side pods each holding thirty-two 57mm rockets, the gunships first orbited for five minutes and then, the lead craft taking the initiative, dropped in low for the attack. Firing their rockets, the helicopters rose quickly as spiralling clouds of smoke and dust following the explosions suddenly enveloped the mountainside. The defiant firing of a heavy machine gun in the distance was a feeble response to these intimidating metal monsters that have sown terror even among the considerably better armed guerrillas in Angola and Eritrea.

By the end of July, the offensive had virtually petered out. Once again, the resistance was in control of much of the valley. Despite the Red Army's overwhelming display of sophisticated military hardware, this modern but cumbersome force had failed to make any headway whatsoever against an elusive and highly motivated guerrilla force.

In early September 1982, a joint Soviet-Afghan contingent of 10,500 troops, including police units, tried for the sixth time to establish a foothold in the valley. As before, the Panjshair was heavily strafed and bombarded. But within a few weeks, most of the Russians had withdrawn with their equipment. Only the towns of Rokha and Onawa remained in communist hands. According to both resistance and Western diplomatic sources, Soviet losses by the end of the 1982 campaign stood at well over 2,000 dead and wounded, with 1,200 Afghan soldiers killed, captured or defected. On the resistance side, it was the civilians who, as usual, suffered the most; well over 1,200 are believed to have been killed, while mujahed losses stood at roughly 180 dead.

Soviet-guerrilla Truce: A Precedent?

At the beginning of 1983, Ahmad Shah Massoud agreed to an unprecedented truce with the Soviet occupation forces. A controversial issue, it prompted violent reactions among resistance circles both inside and outside the country. Some argued that the Panjshair leader had sold himself to the communists in order to make a special deal with the Kabul regime. This was supported by rumours suggesting that Massoud had agreed to collaborate in return for a regional governorship. Others, who did not suspect such devious motives, simply complained that, by coming to an arrangement with the Russians, Massoud was allowing them to free their troops for use against resistance groups elsewhere. For many Panjshair sympathisers in Peshawar, there was uncertainty as to the nature of Massoud's manoeuvring.

By playing chess with the Russians, Massoud was trying, amongst other things, to gain a much-needed respite for his people. Without doubt, the Panjshair had suffered more than its fair share of Soviet attention. Much of the valley lay in ruins, up to four-fifths of its houses reduced to rubble. The invaders had looted or destroyed food stocks, ruptured irrigation channels, chopped down fruit trees and machine-gunned sheep and cattle. Many farmers, except those in the upper regions of Parian, were unable to plant new crops. With little to harvest, the surviving 40,000-50,000 inhabitants (almost as many had fled to Pakistan or Kabul) faced serious food shortages. Medicines, too, were running out and there was a desperate lack of winter clothing. Possibly worst of all, ammunition supplies were nearly exhausted.

The security forces were not doing that well either. Afghan military and administrative outposts left behind by the Soviets were falling to guerrilla harassment. Those that remained were already under siege and, once again, it looked as if the authorities would fail to assert their presence. Toward the end of 1982, in an attempt to end the stalemate and establish a modus vivendi with the Panjshairis, senior Afghan government officials sent letters to Massoud requesting a ceasefire. This the guerrillas summarily rejected, disdainfully maintaining that the Kabul regime 'has no power at all, so it is useless to speak with them'.

Overriding the Afghan authorities, the Russians themselves decided to approach Massoud toward the end of December. This caused considerable concern among Parcham officials, who feared that the Kremlin might start making a habit of working out its own deals with the guerrillas. It was felt that the Russians, who were known to be dissatisfied with the inability of the regime to achieve respect^ble grassroots support, might start looking elsewhere.

As a gesture of 'good faith', the Soviets unilaterally observed their own cease-fire by halting the daily bombardments and confining their troops to camp. Massoud consulted with the valley's religious leaders and local resistance councils before agreeing to enter into negotiations. In early January, 1983, a high-ranking Russian official entered guerrilla territory not far from the last government outpost to meet the Panjshairi commander. Tense bargaining over tea in the customary Afghan manner resulted in a six-month truce. As part of the agreement, the Soviets were assured a peaceful withdrawal of all their forces and equipment. As the troops pulled out, the Panjshairi guerrillas moved back in.

For the mujahideen, the fact that the Soviet authorities had agreed to talk directly with a bunch of 'bandits' represented a de facto recognition of the Afghan resistance. It also set a precedent for direct Soviet-Afghan resistance talks should the Russians ever seriously consider leaving. Most important for the Panjshairis, however, the truce enabled them to rebuild their mosques, homes and shops, cultivate their fields and restock with supplies. The shops were full again and the road to Kabul was open without restriction.

Bizarrely, the Russians still maintained a base at Onawa with the busy main road passing directly through it. Their 800 troops at the base were not permitted to move beyond its perimeter and had to be supplied by helicopter. Only at the mouth of the valley could Soviet checkpoints stop buses and other vehicles entering or leaving the valley. Mujahideen travelling with weapons simply disembarked beforehand and moved around the checkpoints, a blatant fact to which the Russians turned a blind eye.

By establishing a truce with Massoud, the Soviets were hoping to achieve at least two objectives. First, in a rudimentary manner, to show the Panjshairis that material gains could be obtained through peace with the government. A return to normalcy might persuade the local population that war was not worth it, particularly if the authorities were prepared to leave them alone, at least for the moment. Second, to show that even the most famous guerrilla commanders were willing to talk with the Soviet authorities, thereby attracting further candidates or sowing dissension among the resistance ranks, which they did during the early stages of the truce.

In the end, it was Massoud who brought the Red Army to check, although by no means mate. This was conceded by the Russians, who terminated the cease-fire some sixteen months later by launching their seventh, and largest offensive, against the Panjshair. During the interim, however, Massoud not only gained the respite he needed to reorganise his forces and restock on supplies, but he also exploited the opportunity to lay the groundwork for one of his dreams: the creation of a firm resistance alliance in the north.

5 SOVIET INFLUENCE IN AFGHANISTAN

Direct Soviet involvement with Afghanistan dates from the Soviet-Afghan Friendship Treaty of 1921 through which the USSR sought to consolidate a hold over the now fully independent Afghanistan. Until the assassination of King Habibullah in 1919 Britain had controlled the country's foreign affairs. Not only did Moscow establish five consulates in Afghanistan's major towns (there were six Afghan ones in Soviet Central Asia), but its first present to the new government of King Amanullah Khan hinted at things to come: two fighter airplanes to help found the Royal Afghan Air Force. By 1925, the Air Force was completely under Russian control with Soviet pilots flying all twelve aircraft, some of which were used to help put down recalcitrant tribesmen. The Soviet regime reportedly also provided King Amanullah with an aid grant totalling half a million dollars a year from 1921 to 1924.

Under Amanullah, Afghanistan adopted a nationalist, reformist and anti-imperialist approach. Like his father, Amanullah disliked the way the British had treated Afghanistan as a vassal state, but through them he had become fascinated by European scientific and industrial achievements. As a result, he introduced electricity, the telephone, the telegraph and other 'products of progress' to his fellow countrymen.

In the new Afghan king, the Soviets recognised a potentially firm ally because of his declared intention to remain neutral and to help India obtain its freedom from Britain. Afghanistan's relationship with the Soviet Union could serve as a model to the Indians. Furthermore, the Kremlin, determined to crush the Muslim liberation movements in Soviet Central Asia, needed Afghanistan to prevent any renewed anti-Russian spillage across the border. Already in 1920, the USSR had begun sealing off its frontier with Afganistan and by World War II had succeeded in blocking most traditional traffic (including nomad migration).

In contrast to their policies of exporting revolution to China, Mongolia, Iran and other 'ripe' countries, the Bolsheviks made little effort in Afghanistan. Nearly half a century was to pass before Afghanistan had its own communist party. One of the reasons why the Russians did not consider it pertinent to establish a party in Kabul, or, as had been planned, a forward propaganda base for Indian nationalists, was to avoid invoking the wrath of the British. The Soviet Foreign

Office even warned its representatives in Afghanistan 'not to commit the serious mistake of implanting communism in this country'.

Under Stalin, the USSR continued its policy of economic, military and technical assistance to Afghanistan until the overthrow of King Amanullah in 1929, by rebel brigand Habibullah Khan, otherwise known as Baccha-i-Saqao, the son of the watercarrier. Like Ataturk in Turkey, Amanullah had sought to release his country from medieval stagnation. But this modernisation programme met with deep suspicion from the peasantry, who regarded the reforms as an attempt by the central authorities to impinge on their traditional independence. Furthermore, many Afghans, notably the clerics, considered Amanullah's policies 'unislamic'. By the autumn of 1928, the mullahs, tribes and ethnic groups were in revolt. Within weeks, angry insurgents swept aside token Afghan army resistance and headed for Kabul. On 3 January 1929, Amanullah cancelled his reforms, but it was too late. Nine days later, the first rebels entered the outskirts of Kabul forcing the king to abdicate. Aided by loyalists, he escaped and made his way to exile in Italy.

Baccha-i-Saqao, an illiterate Tadjik, proclaimed himself the new Emir. Not being a Pushtun, however, the traditional guardians of the Afghan throne, he had little chance of holding on to his crown. At the most, he could claim only two or three regions under his actual control. Both the British and the Russians, the latter firmly believing that the British had been involved in Amanullah's overthrow, jockeyed for position in the resulting political turmoil. The Soviets even went so far as to send a Red Army expedition of Central Asian soldiers into Afghanistan. Led by Ghulam Nabi Charkhi, a former Afghan ambassador to Moscow, the force included a handful of Afghan students and military cadets and was received enthusiastically by the local population. Nevertheless, it withdrew after several months, possibly because of growing complications in the overall situation.

Nine months after Baccha-i-Sagao's takeover, Nadir Shah, a Durrani Pushtun like Amanullah, entered Kabul at the head of a horde of tribesmen to oust and kill the watercarrier's son. The British granted Nadir Shah tacit backing by allowing him to cross India on his way to Afghanistan, but, unlike the Soviets who had used Red Army soldiers disguised as Afghans during the Charkhi expedition, they did not provide him with any other means of support.

Ruling with his brothers, Nadir Shah was a stern autocrat who tolerated little opposition. He was not totally against modernisation, but he realised that it would have to be a gradual process. Annulling some of the more provocative of Amanullah's reforms, he nevertheless sought assistance from foreign (mainly European) development advisers and contented himself with keeping his country on a neutral basis.

For the Russians, Nadir Shah's regime represented a setback. Some Comintern members considered the new monarchy part of an imperialist plot to encircle and later attack the revolutionary mother country through the establishment of military bases in India and Afghanistan. More realistically, the Kremlin decided to pursue favourable ties with Afghanistan by signing a mutual non-aggression pact in 1931. However there were still problems in Soviet-Afghan relations. In late 1932, Nadir Shah had Charkhi (who had returned from exile a year earlier) executed for insolence. Considering Charkhi its protege, the Kremlin was scarcely pleased. At that time, a group of nationalists, called the 'Young Afghans,' made its appearance in Kabul. Demoralised by the total failure of Amanullah's reform programme, they accused the anti-liberal Nadir Shah of being a British surrogate. Centred on the German-run Nejat high school in Kabul, the 'Young Afghans' had no apparent Marxist-Leninist orientation but are believed to have been encouraged by the Soviet authorities.

Their activities led to a number of assassinations, including that of the king in 1933 as he was handing out prizes at a school ceremony. With the king's death, it was feared that the country would be plunged into a Pushtun-style blood feud, but Nadir Shah's younger brother, Mahmud, saved the situation by using his near-absolute powers as Minister of War to quash any rebellion. This assured the peaceful succession of the dead king's 19-year-old French-educated son, Zahir Shah.

Closely counselled during the pre-war years by Prime Minister Hashim Khan, another of Nadir's brothers, Zahir Shah went on to rule Afghanistan for forty years until his overthrow by Mohammad Daoud in 1973. Under Hashim Khan's influence, Zahir Shah's Afghanistan was run like a police state and all political opposition was crushed. At the same time, the new monarch's attitude toward the Russians was even more antagonistic than his father's. For a long time, he spurned their offers of aid and refused to allow them to open a trade mission in Afghanistan.

Instead, he signed a Friendship Treaty with the United States and sought development assistance from Germany, France, Italy and Japan. During World War II, Afghanistan tried to remain completely neutral and at first refused the British demand to throw out the Germans. But when the Soviets joined the war on the Allied side, they too put pressure on Kabul to rid the country of the Axis presence. The British and Soviet governments plainly indicated that Afghanistan might suffer the same fate as Iran, which had been occupied protectively by both Allied Powers. Zahir Shah acquiesced, but he maintained his country's dignity by ordering only German, Japanese and Italian nationals without diplomatic status to leave. According to some reports, it was also during the war period that the first active pro-Soviet clandestine movement came into being.

Postwar Relations

When Shah Mahmud became Prime Minister in 1946, Afghanistan was allowed a limited form of democracy; more of a liberal than his brother, Shah Mahmud considered it prudent to make certain political concessions. Apart from releasing political prisoners, the new Prime Minister announced the holding of parliamentary elections, thus relieving some of the pent-up frustrations of the more liberal middle class. Educated largely in the French, German, American and other internationally-run schools in Kabul, the middle class aspired to much greater participation in government. Their thirst for change was plainly reflected in the 1949 elections, when no fewer than 50 reformists were voted in to the 120-seat assembly, now referred to as the 'liberal' parliament.

One of the first political-intellectual movements to appear after the war was the progressive-liberal Wikh-e-Zalmaiyan (Enlightened Youth). The spiritual heir of the 'Young Afghans,' it followed nostalgically in the footsteps of King Amanullah by attracting educated, mainly young Pushtun progressives. Emulating the 'Young Afghans,' Wikh-e-Zalmaiyan activists were fervently anti-imperialist and criticised what they considered to be American interference in the region. For many, Britain's withdrawal from the Indian subcontinent had simply been replaced by American interests. With calls for the return of the Pakistani tribal lands already evoking widespread popular support, the Wikh-e-Zalmaiyan took to promoting the Pushtunistan issue as one of its main platforms.

The Russians were quick to encourage such sentiments. Both Kabul University (which now had an active student union) and the civil service became pivots of Afghan liberal dissidence with critics loudly condemning the Royal Family for nepotism and corruption.

In 1953, Lt. Gen. Mohammad Daoud Khan, the 43-year-old first cousin and brother-in-law of the King, was installed as Prime Minister.

A former War Minister, head of the police and commander of the Kabul Central Armed Forces, Daoud instigated a new modernisation programme. This involved five-year economic plans, a restructuring of the armed forces and an attempt to diversify economic ties by looking not only to the United States and the West, but also to the Eastern bloc. Instead of implementing a rash of modernist social reforms, as many educated Afghans had hoped, Daoud decided to progress gradually. He also refused to allow the return of the heady days of liberalism; despite his previous affiliations with the Wikh-e Zalmaiyan, he kept both student and intellectual circles under close surveillance.

With the independence and partition of India in 1947, the haphazard relationship that had existed in the region between the British and the Russians came to an end. The resulting power vacuum caused the Afghan government considerable concern. Although London warned the Soviet Union not to violate Afghanistan's territorial integrity, many Afghans wondered whether they would now be in a position to stave off Soviet advances. The USSR's reluctance at the end of World War II to relinquish its hold over northern Iran as well as its iron grip on Eastern Europe showed only too clearly where Soviet interests lay. With the British counterbalance gone, Afghanistan could no longer use conventional diplomacy by playing off East against West as a means of survival. Daoud therefore tried to exploit US-Soviet rivalry in the hope of establishing a new equilibrium. But it was a stratagem that ultimately cost him his life and Afghanistan its independence.

Washington, for its part, had never understood the strategic importance of preserving Afghanistan as a buffer state. According to John Evarts Horner, the US deputy chief of mission in Kabul from 1951 to 1953, the State Department showed 'absolutely no interest in East-West relations' in Afghanistan during this period. Within the State Department bureaucracy, Afghanistan came under the South Asian Division, where attention was focused on India, Ceylon and Pakistan. 'There was no recognition of its central position; no apparent knowledge of the historical precedents which affected British-Russian relations for better or worse on this frontier', he noted.

Friction was caused by repeated rejections, or offers tied to unacceptable conditions, of Afghan requests for arms. When Daoud, who wanted to ensure his country's continued non-alignment, refused to join the Baghdad Pact (later the Central Treaty Organisation – CENTO) with Pakistan, Iran, Iraq, Turkey, Britain and the United States, the Americans opted for the Pakistanis (also a member of the South-East Asia Treaty Organisation – SEATO) to whom they regularly supplied weapons and other forms of support. With the Push-tunistan issue once again to the fore, Washington was reluctant to grant weapons to the Afghans if they were going to be used against its new ally. When the Americans refused one last bid for arms through Daoud's brother and Foreign Minister, Mohammad Naim, the Afghan leader turned to the USSR.

Expanding Soviet Aid

In 1954, the USSR had granted a $3.5 million loan for the building of two highly visible grain silos and bakeries. Following a short visit in December 1955 by Khruschev and Bulganin, the Kremlin offered Kabul a huge $100 million loan package. Designed to help finance and organise a major part of the infrastructure for Afghanistan's first Five-Year (1956-1961) Plan, this included the construction of the main highway (and the strategic Salang Tunnel) from the Soviet border to Kabul as well as the construction or expansion of airports at Mazar-i-Sharif, Bagram and Shindand, all of which proved enormously valuable in the staging of the 1979 Christmas invasion.

Most significant of all, the Russians stepped in to provide Daoud with the weapons he so dearly wanted. In 1956, he signed a $25 million arms deal with Moscow. Together with Czechoslovakia, East Germany and other COMECON nations, the USSR agreed to take over the restructuring of the armed forces by supplying Kabul with T-34 tanks, MIG-17 jets, helicopters and small arms. Although Turkey, the United States and Germany had traditionally assumed the responsibility for training Afghanistan's officer corps, it was the USSR and its allies which now took the lead. In 1961, the first contingents of Afghan officers and cadets left for instruction in the Soviet Union and Czechoslovakia. Within a decade, an estimated 7,000 Afghans had gone through Eastern bloc training programmes, whereas less than 1,000 had gone to the United States, Turkey and elsewhere.

US-Soviet Competition

Overall, the Russians had adopted a far more effective, and subtle, long-term approach than their American counterparts. In many respects, they treated their southern neighbour as an experimental 'economic Korea', to test to what extent Washington was prepared to compete under pressure in a non-aligned Third World country.

Because of its proximity, Afghanistan obviously represented a greater interest for the USSR than it ever could for the United States. Intent as always on increasing their influence, the Soviets directed their assistance to projects which would provide political gain almost immediately because of their tangible impact on the local population: the paving of streets in Kabul (less mud and dust), the building of grain silos and bakeries (fresh bread), housing (comfort) and power stations (electricity).

Apart from major road construction in the south, many US development projects were less evident to the public eye: health programmes, education, Peace Corps volunteer work and agricultural reclamation. Some of these projects were also in conjunction with international aid programmes, thus displaying UN rather than US insignia. The Americans had also established a poor reputation among many Afghans after the failure of the Helmand River irrigation project. Their construction of the $15 million airport at Kandahar further demonstrated a lack of foresight and unnecessary extravagence. Designed as a major re-fuelling station between Europe and Asia, it would have shortened the flying distance between Tehran and Delhi by 900 kilometres. By the time it was completed, however, propeller airplanes were being replaced by jets which did not require such stopovers.

Ironically, competition between the Soviet Union and the United States also forced them into a form of development co-operation. Former US ambassador Robert Neuman noted that, although this co-operation was completely unofficial, it was good and effective. 'This detente in Afghanistan prefigured the global detente which was to follow during the 1970s.' While the Russians surveyed and aerially photographed the northern third of Afghanistan for maps (thus laying the groundwork for the invasion), the Americans did the same in the south. At Kabul airport, the Russians helped construct the landing strips and buildings, while the Americans equipped the electrical and communications facilities. The Russians built the roads in the north, the Americans those in the south with the two meeting at pre-arranged points.

By 1970, however, it was the USSR, which acted as the dominant power in Afghanistan's military and economic development. Moscow was absorbing roughly 40 per cent of Afghanistan's exports. Unlike the Americans, who offered mainly grants, Soviet aid was in the form of long-term, low-interest loans. During the first two Five-Year Plans (1956-66), Moscow had loaned or bartered the equivalent of $550 million worth of military and economic aid. The United States, on the other hand, had provided a mere $500 million in assistance during the first twenty years since the end of World War II, a period twice as long. From 1966-76, Soviet aid jumped to $750 million, whereas US assistance for the same decade had plummeted to $150 million. From 1976 to the December, 1979 invasion, Soviet military and economic aid came to roughly $1 billion. Judging by the size of this aid bill, it soon became apparent to most observers in Kabul that, if the Afghans could not repay their debts in cash or kind, they would eventually have to do so politically.

Towards a Communist Party

Following independence in 1919, no Kabul government had recognised the 1893 British-imposed Durand Line dividing Afghanistan from colonial India. Prior to British withdrawal from the subcontinent, the Afghans demanded that all Pushtuns in the Northwest Frontier region be given the right to decide their own future: to join the new state of Pakistan, to opt for independence or to merge with Afghanistan.

From the post-World War II years onwards, Daoud, first as Minister of War, then as Prime Minister, knowing a popular issue when he saw one, fanned the flames of both Pushtun and Baluchi nationalism in Pakistan through internal political agitation and even armed cross-border forays by Afghan frontier tribesmen. The Pakistanis retaliated in 1950 and 1955 by closing the overland transit routes from the free port of Karachi to landlocked Afghanistan, a sharp reminder of how dependent the country was on the goodwill of its neighbours.

In the late summer of 1961, a protracted border crisis arose when Pakistan suspended not only normal commerce but also the rights of nomads who had traditionally moved between the two countries in search of pasture for their camels, sheep and goats. The blockade, which lasted until June 1963, led to severe economic hardship and political unrest. Afghanistan was now almost totally dependent on the USSR for its foreign trade. The Russians shrewdly benefitted from this situation by airfreighting Afghanistan's fruit harvests, which were in danger of rotting on the ground, to the USSR. The gesture greatly impressed local farmers and Moscow's prestige grew. What the Afghans were not told, however, was that the enormous cost of the airlift was later tacked on to the country's burgeoning national debt to the Soviet Union. The blockade crisis ultimately led to Daoud's resignation in 1963, and his departure made way for another shortlived experiment in democratic liberalism. Resurrecting parliamentary institutions, Zahir Shah created what seemed to be a more authentic constitutional democracy and prohibited any member of the Royal Family from holding a government position. Under the new constitution, the formation of political parties was technically allowed, but the King never signed the necessary parliamentary legislation. As a result, parties were neither permitted nor forbidden. But the new 'liberalism' did imply the return of a relatively free press, thus enabling the political movements to raise their heads once again.

The PDPA

Until then, the People's Democratic Party of Afghanistan had existed as a clandestine group of a few dozen university lecturers, civil servants and teachers. On New Year's Day, 1965, twenty-seven participants gathered at Nur Mohammad Taraki's house in the middle class Karte Char district of Dabul to officially found the party and hold its first congress. They elected a nine-man Central Committee with Taraki as Secretary General and Babrak Karmal as his deputy. Among the Committee members were Ghulam Dastagir Panjshairi, later chairman of the post-1979 Party Control Commission, and Sultan Ali Keshtmand, Prime Minister under Babrak. The PDPA programme, which was published more than a year later in *Khalq*, (Masses), the official party weekly, called for the creation of a patriotic national and democratic front incorporating workers, peasants, progressive intellectuals, small landowners and the lower middle class to help the country rise from its 'social misery'.

With no mention whatsoever of Marxism-Leninism, the PDPA proposals were remarkably similar to those put forward by King Amanullah. Its full communist identity was kept secret until 1978; a necessary subterfuge, for the party could have expected harsh reactions had it been more candid about its true pro-Soviet nature. Indeed, *Khalq* lasted a mere five weeks before being banned by the authorities.

During the autumn 1965 elections, however, only twenty progressives, including four PDPA members who had campaigned as independents, were elected to the 218-seat parliament, a significant drop compared to the 'liberal' assembly of 1949. One of the reasons behind this was the fact that Afghanistan's traditional tribal, ethnic and religious leaders, less than a third of whom could read and write, had recognised the advantages of sitting in parliament and therefore participated in the polls with vigour. It was not without some satisfaction, however, that the PDPA saw at least half its candidates succeed. All those elected were future members of the Parcham faction and, thoroughly unusual for the time, included one woman, Dr Anahita Ratebzad, a brilliant politician and Babrak's close companion. From then on, the PDPA

decided to concentrate on the main task of expanding party membership and influence.

By the late 1960s, the constitutional monarchy had become a farce.
Parliament once again served as nothing more than democratic window
dressing, while nepotism in both business and government remained the
prerogative of the ruling establishment. Amid growing frustration,
civil servants and army officers found themselves unable to advance
their careers for lack of the right family ties. Even more disastrous, economic development had slowed down and a congested labour market
no longer offered the openings, to what young high school and college
graduates had once expected.

Many blamed the Royal Family for the social and political stalemate, and turned to the extreme left-wing or the nationalist and fundamentalist right-wing parties in hope of change. Reaping the benefits of
urban discontent, it was here than the expanding PDPA found its base.
Between 1968 and 1970, Afghanistan was marked by an era of violence
in which the PDPA and other left-wing parties played a leading role.

Rift Within the Party

Formally starting off as one party, the PDPA did not split publicly into
separate Khalq and Parcham factions until 1967. But their division was
apparent already well before. Foremost were the personality differences
between the two leaders: Taraki, the rural Pushtun and self-made man
of humble background, and Babrak, the younger, almost fashionably
left-wing activist from a well-connected upper middle-class family.
These differences were strongly reflected not only in their strategies but
in the make-up of their factions.

Both men were at odds on how best to apply the revolution to such
a conservative and backward country. Taraki was intent on creating a
Lenin-type workers' party (there were only 40,000 workers in Afghanistan at the time), but which would incorporate anyone, regardless of
class, who was prepared to support radical change. As the Khalq found
its roots among the primarily rural Pushtun middle class, he also backed
the Pushtunistan issue. Babrak, for his part, did not consider the
Afghan population ready for anything as drastic as a Marxist-Leninist
revolution. Enjoying a mainly intellectual Tadjik and non-Pushtun base,
he saw Afghanistan as a mosaic of ethnic and tribal groups rather than a
nation and looked to the Soviet Union as a model. He therefore
favoured a more gradual, evolutionary approach, using existing parliamentary institutions. While Taraki's Khalq refused any form of co-operation with government, the Parcham faction soon became known as the

'Royal Afghan Communist Party'.

Nur Mohammad Taraki

Nur Mohammad Taraki was born a member of the Pushtun Ghilzai tribe in 1917 in Mukur, a small village situated between Kabul and Kandahar. His father was a small merchant. Taraki went to the local primary school before attending high school in Kandahar. From 1935 onwards, he worked in Bombay as a clerk for the Pushtun Trading Company. He continued his education, notably in English, at night school but it was also here that he made his first contact with Marxist-Leninist groups such as the Red Shirt movement, forerunner of the Indian Communist Party. On returning to Afghanistan in 1937 or 1938, he went to live and work in Kabul, where he also obtained a degree in law and political science at the State College for Government Employees. Through connections, he took up a position in the Ministry of Economics, but was later dismissed for misappropriating funds from a government co-operative as well as building materials from a leading Afghan businessman. He eventually ended up as deputy chief of Bakhtar, the Afghan news agency.

Steadily more politically active, Taraki joined Wilk-e-Zalmaiyan in 1948 and began writing short stories and poems in his spare time. He soon established a considerable reputation as a Pashto writer of 'new realism' describing simple rural life and social improvement. Following the government's crackdown on the liberal opposition and press in 1952, he was banished to Washington as press attache at the Afghan embassy, but was relieved of his duties six months later after giving a provocative press conference in which he strongly criticised the Daoud regime.

Over the next three years, his movements remain vague; some reports say that he returned to Afghanistan via India and Pakistan, others that he also made a long trip through Europe and the USSR. At any rate, in 1956, he was hired by the US embassy and AID mission in Kabul as a translator, but then established his own agency, the Nur Translations Bureau, while still pursuing a literary career. From 1963 onwards, he is believed to have concentrated full-time on the organisational activities of the party. Some observers suggest that somewhere along the line, possibly following his departure from Washington, he may have become a paid agent of the KGB. Already in the late 1950s, he was known to have made regular visits to the Soviet embassy in Kabul, but there is not sufficient evidence to confirm the extent of these pre-PDPA Soviet ties.

Babrak Karmal

Babrak Karmal is a completely different political animal; certainly more dynamic and talented than Taraki. Born in 1929 in Kamari near Kabul, Babrak's well-to-do family background gave him the sort of security Taraki never knew. His father, Mohammad Hussein, was a senior officer in the army, who finished his career in 1965 as a general followed by the governorships of Herat and Paktya under Daoud. Claiming to be Pushtun, the family spoke Dari as its first language and may have been of Tadjik descent. As a high school pupil, Babrak (he later took the name 'Karmal' meaning 'friend of labour', or, according to some, a Dari version of Kremlin) attended the German-language Lycée Nejat (also known at times as the Amani Lycée), where he may have come under the influence of teachers active during the days of the 'Young Afghan' movement.

He was considered less than average as a pupil and failed his entrance examination at the University's Law and Political Science Faculty in Kabul. After a second attempt, he qualified in 1951, but he had by then become an active left-wing militant and accomplished orator as a member of the fiery student union. During the 1952 repression, he was imprisoned but released three years later (after recanting his views), none the worse off; other prisoners experienced a much harsher time.

On his release, Babrak worked as a German-Dari translator, probably for the Afghan government, until he was conscripted into the army for the usual two-year stint. Although not able to function publicly as a political activist, Babrak (like Taraki) continued to participate in private political meetings with students, civil servants and army officers until the fall of Daoud. In 1959, he returned to university to complete his law and political science studies. Thereafter he worked again as a translator, primarily for the Ministry of Education. In 1964, he turned his full attention to politics.

According to some sources, Babrak may have been recruited by the KGB during his early student days. He too was a regular visitor at the Soviet embassy from the late 1950s onwards and even made uninhibited use of official Soviet medical facilities in Kabul. Furthermore he lived in the modern, Soviet-built Microrayon housing complex, then, as now, the home of government officials, army officers and Russian advisers.

Once the political split between Taraki and Babrak had come out in the open, Babrak founded his own newspaper, the *Parcham* (Banner), which gave its name to the faction. The first issue appeared in Pashto and Dàri in March 1968. It managed to survive for more than a year before being banned in July 1969 prior to the new parliamentary elections.

The Failing Monarchy

The years immediately preceding Daoud's 1973 coup d'etat were characterised by a violently conservative and religious reaction to the influence of the left-wing parties. Demonstrations in the towns developed into riots, with mullahs, notably those from the countryside, protesting against insults to Islam, modernisation and loose moral values. Fanatics in Kabul, for example, attacked unveiled women in Western dress by throwing acid in their faces. In some areas, there were even minor armed revolts which were quickly put down by the army.

Islamic opposition to the left was not a homogeneous phenomenon, however, while the more traditionalist, rual-based elements of society repudiated anything that threatened their lifestyles, fundamentalist educated urban groups held nothing against modernisation but rather the moral degeneration that came with it. From 1970 onwards, the idea of Islam as a political doctrine instead of just a religion began to galvanise support among the high schools, colleges and university. Some supporters, as part of a 'return to roots' movement, began touring the countryside and villages to preach a more politicised, progressive form of Islam.

Politically the country was increasingly unstable. One government followed another, and the King refused to devolve the necessary constitutional powers which might have calmed the situation. He also failed to support his Prime Ministers, in times of crisis; according to some analysts, it was not the King who was at fault, but the selfishness or poor quality of his advisers, virtually all members of the Royal Family.

Furthermore, Afghanistan was struck by a severe famine in 1971-2. According to some estimates, as many as 100,000 people may have died. Despite the availability of 200,000 tonnes of American-donated wheat, the government neglected to take proper action. A quarter of the wheat may have been held up by the Indo-Pakistani war, but there were numerous scandals of hoarding or re-sale on the black market by corrupt government officals and distributors.

The Return of Daoud

It was during this famine that Daoud is believed to have begun preparations for a coup d'etat. As allies, he chose both liberal and left-wing activists, including a number of well-placed Air Force officers, some trained in the USSR who also played prominent roles during the 1978 communist takeover. Daoud's close ties with members of the Parcham and Khalq led many Western observers to speculate that the coup was backed and perhaps even planned by the Soviet Union.

When Daoud finally launched the coup on 17 July 1973, he proclaimed Afghanistan a republic and formed a government which included four Parcham party members as ministers. For the Soviet Union, his return to power was a cause for rejoicing. For others, it was the beginning of the end of Afghanistan as an independent and non-aligned state. By co-operating with Daoud, the Soviet-backed Parcham no doubt hoped that he would be a political figurehead with the communists calling the tune. Early on he pursued policies, both domestic and foreign, that won the support of the communists, but it soon became clear that he had other ideas.

To the dismay of the PDPA and the Soviet Union, Daoud began mending his fences with Iran and Pakistan. By edging closer to the Shah, he managed to secure a $1 billion aid offer only one year after the coup; the Shah, who was seeking to create a Pan-Islamic Union of non-Arab nations stretching from Turkey to Pakistan soon raised it to $2 billion, more than all of Afghanistan's foreign assistance over the previous two decades. The Iranian proposals included a commitment to build a railway link from Kabul to the Iranian border via Kandahar and Herat. This would indirectly link the Afghan capital with the Gulf and thus relieve the country of its overdependence on the USSR and Pakistan. By 1976, Daoud's support of the Pushtunistan issue, also strongly encouraged by the two communist factions, had dissipated visibly, resulting in friendly meetings between him and President Bhutto of Pakistan.

Even more disconcerting, Daoud signed three aid agreements with the United States totalling over $40 million. There was nothing to suggest, however, that he was seeking to join the Western bloc. In fact, he seemed to have assumed a healthy wariness of both Moscow and Washington. According to Kuldip Nayar, a leading Indian journalist and writer, Daoud had told him in an interview in April 1974 that he 'preferred' Indian to American and Soviet advisers. Between 1973 and 1976, he reduced the number of Soviet advisers from roughly 1,000 to 200, replacing a significant number of them with Indians.

Such developments could hardly have infatuated the Soviet Union. Domestically, too, things were not going quite the way the two PDPA factions had envisaged. By 1976, Daoud had purged his administration of Parcham ministers. A year later, he called a Loya Jirgha, a traditional Afghan gathering of tribal, religious and political leaders representing the entire country, to approve a new constitution and elect him President for the next six years. Few, if any, of the Jirgha participants were left-wing. During the last year of Daoud's rule, a series of political assassinations, committed by both left and right-wing dissidents, gave notice of things to come. But it was the murder of Mir Akbar Khyber, a leading Parcham theoretician, in mid-April, 1978 that prompted the communist takeover, the so-called Saur Revolution.

Preparing for Power

Whether the Soviets had ever intended a communist takeover remains open to question. Most indicators suggest that the 1978 putsch was not only premature, but that events had forced the Soviet hand into supporting it. Relations with Afghanistan during the 1920s and later the 1950s and 1960s had shown that it was not necessary to have an ideologically compatible regime in Kabul in order to exert influence. Although Moscow had sustained the PDPA over the thirteen years prior to the Saur Revolution the Soviets may have regarded the party simply as a means of putting pressure on the government through political agitation. This changed during the latter days of the Daoud era when they realised that a pro-Moscow putsch might prove the only solution.

The two party factions presented the Soviets with a choice. The Parcham would allow them to influence Afghan policy in a constitutional manner, while the ostracised Khalq had already infiltrated the armed forces, the administration and the educational system providing a cadre with the necessary organisation and clout to act against Daoud. It also enabled the Khalq to assure its dominance over the Parcham during the first 20 months of communist rule.

Hafizullah Amin

The key man behind the Khalq's politicking in the armed forces was Hafizullah Amin. Born in 1929 in Paghman, a Gilzai Pushtun like Taraki, Amin studied mathematics and physics at Kabul University before becoming an instructor at a teachers' training college. He went on to serve as headmaster at the prestigious Avesina High School and then left for the United States in 1957 where he gained an MA in education at Columbia University. He returned to Kabul to teach and it was at this time that he met Taraki. In 1962, he went back to New York to obtain a doctorate in education, but dropped out in favour of politics. By 1965 he was back in Afghanistan, and although he had missed the founding congress of the PDPA, he became an associate Central Committee member in 1966. He was also the only Khalq to win an election by taking the Paghman seat in the 1969 parliament.

As a highly effective organiser, Amin began actively recruiting for the Khalq among the armed forces back in 1973. Five years later, the Khalq commanded twice if not three times as many (perhaps 300-500) followers as the Parcham in the army, air force and police. While most senior officers, who were of upper middle-class background, were attracted to the Parcham, the Khalq found its adherents among the more numerous middle and lower rank officers. Within the civil service Parcham continued to have greater support.

Through the insistence, and eventual arbitration, of the Soviet embassy, the two communist factions were persuaded in July 1977 to bury their differences and join together again in a tactical reunion. Whether the Soviets were at this stage contemplating a coup must remain a matter of speculation. The renewed relationship was a precarious and temporary one. Without doubt, the Khalqis, who had always clamoured for radical rather than evolutionary change, were better equipped to precipitate a coup and, although the Parcham participated in its preparations, the takeover was primarily a Khalqi operation.

On 17 April 1978, Mir Akbar Khyber was 'mysteriously' assassinated by a salvo of automatic fire in the street outside his house. While some have suspected the hand of the Soviets behind the shooting, others have pointed to the Daoud regime or Muslim activists. More likely, however, the murder may have been a bid by the Khalqis to provoke civil unrest and rid themselves of a prominent Parcham leader.

Two days later, thousands of demonstrators — civil servants (mainly from the Ministries of the Interior and Finance), students and other left-wing sympathisers — marched silently at Mir Akbar's funeral with Taraki and other communist leaders at the head of the cortege. At his grave, they delivered speeches virulently attacking the Daoud regime. On 26 April a number of leading PDPA figures, including Taraki and Babrak, were arrested and thrown into prison. But not Amin; only ten hours later did police arrest him.

With remarkable rapidity and efficiency, Amin had used the interval to set the coup d'etat in motion by issuing handwritten orders throughout the night and early morning to his contacts in the armed forces. According to some reports, these were photocopied late at night using machines at the Soviet embassy. Others maintain that Soviet pilots flew planes in the attack against the 'Arg,' the presidential palace. Whatever the truth, by the evening of 27 April it was all over. Daoud was dead and the PDPA had proclaimed Afghanistan a Democratic Republic. The communists had taken control.

The 'Saur' Revolution

Whereas the Russians may have advised initially against a putsch, they were now prepared to support it to the hilt. On 30 April the USSR was the first country to recognise the new regime. In the days that followed, India, Bulgaria, Outer Mongolia, Czechoslovakia, Cuba and Vietnam followed suit.

The PDPA was quick to deny that it was in any way beholden to the Soviets; it obstinately insisted that it, and it alone, had carried out the *coup d'état*. Nevertheless, within two months, the number of Soviet advisers had risen from roughly 200 to several thousand, while all major Iranian and Arab-sponsored projects were halted. Moscow also promised to provide more than $1 billion worth of economic aid over the next five years. In fact, hardly a week went by without the signing of one Soviet-Afghan treaty or another; by November, 1978, no less than thirty such agreements had been concluded.

At the time of the coup, neither the Khalq nor the Parcham could count on more than 6,000 adherents. Even fewer had been aware that a coup was in the making. For many Afghans living in urban areas such as Kabul, the new regime represented a welcome change from the Daoud dictatorship as well as hopes for a speedy modernisation of the country. Poor, underdeveloped and plagued by a high rate of illiteracy, Afghanistan was still in desperate need of social and economic improvement.

Yet there was no particular public expression of joy or disappointment in the streets. A general wariness of PDPA motives led to many adopting a 'wait and see' attitude. 'We were actually quite pleased that Daoud was gone. It was clear that people wanted change, but we had no idea what the Khalqis were going to do', said a student from the Lycée Istiqlal, now a junior resistance commander in the Kabul region.

It was soon obvious that the PDPA lacked the appropriate popular support to assume effective power. The new communist order rapidly came to smack of mediocrity and corruption, far surpassing that of the Daoud regime. Trusted political but often incompetent appointees (primarily Khalqi) were brought in to take over from skilled technocrats and administrators. Only three of the new Ministers – Babrak, Amin and Anahita, who had been appointed Minister of Welfare – had had any previous parliamentary experience. Although the bulk of

Taraki's 21-member cabinet (11 Khaqli, 10 Parchami ministers) had had administrative experience, most of them had been lower or middle rank civil servants.

It was even worse in the provinces, where those who took control of government offices had few if any qualifications whatsoever. Many were quite simply ignorant thugs or opportunists who used their newly acquired positions to improve their social standing, settle old rivalries or feather their nests through self-bestowed privileges and bribes.

The patched-up reunion of the two PDPA factions disintegrated rapidly during the first few months of the Revolution. Internecine strife had already broken out on the night of the coup, when Taraki and Babrak quarrelled over who was to read the official proclamation of the putsch over nation-wide radio. Eventually, a military officer performed this politically sensitive task.

Although the factions clashed bitterly over policy, there was an attempt to present both sides as equals in public, at least until the end of May. When newspapers resumed publishing in the aftermath of the coup, there were numerous photographs of all the leaders. But the Khalq soon began to assert their dominance. Even before active anti-communist opposition had a chance to manifest itself, the Khalq had launched its purges against the Parcham with the first arrests only six weeks after the coup.

Six of the Parchami leaders were banished in the traditional Afghan manner by sending them abroad as ambassadors. One of the first to go (to Iran) was Dr Najib, or Najibullah. A 31-year-old physician and Parcham Central Committee member, he later became head of the dreaded KHAD (security service) under the Soviet occupation. Then, on 5 July, the official English-language newspaper *The Kabul Times* announced that Karmal had been relieved of his duties as First Deputy Prime Minister and named Ambassador to Prague. Anahita Ratebzad and Interior Minister Ahmad Nur were similarly exiled to Belgrade and Washington respectively.

Toward the end of the summer, the Khalqi discovered an elaborate plot to overthrow the regime, in which dozens of Parcham leaders and supporters were implicated. These ranged from the six Parchami ambassadors to Defence Minister, Lt. Gen. Abdul Qadar, Planning Minister Sultan Ali Kishtmand and Public Works Minister, Major Gen. Mohammad Rafiee. According to the alleged details, the Parchami had planned to stage nation-wide civilian demonstrations and then seize control of key military and administrative positions.

The Khalq reacted harshly by secretly sentencing several of them to death including Keshtmand and Qadar, who had played a major role in both the 1973 and 1978 coups. Only Gen. Shahpur Khan Ahmadzai, the army chief of staff, and Dr Mir Ali Akbar, a minor political figure and director of Kabul's Jamuriat Hospital, were actually executed. The six ambassadors resigned and went to live in Eastern Europe and the USSR, where the Soviets kept them in political cold storage.

Reign of the Khalq

Why the Kremlin permitted the pro-Soviet Parcham to be ousted by the more nationalist Khalq is unclear. It is certain that the Soviets disapproved of the witch-hunts against the Parcham, yet publicly they demonstrated no sign of disenchantment with the Kabul regime. The Soviet embassy might have been able to bring pressure on the Khalq, but it is debatable whether this could have been achieved without taking drastic action.

By October 1978, most of the top Parchami had been pushed aside, imprisoned or exiled. Under Taraki the Khalqi government started to impose its reforms with vigour. Much of the programme was admirable with its passionate proclamations of justice and equality. Some of the policies including the reduction or cancelling of debts and mortgages owed by small landowners or landless peasants (Decree N.6), the establishment of equal rights for women and the abolition of arranged marriages and dowries (Decree N.7), and above all, the land reform (Decree N.8), might have worked had they been carried out with care and foresight and over a long period.

But such changes struck at the heart of the Afghan way of life. Khalqi determination to impose them immediately with complete lack of respect for community, particularly Islamic, traditions shocked even the Russians. Upheaval and revolt could not fail to be the result.

6 THE COMMUNIST OVERLAY — REPRESSION AND CONTROL

'A million Afghans are all that should remain alive — a million communists. The rest, we don't need. We'll get rid of all of them,' Sayed Abdullah, Khalqi commander of Pul-e-charkhi prison in Kabul.

All that remains are three barely distinguishable mounds in the field where they bulldozed the bodies. As for Kerala, it stands almost deserted. Most of the women, children and the 200 or so men who survived the shooting fled shortly afterwards to Pakistan. Since then, tens of thousands, perhaps hundreds of thousands, of human beings, have died in Afghanistan, and Kerala is only a feeble memory.

It was Friday 20 April 1979, almost one year after the launching of the Saur Revolution.A slow-moving column of government tanks and armoured personnel carriers rumbled up the eroded dirt road toward the small mud and stone town in Afghanistan's eastern Kunar province. Kerala, a farming community of some 5,000 mainly Pushtun inhabitants, is located only 12 miles as the crow flies northwest of the Raghani Pass on the Pakistani-Afghan frontier. To reach the town, one must follow the ancient mule track that leads through the pass and the pine-forested mountains overlooking the banks of the Kunar River. On the other side, where its tributary the Pech runs into the main stream from a broad valley of irrigated wheat fields and fruit trees, lies Kerala.

The townspeople quietly watched the approaching force. There was nothing unusual about the troops. Despite increasing guerrilla attacks, the government still controlled the main road running alongside the river. Soldiers often came to the town. There had been much fighting during the previous weeks between rebel groups hiding in the surrounding mountains and the Afghan military garrison stationed in the valley. Only the previous day, local mujahideen had attacked the Khalqi stronghold at Chagaserai, one of the main security bases in the province.

Today, however, was the Muslim sabbath, a day of peace and prayer. A tacit agreement between the two sides more or less existed not to fight on Fridays. Although most of the communist party members in the army were 'Kafirs', non-believers, almost all the conscripts were good Muslims. The vehicles took up position in and around the town.

107

Some 200 armed soldiers and policemen had come with the convoy. While some stood vigil near the tanks, others quickly spread out into the town. Mingling in the background were also twenty Soviet advisers in Afghan uniform. 'All the men were ordered to come to a 'jirgha' (meeting) to discuss the rebel fighting in the area', remembered Abdul Latif, a former policeman who later fled to Pakistan. 'None of the men were armed. The women and children were herded into the mosque. There they could hear and see everything that was going on.'

When most of the male population had been gathered in the field for the 'jirgha', the Afghan officers with the Soviet advisers standing behind began to berate them loudly for aiding and abetting the guerrillas. As with most towns, villages and hamlets in the province, a certain number of menfolk operated as farmers by day, insurgents by night. 'The government soldiers were very annoyed about the mujahed attacks', said Khalil Ullah, a teacher and one of the male survivors. 'They knew very well that we had been secretly giving the mujahideen food, ammunition, shelter and money.' Abdul Hadi, another teacher, recalled: 'They were particularly angry because the governor of Kunar had previously called on us all to take up arms against the rebels, but we flatly refused.'

With the tanks blocking access to the river, the soldiers aimed their Kalashnikovs at the men. The officers then commanded the tribesmen to shout pro-communist slogans. Instead, they all defiantly replied: 'Allah o akbar! God is Great!' Incensed, the soldiers roughly shoved the men into line. An army officer stepped forward to take a photograph of the group, a picture later used for propaganda purposes to show what happened to those who collaborated with the rebels.

Nabi Madez Khan, a short and stocky schoolboy who lost his father, uncle and four cousins in the massacre, described what happened during the final minutes. Wearing a brown Chitral cap perched on the back of his closely cropped head, he looked younger than his eighteen years as he stood in front of a large gathering of Afghan refugees in Pakistan's Northwest Frontier Bajaur Tribal agency some ten months later. 'I accompanied my father to the field to the meeting', he said softly in Pashto. 'People were afraid that something was going to happen. Some of the men tried to join the women and children in the mosque, but they were turned back at gunpoint.'

Suddenly, a military helicopter emerged from beyond the river and hovered over the field, throwing up dust and blowing the men's hair in their faces. A senior Soviet adviser, a dark blond, green-eyed Slav, who was known to some of the inhabitants from previous visits to the town, conversed rapidly by field radio with the helicopter. 'I became scared and wanted to leave', Nabi said. 'I tried to ask the commandant (Soviet adviser) if I could go, but he ignored me'. Nabi turned away anyway and started to hurry toward the mosque. No one stopped him in the confusion and he looked back several times. The helicopter swerved away abruptly. Orders were shouted and the men were sharply told to crouch down facing the tanks. Some of them began praying. Behind them stood the Afghan soldiers with their rifles cocked; several of the Soviet advisers including the senior officer placed themselves to the rear. Then the shooting started.

'I was running but turned to look back', explained Nabi. 'I saw everything. The soldiers were firing their guns and the men were falling to the ground. I could not see my father.' When the women saw their menfolk being executed, they started screaming and flailing their arms. They ran forward holding up Holy Korans in their hands for the soldiers to see and pleading for mercy. Trying to break through, they were warned back by the guards who shot in the air. According to one of the many women interviewed in Pakistan, the chief Soviet adviser, who was quietly looking on, turned to them and said: 'You can be sure that next year's potato crop will be a good one', or words to that effect.

'When the shooting started', said Bibi Rakhara, an unveiled, wizened old woman who lost her husband, four brothers, one son and two nephews in the slaughter, 'we could see our men falling. We had known what was going to happen. We wanted to reach them . . . to touch them . . . but the soldiers stopped us.' In the mêlée the young Nabi, possibly because of his small stature, made his way to the mosque without being noticed. A few men quickly handed him female clothing. Several other men had also managed to slip in and tried to disguise themselves in dark chadors (veils).

A few minutes after the shooting, a bulldozer appeared on the scene and began ploughing the bodies into the soft earth of the field. Some were still alive and moving. Several women noticed the army photographer taking more pictures. The security forces then fanned out into the town to track down the remaining men. Some entered the mosque and tore away the veils of suspects. Three or four men were discovered and dragged screaming down to the field where they were unceremoniously added to the carnage. Only a few escaped. 'I was in my house when I heard the shooting', a male refugee said. 'I could hear the women screaming and realised what was happening so I ran.' Near the river, he hid among the trees. Latif, the policeman, only survived because, as a government official, he was assumed to be loyal to the Khalq. Three days later, he fled across the border.

Within hours of the massacre, tearful groups of old women and children as well as a handful of stunned male survivors emerged. Dozens of men were fortunate to have escaped because they were out of town at the time. They crossed the Kunar river by the small ferry and then walked to Pakistan through the mountains. A Pakistani army major watched some of them arrive. 'It was a tragic sight', he said. 'I watched all these wretched women and children gradually trickle in over a period of days into Bajaur. They were all weeping. There was hardly a man among them.'

All in all, an estimated 1,170 unarmed males, including boys in their early teens, were callously murdered at Kerala, more than the equally brutal massacres of Lidice, Czechoslovakia, or My Lai, when American troops shot down over 100 Vietnamese civilians in cold blood. Although rumours of reprisory killings had circulated almost from the very beginning of the Saud Revolution, Kerala was the first to be reported in detail by Western journalists (albeit nine months later; first accounts in the Pakistani press two weeks after the incident were ignored) based on the corroborating evidence of some fifty survivors and witnesses. Kerala was also one of the first clear indications that Soviet military and political advisers were involved in such practices designed to prop up the Khalqi dictatorship. Since then scores of slaughters, committed during both the Taraki-Amin and Babrak periods have been confirmed, ranging from the deliberate drowning of some 300 Hazaras in the north to the mass executions of political prisoners on the outskirts of Kabul.

No one can ever know how many Afghans have died in bombardments, military assaults, executions, imprisonment and other forms of repression since the communist takeover in 1978. The figure of several hundred thousand victims appears to be a reasonable estimate although some sources maintain that as many as one million people have succumbed to the repression. Following the Soviet invasion, Babrak himself, in an attempt to discredit the previous Khalqi regimes, claimed 1.5 million killed under Taraki and Amin.

First Repression

While initial Khalqi persecution was directed at the Parcham, the

Taraki-Amin regime soon turned its attention to dissenting non-communist elements. When Khalqi terror first gripped the cities, in the summer of 1978 gradually spreading through the provinces, the people opposed the government in the traditional Asian manner. With passivity. Many Afghans also remained indifferent as long as the hand of the Khalq did not affect them directly.

Within weeks of coming to power, the communists ordered the arrests of mullahs and prominent landowners in the key eastern provinces. Some were picked up by the police as they prayed in the mosques; others were simply dragged into the village squares and beaten. Such outrages were designed to show the peasants that they were no longer at the 'mercy' of their 'reactionary exploiters'. Consisting largely of military officers and teachers from a rural background, but also of frustrated high school students, rootless radicals, opportunists and criminal delinquents, the Khalqi rank and file was united by a superficial knowledge of Marxism-Leninism and a contempt for anything representing the past. The regime's attitude was that the people had to be liberated from their 'miserable existence' even if that meant shoving the new order down their throats. 'The way the Kalqis reacted was both despicable and disastrous', a senior Parcham diplomat noted in late 1983. 'They showed absolutely no respect. They ruined the Revolution and it is because of them that we are having such enormous difficulties today.'

Backed by armed soldiers and police, militants sent into the provinces sought to put into practice what the party preached. Misguidedly, they believed that by destroying the feudal and landowner classes, they could gain the support of the peasantry, the masses. What they were in fact doing was attacking traditional village spokesmen. When, at the end of land distribution ceremonies, government officials invited farmers to spit on their expropriated landlords, many refused. When the farmers continued to resist Khalqi demands, even under threat, they were physically assaulted and sometimes killed. Adding insult to injury, the militants denigrated social and religious customs by burning religious books, tearing the veils off women and mocking villagers at prayer. 'The Khalqis have no prophet, no God!' angrily lamented one Kunar farmer, now a refugee in Pakistan. 'You know what they said when they saw us pray? They said: "Are you doing sports?" These people tyrannized us!'

A Misguided Agrarian Reform

The Khalqis revealed not only total unfamiliarity with the country's social and economic realities, but complete inability to understand the complex nature of the land tenure system. According to some analysts, Afghanistan was not suffering from a major absentee landlord problem at the time of the communist takeover. Nevertheless, they noted, the traditional tenure system did foster a variety of malpractices that could be corrected by appropriate reform.

Traditionally, agricultural production is dependent on five factors: land, water, seed, animal or mechanical power, and human labour. Whoever contributes one of these elements theoretically receives one-fifth of the resulting crop. In most cases, it was the landowner who provided everything but human toil. Although the local 'malik,' or headman, often took advantage of his position, extorting unreasonably high shares from his villagers, American ethnologist Louis Dupree, a leading authority on Afghanistan, observed that

> all landlords should not be stereotyped as mercenary tyrants. Viewed from within the cultural milieu, the landlord becomes a major entrepreneur, juggling extensive operations and tremendous capital. . . But the relationship between landlord and tenant, landlord and overseer, and overseer and tenant involves much give and take. Many landlords in Afghanistan take a paternalistic interest in their peasants.

As rural Afghans have always regarded the Kabul authorities with distrust, they were often quite content to have the local landlord represent their interests in the big city and serve as a buffer against government demands.

As part of the new regime's land redistribution programme, the Kalqis decreed that private property was to be limited to the equivalent of six hectares of cultivated and 60 hectares of fallow land. But simply handing land over to the peasants was not the answer. Farmers who accepted confiscated property found that there was no structure to go with it. No seeds, no machines, fertiliser, credits or water rights. To their dismay, they soon discovered that nothing had in fact changed. Once again, it was the traditional landlord who had to deal with the Kabul authorities and provide them with basic agricultural necessities in return for part of the crop.

Six months after the invasion, I travelled by pickup truck to the Chagai Hills in Helmand Province in southern Afghanistan with a group of Baluchi tribesmen. There, I was taken to a hidden desert camp just south of the Helman River. The guerrilla commander who received me had been a principal landowner before the confiscation of his properties in a semi-arid but fertile agricultural region roughly three hours jeep ride away. The several hundred mujahideen with him were all tenant farmers from villages formerly under his control. As we chatted over tea in a long, dried mud and reed guest-house, I witnessed a scene that could easily have taken place in the last century.

A steady stream of followers entered the hut to consult with their chief. An aristocratic, finely featured man in his mid-fifties with a magnificently groomed beared, he listened quietly to their problems one by one, dispensing advice with the air of a Solomon. One farmer wanted to know whether it was better for him to send his family to Pakistan. Another wanted permission to go to Dulbandin across the border to buy supplies. The tractor had broken down, he explained, and there were no spare parts in the camp. A father wanted his son, who had come of age, to participate in the next raid against the 'Khalqis', as many Afghans continued to call the Babrak regime. At the end of each parley, the follower knelt down to kiss the landlord's hand in respect. I later asked a tribesman whether the government had not tried to distribute his master's land. Yes, said the man, that was so. Was he not pleased with the prospect of having his own land? He looked up in surprise. 'Yes, but that would be stealing. In Islam, one man does not steal from another.'

First Revolt

Within months of the takeover, the Khalqis seemed to be doing everything possible to antagonise the Afghan population. They had already initiated a policy of bloody reprisals for non-co-operation. In the late spring of 1978, for example, government security forces burned down the village of Solayman Khel in Kunar province for hiding a Hezb-i-Islami militant. Such actions only served to further incite local communities. When villagers returned to the smouldering ruins of their homes, they told the militant, who had managed to hide during the foray: 'We are not for your party. We don't know what you do. But we support you against this government of Kafirs.'

By mid-summer, 1978, the first armed opposition to the Khalqis broke out in Nuristan, a wild mountainous region of deep valleys, swirling torrents and unexpectedly dense pine and oak forests, whose 100,000 inhabitants were forcibly converted to Islam in the late nineteenth century. At roughly the same time, farmers and villagers rose up in revolt against the authorities in the Panjshair. Government retribution was swift and vicious. For days on end, MIG-17s and Mi-8 helicopter gunships indiscriminately strafed and burned settlements. In Nuristan, the newly appointed communist governor ordered the closure of all the mosques and forbade the observance of Ramadan, the Muslim period of fasting.

Such measures did not go down well with the Nuristanis. Third-generation Mohammadans, they practise their religion with the fervour of the newly converted. Following a riot in the regional capital of Kamdesh, they chased out the governor and ransacked the local police arsenal. In September 1978, government troops tried to re-enter the region, but were repelled. The Khalqis then launched a series of aerial bombardments, which included the use of phosphorous incendiary bombs and, according to some reports, napalm. Much of Kamdesh, renowned for its distinctive magnificently sculptured house façades and portals, was devastated. Nevertheless, the communists failed to recapture the region and by the end of the month, Nuristan had declared itself 'independent'.

On 14 February 1979, American ambassador Adolphe Dubs, an extremely well informed member of the Western diplomatic community, was held hostage at a downtown Kabul hotel by four armed members of the Settam-e-Melli, an extreme left-wing, Maoist-influenced group formerly associated with the Parcham. Not only did this incident indicate the growing lack of security in the capital but its outcome led to a serious deterioration in Afghan relations. During the rescue assault by Afghan police (in which Soviet advisers played an obscure role), the ambassador was killed in the crossfire. Amidst rumours of a plot by either the Afghans or the Soviets, or both, to rid themselves of Dubs, Washington refused to replace him (the embassy has since been run by a chargé d'affaires) and drastically cut back its foreign aid programme from $27 million in 1978 to a mere $5 million.

The Spreading Insurgency

Revolt was now erupting throughout the northern, central and eastern highlands. Desperately trying to reassert its authority, the regime was involved in major anti-insurgency operations in no less than a dozen provinces. With some prodding from the mullahs, rebellion broke out in the Hazarajat in February 1979. Using old guns, swords, axes, shovels and sticks, peasants and townsfolk alike swarmed against Khalqi offices and military garrisons at the 'Ulus Walis' (regional government seats) at Darai Suf, Joghori, Nawur, Waras, Behsud and Yakaolang. Within three months, the rebels had seized the strongholds. Most of the Hazarajat was now 'liberated' with the exceptions of Chagtcharan and Bamiyan.

The Hazaras succeeded in taking Bamiyan in July that year, when some 200 mujahideen armed with only 42 guns attacked under cover of darkness. Aided by rebellious soldiers, they broke into the town arsenal, capturing 500 rifles which were immediately distributed among the partisans. The government re-occupied the town shortly afterwards, but it was grabbed back by the resistance in the early summer of 1980, when the entire Bamiyan garrision defected to Tadjik guerrillas who had been harassing the communists from the east. Three days later, it changed hands yet again. It finally took a combined Soviet-Afghan government force supported by 400 armoured vehicles and heliborne troops to do the job.

Kunar witnessed its first anti-communist revolt in March 1979. Angered by communist disrespect for Islam and local traditions, Abdur Raouf, commander of the government garrision in Asmara, took matters into his own hands by killing four Khalqi officers and joining the rebellion with most of his men and arms. Faced with increasing revolt in other parts of the valley, the government ultimately reacted with the Kerala massacre.

The Herat Incident

It was in Herat province that the Taraki-Amin regime faced one of its most dire threats. In mid-March 1979, reports began to reach Kabul of riots and mutinies among the troops, probably sparked off by the enforced participation of women in government literacy programmes. Then came the news that telephone communications between Herat, Afghanistan's third largest city, and the capital had been severed and that its 200,000 inhabitants had risen against the regime. The government media tried to blame these 'disturbances' on an alleged 4,000 Iranian infiltrators who had entered the country surreptitiously to spread dissent.

For two days, screaming mobs armed with weapons plundered from government arsenals hunted down Afghan communist officials and officers and Soviet advisers. At least 50 Soviet advisers and members of their families are reliably reported to have been killed. One Western development worker, taken for a Russian because of his blond hair and blue eyes, was almost hacked to death; only the opportune intervention of an Afghan friend in the crowd saved his life. The degree of hatred for the Russians on the part of the crowds indicated the extent to which the population had come to associate the Soviet Union with the Khalqi regime.

When the Taraki government called in the air force, only a few of the remaining pilots, who had not defected, agreed to fly against their own people. Those who refused were subsequently executed. It was then that the Russians intervened by dispatching squadrons of bombers, probably Ilyushin Il-28s, from Dushanbe, capital of Soviet Tadjikistan some 300 miles to the north, to bomb the rebels. By 20 March loyal Afghan troops, supported by tanks, assault helicopters and Soviet military personnel, had entered the turmoil-ridden city, where they confronted the surging crowds, mercilessly shelling and machine-gunning anything that moved. By the time the revolt was suppressed, at least several thousand people had been killed or wounded, with some reports quoting as many as 30,000 – 40,000 casualties.

Towards a Police State

By the first anniversary of the Saur Revolution, much of Afghanistan was beginning to take on the characteristics of a nation under siege. The curfew imposed in April 1978 had never been lifted and foreign residents were restricted to a radius of 35 miles around the capital. Soldiers guarded all important government buildings, while searchlights scanned the Kabul surroundings at night (still very much in effect in 1984). The American Peace Corps had left in the wake of the Dubs affair and in an atmosphere of growing tension UN technicians were sending their families home. As under most totalitarian regimes, Afghan residents were warned not to speak to foreigners. For the first time, Radio Kabul was admitting officially that trouble was being caused by 'reactionary counter-revolutionaries and imperialist lackeys.'

Increasingly dependent on the USSR, the Khalqi regime now hosted roughly 4,500 Soviet advisers, a third of whom were involved in military activities. According to Western intelligence, an estimated 100 Soviet military advisers had been killed in clashes with the guerrillas during the first year of communist rule. There seemed little doubt that the Russians, on whom the lynching of Soviet citizens in Herat had had a traumatic effect, recognised the dangers of a regime which continued to suffer from bitter internecine strife and growing popular resentment. It was also difficult to imagine how Afghanistan's internal degradation could benefit Soviet policy.

On numerous occasions, Soviet officials tried to persuade the Khalq to be less doctrinaire. In particular, Vassily Safrontchuk, a senior Soviet diplomat and the KGB resident who advised Taraki on a daily basis, exhorted the President to form a more representative administration and to halt further alienation of the population. Yet Taraki and Amin (the latter appointed Prime Minister while Taraki retained the presidency) were themselves caught up in their own power struggle and refused to heed Soviet warnings. Apart from a few mollifying gestures such as the holding of a massive demonstration on the prophet Mohammad's birthday in February 1979, they refused to roll back the reforms.

Instead, both leaders regarded repression as the only means to crack down on dissent. 'Those who plot against us in the dark will vanish in the dark', maintained Taraki. This meant the creation not only of a ruthless secret police apparatus, but also a politically motivated (and well-paid) militia. As the insurgency spread, the army was proving less and less reliable. Only reluctantly did soldiers go into battle against their own people. They defected readily, often killing their Khalqi officers and occasionally Soviet advisers in the process. Party militants, on the other hand, could usually be counted on to fight for the Revolution.

Paradoxically, even though the Russians did not seem to favour Khalqi methods, they supported the dictatorship by providing it with the necessary technical expertise. From the early 1950s, West Germany had trained Afghanistan's civil police, but when the force backed Daoud against the communists, it was one of the first departments to be purified by the new regime. Under the guidance of security advisers from the USSR and East Germany, which had established an embassy in Kabul following the 27 April coup, the Khalqis created, in addition to a new civil police, a secret security organisation known as the AGSA. With interrogation and torture centres established in the basements of various ministries and confiscated houses in the Afghan capital, the AGSA (to become the KAM under Amin and the KHAD under Babrak) soon emerged as one of the most heinous instruments of Khalqi repression.

Towards a Fully Fledged War

On August 5, 1979, rebels made their first attempts at organising a nation-wide insurrection, but it failed in tragic disaster. For weeks before rumours of an impending revolt had circulated. Almost two months earlier, there had been an attempted uprising in Kabul when the primarily Hazara population of Chandul rampaged through the streets, attacking police stations. Within hours, the security forces arrested an estimated 7,000 demonstrators; many were imprisoned, never to emerge alive.

As frustration and anger against the regime deepened, the opposition felt that something had to be done. 'The government installed by the Kremlin was becoming more and more terrorist and arbitrary', recalled Farid, member of an urban resistance group and a high school student at the time. Tracts were distributed warning the people to prepare for revolt. The centre of operations was to be at the Bala Hissar fort, which would give the signal for the insurrection. With the Jabha Mobarezin e Mujahidin e Afghanistan (Militant Front for Mujahed Fighters of Afghanistan), a small but progressive resistance movement, playing a significant role, the plan called for the takeover of Radio Kabul and the co-ordination of simultaneous revolts throughout the country. Key officers in the armed forces, including dissatisfied communists, led by Col. Sayed Gul Ahmad were also involved, some having deliberately lengthened their commissions in order to participate.

The uprising was planned for mid-day. A pre-arranged interruption in a Radio Kabul broadcast was to be the sign for fighters in other towns and provinces to gather at the mosques. Because of martial law, religious centres were the only places where the population could congregate without arousing suspicion. The crowds were then to march through the streets shouting slogans such as 'We will make Afghanistan the cematery of the Russians' or 'Death to Russian social-imperialism'. As the demonstrations expanded, Afghan soldiers were expected to join in and distribute weapons from the state arsenals.

Unfortunately for the plotters, three AGSA informers had penetrated their number. Forewarned, the authorities brought in extra troops and reinforced security around the radio station. Unable to move against this vital objective, the rebels were never able to broadcast their signal. Nevertheless, Gul Ahmad went ahead with the operation. Fighting broke out at Bala Hissar, with the rebels killing most of the Khalqi officers and Soviet advisers inside.

By one o'clock, the insurgents, now armed with captured tanks and heavy weapons, sought to leave the fort's precincts and join up with the population outside. But the government forces, openly directed by Soviet military advisers, were waiting. While tank-supported troops stood back, planes and helicopter gunships bombed the fort and its surroundings for six hours, resulting in several thousand rebel and civilian casualties. Many of the officers surviving the mutiny were arrested and, if not executed on the spot, dragged off to prison where they were tortured and killed. Meanwhile, in the provinces, the planned mass demonstrations never occurred when no news came through. Despite the debacle, the Bala Hissar incident has now come to have similar connotations in Afghanistan to that of 'The Alamo' in the

United States.

Purges and Insecurity

By the time of the Amin coup against Taraki in September 1979, the determination to resist communist rule was hardening. Civil servants, university professors, doctors, students and other members of the educated elite, including members of the Parcham faction, continued to disappear from the bazaars, their homes and places of work. Many whose lives were in danger or who saw no future in staying began fleeing abroad, some to Western Europe and North America, others to Pakistan to join the resistance.

There were also problems within the government itself. Apart from his continued purges against the Parcham, Amin angered many members of his own faction by launching a frenzied crackdown on Khalq, mainly Taraki, supporters suspected of political deviation or conspiracy. By the time the Soviets stepped in at the end of December 1979, the Khalq itself had suffered a major rift.

During the three months of Amin's rule, security crumbled even further. Travel by road between the cities had become outright hazardous. Mujahed activities often closed the main highways for several days at a time. Vehicles travelling on the Kandahar and Herat routes could move only in heavily armed convoys which would wait on the outskirts of the cities until the roads were reported clear. But these precautions did little to prevent the rebels from sniping at the convoys. Added confusion arose with some Afghans, as often as not conventional bandits, taking advantage of the situation and passing themselves off as 'mujahideen' in order to accumulate booty.

The guerrillas were becoming less selective in their attacks. 'Previously, they would choose their cars or buses, usually ones they knew were carrying communists', one West European diplomat told me in late September 1979 in Kabul. 'Now they are shooting anything in sight. This has alienated a lot of people. Women and children are being killed without the rebels asking whether they support the insurgency or not. People are afraid to move.' The mujahideen, however, were achieving their aim of forcing the government, unable to guarantee security, to relinquish its control of the countryside.

Even foreigners were being hit. In one incident, a vehicle of the Magic Bus Company in Amsterdam, one of the last tour operators on the overland 'hippy' route to India via Afghanistan, was attacked in the southern part of the country; a Swiss and a Canadian were shot dead and an Australian seriously injured as bullets fired by unseen gunmen from the surrounding rocks ripped through the windows. In early September, six West Germans were killed while picnicking on the outskirts of Kabul. A British nurse accosted by mujahideen managed to evade a similar fate by crying out: 'BBC, BBC!' thus persuading them that she was not Russian.

The international community in the Afghan capital was pulling out or reducing its diplomatic and development operations. The United States had already withdrawn some of its staff and families following the Dubs affair. The Canadians, West Germans and Japanese had all evacuated their dependants, while the British had trimmed their staff to the point where they could move out all personnel in one emergency flight. Fearing a rise in sporadic violence, Canadian Ambassador Douglas Small in Islamabad, who was also accredited to Kabul, noted that the 'inability of the government to control the rapid deterioration of the security situation has influenced our decision to advise on evacuation.'

American pilots of the PanAm-operated Ariana Afghan national airlines, who had already removed all their personal belongings from the country, said they would fly only as long as conditions permitted. 'I'm clean', one pilot announced with a shrug, 'I can leave anytime'. The American pilots, as well as their Afghan colleagues who seemed to defect every time a plane landed in Frankfurt, were eventually all replaced by Russians. With travel dangerous, many United Nations Development Programme (UNDP) projects were lying idle. 'We're reduced to shuffling papers. We just want to get the hell out of here', said one co-ordinator. A Swiss dairy specialist, who normally drove several times a month to oversee dairy projects in the north supplying Kabul with much of its fresh milk, yoghurt and cheese, had to halt his up-country tours by the end of the summer. Although well-known by local inhabitants, he explained that he would soon have to close shop because 'accidents can happen'.

Police terror, Human Rights Violations and the Kremlin

The development of the secret police since 1978 has been primarily the responsibility of East German security advisers. Under previous precommunist regimes, the Afghan secret services often used extreme brutality and terror but with limited results. This changed with the influence of the SSD, the East German heirs to the Gestapo. Specialising in secret police organisation, the SSD already had an accomplished track record among other Moscow protégés elsewhere in the Third World such as Ethiopia, Angola and South Yemen, and proceeded to do the same in Afghanistan.

First as the AGSA, communist Afghanistan's secret police was directed by Assadullah Sarwari, a much hated Khalqi fanatic notorious for his torture methods against both the Parcham and opposition dissidents. Known as the 'Butcher' or 'King Kong,' he rapidly gave the organisation a reputation for terror. He was also suspected of being a Soviet agent. Shortly after coming to power, Amin replaced Sarwari by his own nephew, Assadullah, and re-named the security organisation the Kargari Astekhbarati Muassessa, or KAM (Workers Intelligence Institute). Amin promised to end the excesses that had existed under Taraki, but then pushed the KAM into undertaking equally reprehensible atrocities.

As early as the autumn of 1978, human rights observers estimated that 50,000 Afghans had passed through or were still in Khalqi detention centres. With no reliable figures available, roughly 20,000 Afghans (as many as 100,000 by some accounts) had been killed in purges, security operations or in captivity. A year later, in September 1979, the London-based human rights organisation, Amnesty International, maintained that at least 12,000 political prisoners were languishing without trial in Pul-e-Charkhi, Afghanistan's most infamous prison. Amnesty's report noted that prisoners were summarily executed; others simply 'disappeared' following their arrest. It found that torture was frequently used. Other accounts referred to regular executions by firing squad, well before large-scale repression began in earnest in early 1979. Some human rights sources in France have quoted the mass live burials of Pul-e-Charkhi inmates during the summer of 1979 in huge, bulldozed pits. When Amin staged his own putsch a month later, he published a list of 17,000 names of persons allegedly killed by Taraki. What he failed to note was that he had personally overseen much of the Khalqi repression at the time.

Following the Soviet invasion, the new Babrak administration sought to cleanse the PDPA's tarnished image by blaming previous 'excesses' on the 'hateful butcher' Amin. Through their Afghan puppet, the Soviets no doubt hoped that Amin's overthrow would earn them both the gratitude of the Afghan people and a clean slate. In addition to rolling back certain reforms, repudiating Amin's anti-Islamic policies and proclaiming its respect for traditional values, the Moscow-installed regime released several thousand political prisoners in a much publicised amnesty in January 1980. Nonetheless, political persecution and atrocities continued just as systematically, if not more so, under the Soviet occupation.

Former prisoners from Pul-e-Charkhi claimed that Soviet or East German advisers were often present during interrogations by the AGSA and the KAM, or were aware of the torture sessions. Government defectors have confirmed these observations. 'We often used to see them in the corridors', said one former political inmate, a university professor released during the Babrak amnesty. 'We used to be questioned (by Afghans) but then they would take their papers with our answers into the next room where there were Russian advisers. We could hear them. We could see them. Some nights they would enter (our cells) to look at us.' Since the Soviet intervention, it appears that the KGB and SSD have taken virtual control of all intelligence activities and dealings with political prisoners. Former internees have also talked of regular visits to the prison by East European 'observers'.

Early in 1980, American orientalist Michael Barry, a Farsi and Pashto speaker with an intimate knowledge of Afghanistan, travelled to western Pakistan on assignment for the International Federation of Human Rights. There he interviewed on tape dozens of refugees, defectors and resistance fighters, questioning them in detail about cases of government repression. His comprehensive report referred explicitly to atrocities that occurred both before, during and immediately after the invasion.

One of those interviewed was Abdullah Osman, a former professor from the Kabul medical faculty, who was arrested in November 1979 duing the Amin regime and released in the Babrak amnesty. He spoke of regular executions of prisoners at Pul-e-Charkhi. 'They had their hands tied, their eyes covered with a black band and they were forced to climb into a truck', he recounted. They were then taken to a field at Pul-e-Goun beneath Mount Char on the outskirts of the capital – a field renowed among Afghans as one of the regime's principal execution grounds, where according to witnesses, prisoners were forced to dig huge ditches which served as their own graves. They were then executed by machine gun, and whether dead or alive, pushed in and buried.

Once Osman watched from his cell window as a group of more than 12 inmates were being assembled for departure.

Before leaving, two prisoners, who had their eyes covered and hands bound, realised what was happening. Supported by those in the truck, they began to resist by appealing to (the Muslim sensibilities of) the guards . . . fighting broke out. Prisoners fought with their bare hands against the armed guards, crying: 'Allah o Akbar. God is Great. Join us. Help us. It's a communist regime. An inhuman regime. They will kill you like us. Group by group they'll kill you all!

Those in the cells could not help and guards fired in the air to intimidate them.

The fighting continued until four in the morning. Most of the prisoners who were supposed to have been taken away were dead ... the five or six survivors, all wounded, were taken to the commander's office . . . where he told them: 'You are nothing but dogs. We're not going to waste bullets on dogs.' He then ordered them to be beaten to death with sticks.

Sayed Abdullah, the jail's callous commander, was himself later killed by a prisoner. According to testimony, a list was always put up on the wall of those to be taken away for execution. When the condemned men were being led to the waiting vehicles, Abdullah was on hand to watch as they shuffled through the gate. One of the men had a knife which he had managed to purchase from a guard for 5,000 Afghanis (circa $120). As he passed, he jumped out of line and stabbed the commander before being shot down by guards; in reprisal, the authorities executed 44 inmates.

Prisoners were also murdered by being thrown into the prison cess pools. When the January 1980 amnesty was announced, women came to the prison with their children to meet their menfolk. When they did not find them, they were shown the pits. 'They surrounded the cess pools and poked for bodies with long sticks', remembered one inmate released at the time. 'They were crying. Weeping.'

Numerous accounts, including the Barry interviews, refer to massacres in the countryside both before and after the Soviet invasion. Toward the end of April, or early May 1979, roughly at the same time as the Kerala massacre, government troops rounded up and tried to drown some 1,500 young men, mainly Hazaras, in the northern province of Samangan bordering the USSR, in retaliation for the assassination of Khalqi officials. According to a member of the Hazara resistance, who previously worked in a senior position in the government cultural service, 'they tied their hands and covered their eyes before throwing them into the Amu Daraya (Oxus river)'. Although it remains unclear how many died, the incident has been corroborated by other witnesses, who maintained that Soviet advisers were present.

The KHAD

Since the beginning of the Soviet occupation, the Khidamat-e-Atla't Daulati or state affairs service, the KHAD has evolved into a formidable security weapon. As with many other totalitarian regimes, the internment or intimidation of citizens by the secret service is only one aspect of the regimes contrivance to crush internal opposition. The KHAD's extensive activities — gathering intelligence, infiltrating the resistance, spreading false information, and processing political prisoners — in many cases have proved more effective against the guerrillas than have massive military onslaughts. Particularly detrimental has been its growing role in effecting Soviet 'divide and rule' tactics.

Immediately following the invasion, the Soviets with the help of the SSD reorganised the KAM into the KHAD and appointed Dr Najibullah, the former Parcham ambassador to Tehran under Taraki, as its director. Also head of the tribal department of the Ministry of Tribal Affairs and Nationalities, he is a powerful member of the PDPA Central Committee and reports directly to the KGB. Disposing of an enormous budget channelled directly to it by the Kremlin, the KHAD is thought to have at least 15,000 — 20,000 full-time trained agents. Many have gone to the USSR or other Eastern bloc countries, notably East Germany, for three to six months instruction. According to Western intelligence sources, this includes training in interrogation and torture methods. An additional 100,000 or more male or female informants are said to be on the KHAD's payroll.

As with the pre-1980 human rights situation, there are no reliable estimates of the number of political prisoners interned by the present authorities or dispatched to camps in the USSR, as some reports indicate. Nor are there any firm estimates of those tortured or executed since the invasion. In both cases, human rights observers believe that tens of thousands have been jailed or deliberately killed by the KHAD and other security organisations. As Amnesty International pointed out in its November, 1984 report on human rights violations, war conditions and the Afghan governments' continued denial of access to international humanitarian organisations and most of the world press have hampered the collection of information and the verification of these allegations.

Torture and Defiance

The threat of the knock at the door or the street sweep remains a constant concern for Afghans living in the Soviet-occupied zones. With the rise in urban guerrilla activities in 1984, security precautions have become steadily more severe. Even remote suspicion of resistance affiliation is enough to land one in a basement interrogation chamber of the KHAD. One pupil from the Lycée Istiqlal, now continuing his studies in Switzerland, was picked up by communist militiamen while trying to escape to Pakistan. He was brought to a KHAD detention centre in Gardez where he was interrogated for four months. Beatings and electric shocks applied to his genitals and other sensitive parts of his body were part of the procedure.

Secret or show trials followed by television appearances of accused admitting to 'CIA crimes' or collaboration with 'imperialist anti-revolutionary forces' are regularly staged to remind the population of what happens to those who continue to oppose the authorities. In March 1982, the KHAD arrested Professor Hassan Kakar, a renowned Afghan historian and head of the Department of History at Kabul University. Seven other academics were also detained on charges of founding a human rights organisation and of disseminating anti-government literature. Their incarceration came in the wake of openly expressed resentment among students and lecturers of the growing 'Sovietisation' of the educational system. This involves the current practice of replacing university lecturers who have been purged or have fled — more than four-fifths of the total by the end of 1983 — with Soviet advisers and usually unqualified Afghan party activists. Pressure has also been put on the remaining non-communist teachers and students to join the PDPA.

The academics denied the accusations, but were jailed without trial anyway. Five of them were eventually freed, after having reportedly made public statements in support of the government. For more than a year, little was heard of Dr Kakar and the two other prisoners as no family visits were allowed. But then in mid-summer, 1983, they were tried in camera for their 'crimes' by a revolutionary court. The two lecturers were believed to have been sentenced to ten and eight years respectively, while Dr Kakar received eight years and was then bundled off to Pul-e-Charkhi. During the hearing, Kakar apparently denounced both the Soviet invasion and the integration of Russian teachers within the higher educational system. He courageously refused to read a prepared statement on national television and condemned the Babrak Karmal regime, to what he referred to as the 'sentence of history.'

Cases of outright defiance, such as that of Dr Kakar, have not been uncommon, but the KHAD can bring often nefarious pressures to bear on prisoners who refuse to co-operate, including torture, harassment of their families, bribery and promises of release or reduced sentence. As

Amnesty International and other human rights organisations have stressed, this repression is directed not only against citizens believed to be involved in active resistance, but also those merely suspected of opposition or who have relatives abroad. At least eight centres of interrogation and torture are known to operate in Kabul, and, apart from Pul-e-Charkhi prison, major detention centres exist in Jelalabad, Kandahar, Faizabad, Herat, Mazar-e-Sharif and other provincial towns.

Most arrests are made at night with armed militiamen or troops surrounding the building where the suspect is known to be before KHAD agents move in. No reasons are given for the arrest, and families are not told where the prisoner is being taken. Many are never seen again. There are numerous cases of people being arbitrarily arrested, held for several months while being interrogated or questioned under torture and then suddenly released without explanation. Some may have agreed to work as informers in return for their liberty, while others are simply informed that a mistake had been made or that they have been used to set an example. In this manner, the KHAD has imprisoned, tortured or killed thousands, ranging from protesting high school pupils to members of urban guerrilla movements such as the SAMA.

One victim, Farida Ahmadi, a fourth year medical student from Kabul, was arrested for distributing anti-Soviet tracts and then released after several months of often brutal interrogation. The young woman claimed that six female party members, all roughly her age, had carried out the main interrogation which involved beatings, electric shocks, being forced to stand for two weeks without moving and being taken through chambers where other victims were being tortured. Other inmates, she maintained, sometimes had their fingers, hands and arms hacked off. Towards the end, she explained, when the women could not break her, male torturers including a Russian were brought in. Once, in order to frighten her, one of the torturers personally gouged out the eyes of a swollen, but still living, body. At human rights hearings in Paris, Geneva and in the United States, Farida provided the names of most of those responsible.

Atrocities

There have been many reports of Soviet or Afghan government atrocities against civilians, but Western observers have only been able to compile a few fully-documented accounts, let alone witness them at first hand. In August 1984, I was present when Soviet MIG-27 ground attack planes deliberately bombed a column of refugees near the

Chamar Pass in northeastern Afghanistan, killing at least forty men, women and children and seriously injuring dozens of others.

Two years earlier, both Swedish and resistance sources revealed the slaughter of more than 1,000 civilians in Logar Province. Relying on information furnished by KHAD infiltrators, the communists acted in reprisal against local collaboration with mujahed forces operating along the strategic Kabul-Gardez highway. In a three-day combined Soviet-Afghan assault, six villages were devastated by helicopters and MIG jetfighters; water and agricultural installations were systematically destroyed, houses burned and livestock killed.

Later that year, the Padkhwab-e-Shana massacre, also in Logar province, came to light, 105 Afghan civilians were asphyxiated and burned alive in an irrigation tunnel by Soviet troops. Apart from the detailed testimony of survivors, the incident was investigated on the spot by a special international human rights commission (a French co-ordinator, an Italian international law specialist and an American ethnologist) sponsored by the second Permanent People's Tribunal on Afghanistan in Paris in late November, 1982. 'We thought that as a commission it was essential to prove at least one refugee story to make a point... to show that what the refugees are saying does correspond to what is actually happening in Afghanistan', observed one member of the commission.

According to both the witnesses and the commission findings, Soviet troops approached the village of Padkhwab-e-Shana at dawn. The victims, both villagers and refugees on their way to Pakistan, hid in a 'Karez', an underground irrigation system, when they saw the soldiers coming. When the Soviets discovered that people were hiding in the canal, they ordered two elderly men to call on them to come out. 'But those inside told the old men that they would rather die than be taken by the Russians', said Habib-ur-Rahman Hashemi, the village head who lost 25 members of his family in the massacre. The occupation troops then dammed up the canal outlet forcing the water to rise. A cistern truck, probably containing petrol, was brought in and a hose inserted into one of the irrigation system openings. A second vehicle then drove up with a dozen men on board, all wearing protective clothing. They proceeded to pour the yellowish-white contents of two 100-litre containers into the canal followed by a sack of white powder. They moved back and several soldiers fired incendiary bullets inside causing a series of explosions.

The procedure was repeated at another 'Karez' outlet further away. The soldiers stayed until three in the afternoon, almost without moving. 'When they were sure that no one was alive in the canal, they all began applauding and then left the village', said Sayed Mortaza, the local mullah. Some forty men who had managed to hide elsewhere emerged and immediately tried to enter the system, but the stench was too strong. Over the next three days, they managed to remove the bodies, most of them burned beyond recognition. As a result of the killings, the entire village, except for five families suspected of pro-communist affiliations, left for Pakistan.

Propaganda and Counter-propaganda

Both the Soviets and the Babrak regime dismiss allegations, whether of torture by the KHAD or the deliberate murders of civilians by the military, as malicious Western propaganda. At a press conference in December 1982 in Paris, visiting Foreign Ministry officials from Kabul insisted that such reports were totally unfounded even when they were confronted by Western journalists, including myself, who had witnessed government operations against civilians. As for the 'so-called KHAD', one Information Ministry official (who, as it later turned out, had interrogated a captured French reporter in 1981 for the KHAD) tried to convince two French journalists filming in Kabul at the turn of the year 1983/84 that the existence of such an organisation was a figment of the imagination.

Instead, communist counter-propaganda, most of it published by the Novosti Press Agency in Moscow and bearing such titles as 'Crimes and Confessions of Counter-revolutionaries' or 'The Truth About Afghanistan: Documents, Facts, Eyewitness Reports', has sought to draw public attention to the purported atrocities of the guerrilla 'bandits'. These include films, books and photographs depicting purported atrocities ranging from the assassination of party officials or the 'destruction of public property' (trucks, buildings etc).

Infiltration

Over the past few years, the Soviets have succeeded in penetrating the resistance organisations by means of the KHAD, not only in Afghanistan but also among the political groups and refugee camps in neighbouring Pakistan and Iran. French doctors clandestinely touring resistance areas have found the houses in which they slept mysteriously bombed two days later. One French TV reporter, Jacques Abouchar, was wounded and captured in September 1984 during a Soviet-Afghan ambush in southeastern Afghanistan, after being informed upon by KHAD agents.

In particular, the KHAD is thought to be responsible for much of the internal rivalry and political divisions that have arisen among major guerrilla fronts. As one mujahed commander complained: 'In some areas, KHAD agents have rendered mujahed groups completely useless by getting them to fight among themselves. Why should the Soviets worry about killing Afghans if the mujahideen do it for them?'

In late 1980, Hazaras recruited by the communist Tudeh Party in Iran in conjunction with the KGB and the KHAD began to filter back to Afghanistan. So did Iranian Tudeh agents purporting to represent Khomeini. Within months, they succeeded — by playing off religious and traditional sentiments — in contributing to the disruption of the 'Shura' (the main Hazara resistance assembly) which was already in conflict with the radical pro-Khomeini Nasr, thus curbing organised resistance activities. Local guerrilla commanders and intellectuals were hounded by the spread of false rumours. Even volunteer French doctors, who were providing basic health care in many villages, were forced to leave the Hazara heartland by clerics persuaded that the Europeans were 'godless imperialists' and anti-Khomeini instigators.

Defenders of the Revolution

KHAD-control of the government militia, the 'Defenders of the Revolution', has also seriously weakened the resistance in certain areas. Although not necessarily pro-communist, militiamen are attracted by high salaries and proper weapons. They dress and look like mujahideen, and in many cases, are in fact mujahideen. 'Defection' to the militia, sometimes on the orders of resistance commanders in order to procure more arms, ammunition and money, is not uncommon. Some return almost immediately to the mountains, while others collaborate with the mujahideen during anti-government operations.

Nevertheless, a sizable hardline element exists among the militia whom the Soviets consider more reliable than the defection-ridden Afghan army, particularly in frontline battle positions. For financial bonuses, they are usually willing to participate in special operations. The Kremlin, via the KHAD, ensures that funds are never lacking. The more militant militiamen, many of them belonging to party-operated 'Bureau Guard' or 'Avant Guard' units, are used mainly for frontier patrols or to scour villages in search of anti-government suspects. Another KHAD tactic is to discredit the mujahideen in the eyes of the local population by disseminating false rumours or by dispatching into the countryside groups of unruly militiamen masquerading as guerrillas.

Paid more than 3,000 Afghanis a month (roughly $40), no small sum in Afghanistan, militiamen receive political and anti-insurgent instruction from Soviet advisers. Promising young militiamen are sent to the USSR for specialised training in infiltration techniques, subversion and intelligence. Once back in Afghanistan, they are encouraged by the KHAD to penetrate local resistance organisations or to 'flee' to Pakistan in order to operate among the refugees. During their absence, perhaps for three or four months, their families are looked after to the tune of 15,000 Afghanis ($200).

As the security situation continued to deteriorate, the Kabul regime announced the creation in the summer of 1981 of new special defence councils at the national, provincial and district level. Faced with growing casualties, defections, political distrust and poor morale, the army and all other security organisations were to be brought under strict party control. At the same time, manpower shortages were becoming so acute that Radio Kabul began appealing to boys, and even girls, as young as twelve years old to join up. While squads of militia-women were activated in Kabul to search cars and individuals, armed males, most of them hardly more than sixteen or seventeen, were deployed at night to man security posts or patrol the streets. Operating like neighbourhood gangs, they had little political motivation, but, frightened and frightening at the same time, they exuded a sense of triggerhappiness and ruthlessness similar to that found among young members of the Nazi-backed French 'milice' during World War II.

State Within a State

For the resistance, dealing with the KHAD will no doubt remain one of its trickiest predicaments. With substantial powers of its own, the KHAD is increasingly a 'state within a state'. Nevertheless, guerrilla leaders are seeking to eliminate rivalry by means of force, persuasion or third-party reconciliation. Just as the KHAD has succeeded in penetrating the resistance, the mujahideen have never lacked collaborators among the government ranks. Tip-offs have led to the rooting out of informers, who are then tried by Islamic courts and often executed, while communist officials or KHAD operators known to be specifically involved in resistance infiltration are, wherever possible, assassinated.

Ironically, despite close KGB management, the KHAD is not as closely controlled by the Soviets as they would like. Much to the KGB's dismay, it is becoming increasingly involved in the internecine strife between the Parcham and Khalq factions. Although the Khalq-dominated Ministry of the Interior operates its own substantial security and intelligence service, it is the Parcham-influenced KHAD that has achieved the central position in the government's repressive apparatus. KHAD agents will often deliberately provide arms or information to the mujahideen in the knowledge that they will attack control posts manned by pro-Khalq militiamen or soldiers. Similarly, some of the assassinations carried out against the Khalqis are thought to be KHAD-initiated while the Khalqis play a reciprocal game against the Parchamis.

The National Fatherland Front

Ever since the invasion, the Babrak regime has been trying desperately to establish its legitimacy with the Afghan people and the world at large. With Soviet encouragement, the PDPA has recognised that, in the long run, the success of·the revolution will depend not on military gains but on whether it can make itself acceptable to the country as a whole. To this end, Babrak officially established the National Fatherland Front in June 1981, which seeks to portray itself as a non-partisan assembly of religious, tribal, ethnic and political leaders.

Six months previously, on the first anniversary of the Soviet intervention, the Kabul government launched an elaborate campaign accentuating the virtues of the Front. By asserting its respect for national liberty and cultural identity, the PDPA sought to convince the population of the need to create a classic united front for the good of the country. Babrak even assured the nation of his 'respect, observance and preservation of Islam as a sacred religion' and expressed his desire for revised land reforms and a general amnesty. Once this was achieved, maintained some PDPA theorists, the next step would be free parliamentary elections. For the Soviets, there were high hopes that this would ultimately prove the most effective weapon in blunting anti-communist resistance and providing the PDPA with a way of broadening its own minuscule popular base.

Coordinating the development of the Front was the newly formed Ministry of Tribal Affairs and Nationalities in which the KHAD has a direct and prominent role. In a gesture designed to appeal to the country's tribal and ethnic communities, the founding Congress of the Fatherland Front was heralded as a contemporary 'Loya Jirgha' (a traditional assembly of tribal, ethnic, religious and nomadic leaders, normally used to obtain a national consensus on historic decisions). Since the invasion, the resistance has convoked its own 'Loya Jirghas' on several occasions.

After several false starts, enough tribal, religious and regional representatives were scraped together, an estimated 1,000 non-party delegates, to justify the massive publicity effort that had gone into its pre-paration. The PDPA also attempted to draft well-known national figures like writers and singers in order to provide the Front with greater credibility. According to Radio Kabul, the celebrated classical singer, Ustad Hussein Sirahang had agreed to participate. But Sirahang reportedly would have no truck with the regime and pointedly refused to sing eulogies of the Saur Revolution or Soviet-Afghan friendship.

The Congress appealed to the nation to work for durable peace and normalisation. In what amounted to the regime's first official general amnesty (not counting its release of several thousand political pris-oners from Pul-e-Charkhi in January 1980), it called upon the resistance not to be 'false and sold-out chieftains who are trampling underfoot the tenets of Islam. Stop serving the interests of the outsiders. Come down from the mountains. Pick up the ploughs and spades which your hands miss so much.' The assembly further invited all refugees to return, thereby contradicting Babrak's earlier assertions that a refugee situation did not exist in Pakistan or Iran. It also warned those who did not come back that they would miss out on the land redistribution.

Composed of twelve PDPA-run institutions representing different sectors of Afghan society such as the clergy, farmers, youth and women, the Fatherland Front has nevertheless failed to have much impact. A further effort by the Ministry of Tribal Affiars to strengthen the government was the reorganisation in 1981 of the administrative and party machinery into eight different zones, each comprising three to four provinces and a number of tribal and ethnic groups. A cabinet minister or member of the Politburo was put in charge of each zone and charged with the responsibility of implementing land reform, indoctrin-ating the masses and adopting special measures to combat the resistance.

Divide and Rule

Since its inception, the Ministry of Nationalities and Tribal Affairs under Parcham Suleiman Layeq, who is also vice-chairman of the National Fatherland Front, has concentrated on winning over some of the hundreds of Pushtun tribes living south of the Hindu Kush, tradi-tionally fertile ground for playing off clan rivalry. Just as the British obtained tribal peace or neutrality through bribes, favours, intrigue or threats, the Babrak government hopes to obtain outright collaboration from the tribes, or at least their neutrality.

The communists have succeeded in winning over, sometimes only temporarily, a number of significant tribal groupings. More often than

not, however, the relationship is one of declared neutrality or a collaboration of convenience rather than committed political alignment.
And in many cases, these truces remain extremely fickle. Some Paktya
tribes, for example, have enjoyed the right to military exemption based
on precedent from previous governments going back several decades.
When the Babrak government tried to annul these rights in early
October 1982 to strengthen the security forces, tribal chiefs already
co-operating with the authorities through non-belligerence agreements
rebelled by holding a large demonstration in the capital. Fearing further
trouble or a switch to the other side, Babrak agreed to cancel the order
a month later.

The resistance has also taken steps to prevent government
approaches to the tribes from coming to anything. In one case, almost
a year and a half after the invasion, officials tried to negotiate a truce
with the Khost and Tani tribes in Paktya province. In return for an end
to support of the resistance, the communists promised to terminate all
military activities in the area, exempt all local men from army conscription and release imprisoned mujahideen. Several days after the arrival
of a ministerial delegation in the provincial capital of Khost, however,
the mujahideen launched a number of assaults against military outposts
in the region to warn off both the government and any locals contemplating collaboration. The situation deteriorated to such an extent that
the delegation was obliged to return to Kabul.

There is increasing evidence that the Ministry's activities have not
been restricted solely to Afghan territory. Divided into three main
departments, the first two deal with Pushtun and Baluchi tribal groups
in Afghanistan and Pakistan respectively, both directly supervised by
Dr Najibullah. Of deep concern to the Islamabad government, the
KHAD has been using its Pakistan department to dispense weapons and
cash to dissident Mohmand, Afridi, Shinwari and Waziri tribes in the
Northwest Frontier area. Only the third department, which deals
specifically with ethnic groups such as the Tadjiks, Uzbeks, Turkmen
and Hazaras in northern and central Afghanistan, is directed by the
Minister himself.

It is certain that the Soviets through their KHAD intermediaries will
persist in such efforts to erode the resistance. War fatigue among the
general population both at home and in the refugee camps is a major
factor that could work in the Kremlin's favour in the years ahead. That
is, unless the resistance and its outside backers take more constructive
steps to remedy the situation. Pakistan, too, can expect greater pressures. Less than a month after his assuming power in early 1985, the

new Soviet leader, Mikhail Gorbachev, insinuated that Moscow might adopt an even tougher stance towards Afghanistan and warned Islamabad that life could become much rougher if it did not tone down its support for the mujahideen.

7 THE SOVIETISATION OF AFGHANISTAN

Since the Soviet invasion, the Democratic Republic of Afghanistan (DRA) has gradually adopted the profile of a Soviet autonomous republic, with the Russians assuming total control of the government and the war against the resistance. It was costing the Soviet Union well over $2 billion, possibly as much as $3 billion a year, in occupation and economic development support by the end of 1984. The Kremlin still promotes the appearance of a non-aligned and sovereign Afghanistan which invited in a limited contingent of Soviet troops to help stave off 'outside counter-revolutionary interference'. But Afghanistan remains an independent nation only in name. Even the PDPA has found its powers of decision reduced to virtually nothing. 'It is quite clear to everyone that the real power lies with Moscow and not Babrak Karmal', noted former Afghan diplomat and UN General Assembly President Abdul Rahman Pazhwak, shortly after going into exile in 1982.

At the time of the invasion, the PDPA was a discredited political minority which had no choice but to rely on massive Soviet assistance. Khalqi PDPA membership barely numbered 5,000 (the Parcham less than 1,000) and there was no conceivable way that Babrak Karmal could have run the country on his own. Since then, Soviet attempts to turn the regime into a legitimate authority have faltered. The PDPA still remains bitterly divided; the Parcham and the Khalq have themselves splintered into smaller factions. Babrak's failure to end the strife has frequently led to rumours that a frustrated Kremlin was angling for another leader, more acceptable not only to the two communist wings but also to the Afghan people. So far, no figure has emerged with the necessary prestige and untarnished reputation to step into his shoes.

Party strength has certainly risen, to more than 80,000 by the end of 1984 according to PDPA officials; but less than half seems a more likely figure. The actual number of members who are pro-Soviet is thought to be no more than 5,000-6,000. A significant proportion of card-holders such as government officials are known to have been forced to join for professional reasons. Others have become apostates because of present political circumstances. Still others, who in private profess pro-resistance tendencies, are in fact attempting to keep a foot in both camps.

Either way, the resistance has benefitted. Both Khalqi and Parcham militants often seem more concerned with destroying one another rather than the mujahideen. Khalqis openly condemn the Parchami as traitors for having brought in the Russians, while the Parchami in turn accuse the Khalqi of disloyalty and collaboration with the resistance. Shoot-outs have become so common that it is sometimes not known for certain whether assassinations have been carried out by the resistance or one of the PDPA factions. Many party members, particularly the more nationalist Khalqis, have become disillusioned and deeply resent the way they are being treated by the Soviets. Anti-Russian sentiment has begun to emerge among Parcham militants angered by high-handed Russian attitudes.

Apart from the presence of Red Army occupation troops, Afghanistan has undergone dramatic changes through the influence of large influxes of Soviet advisers, both military and civilian. Compared to the 3,500-odd advisers present prior to the invasion, their numbers more than doubled within the first month of 1980. By early 1984, they were believed to total well over 10,000 many of them living with their families in specially-guarded enclaves near the Soviet embassy or in the Russian-built suburb of Microrayon near Kabul airport.

The Army: A Demoralised Fighting Machine

Communist propaganda on all fronts, both Soviet and PDPA, was still arguing in early 1984 that the Red Army was not militarily involved except in a supportive role to the Afghan security forces. Nevertheless, attempts to rebuild the Afghan army, air force and gendarmerie into an efficient fighting machine continue to plague Soviet advisers. Morale and discipline remain low, while revolt, desertion and defection among the rank and file have in many respects turned the Afghan military into a burden rather than a boon for the occupation forces.

Overall army strength dwindled from an initial 100,000 in early 1978 to 30,000-40,000 by mid-1980, with many soldiers joining the resistance, weapons and all, or simply returning home to their families. By the end of the year, despite increased conscription efforts, it had plummeted to a mere 25,000. Estimates of present strength hover between 30,000 and 45,000 with battalions experiencing desertions — up to 80 per cent in certain units — at about the same rate as arriving conscripts, some of whom have been drafted several times over. 'The army has become like a room with two doors', noted one resistance commander. Soviet political advisers are attached to the army with the sole purpose of explaining their country's purpose in Afghanistan and the need for the Afghan people to defend themselves against the evils of 'imperialist' and 'reactionary' outside forces.

Such pep-talks have done little to raise confidence in Soviet solidarity. Aware that defectors are a major source of weapons for the mujahideen, the Soviets have continued to withhold anti-air and anti-tank weapons from all but the most reliable Afghan units. Ex-soldiers have reported being forced into battle as cannon fodder with Soviet guns in their backs.

While visiting the Panjshair in mid-1984, I regularly encountered between ten and fifteen Afghan soldiers deserting every day from government bases inside the valley. They all complained of being press ganged off the streets and into the army, where they received between one and two months basic training before being sent to the front. Issued with guns only for guard duty or combat, most already belonged to the resistance parties and wanted to return to their home regions as soon as possible.

Repeatedly, the government has launched conscription drives. These range from the promulgation in August 1983 of revised draft laws restricting the number of military service exemptions, to the use of 'talashi' in which security forces cordon off villages or town sections in search of eligible males. Plainclothed militiamen brandishing Kalashnikovs often roam the streets to press gang hapless male candidates by pulling them off motorcycles or out of buses, or rounding them up in the bazaars. Not only has the regime increased the normal conscription period from two to three years, but it has also resorted to the enforced recruitment of boys as young as fourteen and the recall of disgruntled veterans with completed tours of duty already behind them.

With little advance warning, conscripts are brought to the capital's national stadium where they are processed by senior officers before being flown or trucked to army bases in various parts of the country, preferably well away from their home regions. These intensive efforts have only succeeded in reducing army morale and forcing more young men to join the resistance, flee to Pakistan or go into hiding.

By the end of 1982, military conscription had become a key factor behind public animosity against the regime. Even party militants, some of whom had initially joined the PDPA in order to avoid military service, were finding themselves sucked into the crumbling war effort. Ministries, schools, banks, shops, factories and offices were all showing the effects of the call-up with well over half the available male work force enrolled in the security forces, causing the Khalqi Minister of the Interior, Sayed Mohammad Gulbazoy, to complain in late 1983 that the drafting of reservists was ruining the economy. On top of these manpower difficulties, Soviet military advisers have been seriously hampered by party feuding among the officers. Still dominated by the Khalq, the army has been unable to act decisively on numerous occasions because of disputes. While officers from both factions are constantly jockeying with each other in their attempts to recruit followings among the ranks, the soldiers themselves tend to remain deeply suspicious of party members, Soviet advisers and militiamen.

Another drawback is the poor training of recruits and the lack of qualified officers. In order to raise standards, the Soviets have dispatched numerous junior officers to the USSR and Eastern Europe for crash courses in anti-insurgency warfare and political indoctrination. Requiring all soldiers up to the rank of lieutenant to remain at least three years in the armed services, the authorities offer exorbitant salaries, when compared to what civil servants or teachers earn, to officers and cadets: from 5,600 Afghanis ($80) for junior officers (sometimes after only three months basic training) to 8,000 Afghanis ($115) and upwards for officers with higher education. Further attractions are two-year reductions in the overall liability for reserve service for every extra year that officers stay in the corps.

A Window-dressing Government

On the administrative level, the Soviets maintain direct control of all key departments such as communications. Each minister has at least two Soviet advisers, and according to middle and senior rank Afghan officials who have defected since the early days of the occupation, no minister can make a single decision, even a minor one, without consulting his omnipresent Soviet shadow.

The severe shortage of cadres, resulting from the exodus of qualified personnel and strife within the communist party, has contributed towards more advisers being brought in. Usually Central Asians, the Soviet advisers often leave unqualified party members in visible but powerless government positions while they actually run the show. But increased Sovietisation has itself caused some of the most able Afghan administrators to leave. By the end of 1983, well over four-fifths of the country's career diplomats had quit their posts, been forced to retire or transferred to other ministries. At the Paris embassy, defections among the skeleton staff still continued well into the fourth year of occupation.

The Afghan leadership visits the USSR and other Warsaw Pact

countries regularly, often staying away for long periods at a time. Commenting on Babrak's return to Kabul in June 1983 after almost a two-month visit to East Germany and the Soviet Union where he was believed to have held extensive discussions on PDPA factionalism, one Western diplomat noted:

> Either he is supremely confident of everything being under control — and everyone knows that is not the case — or the Russians have refined their running of the administration to such a point that his absence or presence does not really matter.

Kabul's Foreign Ministry, which is nominally headed by Parcham Shah Mohammed Dost, has its policies unabashedly dictated by the Kremlin. Although Dost has dutifully represented his government at the UN-sponsored talks in Geneva on a political settlement in Afghanistan or delivered speeches at the General Assembly in New York, he is nothing but a pawn. 'Only a building remains and that is just for show', maintained Mohammad Daoud Mohabbat, former director of the political affairs section, after fleeing the country with his family in October 1981. All statements issued by the ministry, which is now composed 90 per cent of party members or officials with high-ranking family connections, are prepared by a special team of Soviet advisers. According to Mohabbat, the May 1980 and August 1981 Afghan proposals for normalisation talks with Pakistan and India were drafted in this manner. 'My department should have written both statements', he said. 'But the first thing I heard of them was on the radio. I clipped them from the newspaper the next morning so I could read the full text.'

For a long time, the real Foreign Minister of Afghanistan was Vassily Sovruntchuk (since replaced), head of Dost's advisory team after the invasion and technically number two at the Soviet embassy. According to opposition sources, he drove up to the Foreign Ministry with a personal bodyguard in a chauffeur-driven car at eight o'clock in the morning. With his office next to Dost's, he was never seen to leave the building until well into the evening. At least eight other senior advisers maintain offices at the Ministry, with three of them constantly in Dost's presence. All telegrams and official documents are shown to them and nothing may be dispatched without a Russian signature.

During the first months of the occupation, secret state documents were systematically sifted by the KGB and then taken away. The

Soviets were conspicuously interested in original maps depicting the Durand Line, possibly preparing a legal dossier for future territorial claims against Pakistan in a resuscitation of the Pushtunistan issue. Moreover, according to Mohabbat and other sources, ten out of fifteen Afghan diplomats posted to Iran, Pakistan and India in the summer and early autumn of 1981 were in fact KHAD agents. Mohabbat said that he had not seen any of them before, and most could not speak English. 'We thought that these countries would not give them visas, but unfortunately they did.'

Educating a New Society

In order to enhance their influence over most sectors of Afghan life, the Soviets have tried to bring the country's educational, cultural and social institutions into complete conformity with those found in the USSR and Eastern Europe. On the whole, however, Sovietisation affects only Kabul and a few other urban centres, with the majority of the population more or less untouched.

Since the intervention, the Kremlin has helped the PDPA set up numerous Soviet-style organisations. One of the first such bodies was the Afghan-Soviet Friendship Society. This resulted in the opening of 'Friendship Houses' in all the ministries, colleges and the university, where civil servants or students can attend lectures on life in the USSR or meet with visitors from north of the border. The largest is the Russian-built complex at Deh-Mazang in Kabul, which boasts concert and meeting halls, a cinema, bar, cafeteria and library. The authorities are in the process of introducing the centres into schools.

Bodies such as the Democratic Organisation of Afghan Youth, the Democratic Women's Organisation of Afghanistan and the Union of Writers and Poets have been formed, with the party and Soviet counterparts issuing guidelines on how each group should operate. They cultivate close ties with their Soviet equivalents and send delegates to each other's conferences as part of Kabul's 'unbreakable' friendship with the USSR. In addition, the Soviets have offered an attractive array of privileges for Afghans willing to collaborate with the regime: chauffeur-driven cars, rapid promotion, housing benefits, higher salaries, bonuses and travel possibilities to the Soviet Union and Eastern Europe.

Learning a lesson from the British, whose frontier military commanders or political agents often developed into noted scholars on tribal customs and behaviour, Dari and Pashto experts from the USSR arrived in the wake of the Red Army troops. Since then, they have ransacked government files and libraries in search of information on Afghan tribal, ethnic and religious characteristics. An intimate knowledge of local culture would undoubtedly prove extremely useful for political or propaganda purposes, particularly if applied as background for KGB 'divide and rule' tactics. 'The Russians are probably just as informed, if not more, as the old British Central Asia and frontier hands who knew every Afghan characteristic right down to the last detail', said one Western regional specialist.

The war has been particularly hard on schools and colleges. Student ranks have been whittled down through flight, conscription, imprisonment and death. Qualified instructors have disappeared for the same reasons. In 1982, for example, only 500 BA students graduated from Kabul University out of an original classs of 2,300. Since 1978, 1,800 had gone missing. 'Sometimes boys and girls critical of the government were taken out of class and never seen again', said Mohammad Nasim, a former trainee teacher from Kabul. Unconfirmed reports have also referred to recalcitrant students being taken to Kabul airport in trucks and then flown to the USSR for forced labour.

To an extent, the refugee exodus has benefitted the resistance by providing it with a small cadre of educated commanders and organisers. Former teachers or engineering students, who are respectfully addressed as 'Mahalem Sab' (Mr Teacher) or 'Enginir', lead guerrilla units into battle or run resistance administrations. Another respected figure, Dr Sayad Burhannudin Madjruh, a philosopher, poet and former rector of Kabul University, directs the Afghan Information Centre in Peshawar. An exceptional and extremely valuable institution, the Centre has sought through its monthly news bulletin to provide an objective and well-informed appraisal of the war situation for editors, journalists, embassies and other observers abroad. Nevertheless, an entire generation of future Afghan doctors, scientists, teachers, leaders and administrators is being denied its right to education – an unfortunate circumstance which promises to retard the country's development still further.

With military service affecting all males between the ages of fourteen and fifty, conscription in Afghanistan is reminiscent of the desperation that existed in Nazi Germany towards the end of World War II. Defections or disappearances in boys schools may begin as young as thirteen, with parents often refusing to allow their children to attend school for fear than they will be taken. In one case in Kabul, a young boy and his mother were stopped at a roadblock by militiamen in search of conscripts. 'Afghanistan needs soldiers, not students', one of the men told them; in the end, the boy was released when the mother convinced an officer that he was under fourteen.

'You are never sure of returning when you leave home. You never know what will happen', said Hamad, a second-year trainee teacher. As with other students on military deferment, he always kept his papers on hand. One evening, while returning home, he passed several checkpoints without any problem, but at one post the officer-in-charge took his documents and tore them up in front of him and then took him by force to a nearby military enrolment office. He was held for two days, but managed to escape. Men lacking proper documents are often sent to faraway fighting fronts without any training. 'Everyone knows the authorities are using such methods', said Hamad. 'But when friends and relatives ask what has happened, officials deny knowing anything about them.'

Even students returning home on vacation from studies in the USSR or Eastern Europe have been told that they would have to serve in the local militia until the next term. When some students in the summer of 1981 said they wanted to return to Russia because security in their villages was poor, they found that their travel papers had been blocked for the holiday period.

Sovietising the Classrooms

By mid-1983, nearly nine out of ten students at Kabul University were women. Overall, roughly ten per cent were members of the PDPA. Most of the anti-communist males had left or been drafted long before. For many students and teachers opposed to the communists, Sovietisation had become an ugly fact of life. Teachers were being forced to conform or be dismissed; some lecturers were even being pressured into going to the USSR for further 'training'. The university engineering faculty, which was established by the Americans several years prior to the invasion, has been re-organised along Soviet lines, while the Department of Economics now consists of narrow specialisations such as the study of the Tashkent industrial and agricultural co-operatives.

It is no different in the schools where the Russians hope to indoctrinate a completely new pro-communist generation. Resistance members with family members still in Kabul have deliberately withdrawn their children from class in order to prevent them from being brainwashed. The only option open for young Afghans wishing to continue an education unadulterated by Marxism-Leninism is to go to Pakistan.

Nevertheless, high schools were among the first educational institutions to protest against the Soviet intervention. According to Jean-Denis Herle, a French teacher at the Lycée Istiqlal who first arrived in Kabul in August 1979 and remained during the first year and a half of the occupation, the pupils were 'profoundly disturbed' by the upheavals in their country.

During the Taraki era, all school buildings were painted red and pupils were obliged to arrive thirty minutes early in order to participate in political instruction. At 8.15 am, the national anthem was played over loudspeakers and pupils were expected to enter their classrooms singing. A picture of the 'Great Leader' (Taraki) hung in the main entrance hall and in most rooms. When Amin took over, the political sessions were abandoned but overall tension in the capital began to prevail. 'Most of them had an uncle, a brother or a cousin who had disappeared, either imprisoned or killed', said Herle.

Hostility toward the Russians grew steadily during the first six months of the occupation, with students going on strike and participating in mass demonstrations. They told their teachers that they would only start working again 'once the Russians have left our country'. By the time classes resumed after the 1980 summer vacation, the quality of education had deteriorated sharply, with numerous schools operating at only forty per cent capacity and with overflowing classes because of the shortage of teachers.

According to most informed sources, regular instruction in the senior classes no longer exists. Seventeen and eighteen year old pupils often complain to their teachers that there is little point in learning if they can be called up at any moment or can enter university without examinations if they join the party. In early 1982, Radio Kabul announced that all 10th grade high school drop-outs who volunteered for two years of military service would be automatically granted 12th grade certificates, while those from the 11th grade could enter university or college without passing entrance requirements on their release from the army. 'Those students who have been rejected by all educational institutes will be automatically inducted into the armed forces', the radio said. As most political undesirables were barred from higher studies, this meant that military service was now being directly equated with education.

'There is hardly any discipline left', said an 18-year old former pupil from the Lycée Istiqlal after his escape to Pakistan in mid-1982. 'Nobody really studies any more. Since the arrival of the Russians, there has been little point. The Parcham want us to be like them.' Hardly 500 pupils remained in the school, he added, less than half the pre-invasion figure. Two or three pistol-carrying party militants were present in every class, but they were shunned by their fellow pupils. Even the headmaster, a PDPA member, came to work with a Kalashnikov slung over his shoulder. According to French and resistance sources, anti-communist pupils demonstrate their antipathy for the regime by pointedly ignoring communist teachers in the corridors or walking out en masse when they try to hold political seminars. Resistance leaflets are clandestinely distributed and anti-Soviet slogans daubed on the walls of the school precincts.

Educational Discrimination: Supporting the PDPA Elite

To purify the system further, the authorities have made it increasingly difficult for non-party members to attain higher education. Exiled Kabul University officials have remarked on the extremely high number of first-year students post-1982 (roughly 15-20 out of a class of 40) who have PDPA affiliations compared to only three or four in the more senior years. 'When we passed the entrance exams only about fifteen per cent – all party activists or relatives of party members – were immediately admitted to the Kabul colleges', said one student now with the resistance. 'The rest of us were told to go provincial colleges. But as we knew there were no colleges in the provinces, we did everything possible to stay in Kabul.'

According to the student, some of their number finally agreed to go to one such fictitious college at Charikar, just north of the capital. There they were received by the local authorities and installed in a large building. In the evening, they were assembled in the courtyard, registered and equipped with Kalashnikovs. Some of the men protested, but were informed that the teaching staff had not yet arrived nor were the facilities ready. In the meantime, they would have to learn something useful such as how to fight. Once college started, they were told, they would have to fight anyway, fight for the Fatherland at night, study by day. When students complained further, party officials offered the following proposal: whoever agreed to serve in the army would receive 1,000 Afghanis ($14) and a college diploma without having to study or pass examinations. 'The next day', the student said, 'everybody started deserting'.

In the face of the massive departure of qualified teachers, the Soviets have sent many of their own instructors, primarily Central Asian Persian-speakers, to fill the gaps and impose their own way of thinking. The presence of Soviet teachers in Afghan schools and colleges is nothing new, of course. Just as American, British, French, German and other foreign teachers have taught in Afghan educational establishments as part of development programmes, so have Soviet Russians, Tadjiks and Uzbeks. Kabul's Polytechnique, for example, has always relied heavily on Soviet staff, but their numbers have increased markedly since the 1978 *coup d'état*.

Ideology Over Religion

Structural changes in the educational syllabus such as the compulsory learning of Russian are rapidly bringing the Afghan system into line with that of the Soviet Socialist Republics. According to Dr Sayed Mohammad Yusuf Elmi, professor of Islamic Civilisation at Kabul University who fled with his family to Pakistan in August 1983, at least four manifestly anti-Islamic subjects have replaced classical studies and are taught by the Soviets themselves: 'Historical Materialism', 'The History of Revolutionary Movements', 'Scientific Sociology' and 'Dialectical Materialism'. He also maintained that the university central library has become a centre of Soviet studies, where Soviet literature is readily available, but that those who ask for non-Russian material are told that 'it is out'. Similarly, the Behaqi Bookshop, the largest in Kabul, offers Soviet publications at extremely low prices.

Textbooks printed in the USSR, including rewritten Afghan histories, have replaced Afghan ones, while Marxist-Leninist tracts are distributed in Pashto and Dari. Political dissidence in class is forbidden (sometimes with little effect), and students are ordered to read 'progressive' books. 'Only by doing this, they told us, could we evolve like the Soviets and emerge from our misery', said a former high school student from Ghazni. 'We used to have books dealing with Islam and its philosophy. Now they have changed all this with books about Lenin and Marxist thought. . . religious science has been repressed.' In this manner, once highly respected institutions such as the Kabul Faculty of Law or the Lycée Istiqlal have been reduced to ideological stage shows.

The French and German high schools in Kabul still operate with a small contingent of European teachers. But the once highly popular British Council and American Centre have been closed down, thus substantially curbing access to Western periodicals and books. The remaining non-communist Europeans, who avoid discussing politics in class, necessarily restrain their association with Afghans. There are obvious dangers; Afghans frequenting foreigners are often put under KHAD surveillance. During the early stages of the occupation, one

British teacher was threatened by the authorities for having explained to her pupils that most policemen in the United Kingdom do not carry guns. Berated for telling imperialist lies by a communist militant, she was reported to the directorate when she refused to withdraw her statement.

The UN in Kabul: Ghost Projects or Aid?

Increased Sovietisation has meant the departure of most Western development technicians and advisers. Certain international organisations such as the World Health Organisation and UNESCO have continued to maintain limited operations in Kabul despite the occupation, but can only function in the government-controlled zones for security reasons. They have also come under considerable Soviet pressure to serve the interests of the PDPA regime.

Still operating primarily educational programmes, UNESCO's take-over of the British Council premises to continue with English-language courses seems innocuous enough. Nevertheless, among the organisation's few remaining projects in Kabul, its association with the regime's controversial National Literacy Programme has aroused the most irritation. Originally designed with UNESCO assistance to span twenty years, it was whittled down under Khalqi pressure to an unrealistic four-year programme. With such a high rate of illiteracy in Afghanistan, the programme was obviously an urgent reform, but its ruthless implementation by the regime undermined all good intentions.

Hundreds of Afghan teachers, who would logically have been involved in the programme under normal circumstances, were hounded out, beaten, imprisoned or killed for refusing to support government practices in applying the reforms. Ordinary citizens were horrified by Khalqi behaviour towards the conservative peasantry. Armed militants forced their way into homes in order to drag women off to class or shot mullahs who protested against Marxist indoctrination in the literacy campaign. It was this sort of physical and moral abuse that provoked the violent Herat uprisings in March 1979. One former student-teacher said:

> There was little to learn in these courses. In the beginning, we thought the communists had a good idea and we were willing to support the reforms. But they were badly organised and textbooks were soon replaced by communist ideology and propaganda. People

began getting suspicious and started calling the instructors 'children of Russia'. That's when the trouble really began.

Today, the programme is no longer applied so ruthlessly, but it is a far more effective form of political indoctrination than before, organised primarily by the Soviets but supported in part by UN funds. At one point, the Kremlin tried with UNESCO acquiescence to swamp one of its adult education programmes by sending 18 Soviet instructors to fill the salaried posts of six teachers designated by the Paris agency. It was only when the UN Development Programme in New York and the US and other governments protested, that UNESCO eventually backed down and a compromise agreement was reached.

Scholarships and Indoctrination

Anxious to construct an ideologically firm base of cadres as soon as possible for the new Afghan order, the Soviets have facilitated academic grants and scholarships to educational establishments in the USSR and Eastern Europe. Already in late 1981, Afghanistan represented the largest contingent of students in the Eastern bloc from any developing country — 8,700 out of some 72,000. By the end of 1983, an estimated 20,000 Afghans had gone there for trainining and further education since the invasion.

Yet even among Afghans already in the USSR, there have been numerous reported cases of disenchantment or outright anti-Sovietism. During the summer of 1980, some 500 Afghan citizens, most of them students, were denied permission to leave for the West instead of returning home. The Soviet Foreign Ministry refused to issue exit permits and there were at least four known cases of forced repatriation of dissidents to Afghanistan where they were executed by the KHAD.

Others have disappeared under more mysterious circumstances. Ahmed Kasim Zariffa, an Afghan student mechanic, was arrested in Moscow by the KGB four months after the invasion and never seen again. Back in Afghanistan, officials informed his family that he had gone insane and had been put into a psychiatric clinic. Afghan students in the USSR have often reported racist attitudes among the Russians. According to one observer, 'the Soviets resent that Afghan boys are studying in the Soviet Union while Soviet boys are dying in Afghanistan'. Such treatment has not been restricted to non-party members.

The Kremlin has concentrated on Afghan youth as its hope for the future. As one senior Paris-based Soviet diplomat, later expelled by the French government for spying, told me: 'It is necessary to create a properly indoctrinated young generation to lead a progressive, new Afghanistan.' According to Western and resistance sources, thousands of children between the ages of six and ten, mainly party offspring, have been shipped to the USSR and the Eastern bloc for 'solidarity vacations' or 'mental recreation'. Commenting on the month-long visit of 800 Afghan children to the USSR in July 1981, Babrak Karmal stated that 'the builders of the country's future should be trained properly and enjoy appropriate facilities'.

According to some reports, a significant number of these children have been kidnapped during military sweeps or picked up as orphans in rural areas and sent to the Soviet Union for a complete education. Some parents have also been persuaded to send their children in return for money or other benefits, and some have acted under threat. Under Amin, 300 children (including 200 orphans) were shipped out, most of whom have allegedly never returned. One of the main organisations involved is the KHAD-directed 'Waltan Palanzai', an educational establishment designed to give both war orphans and the children of party officials a firm grounding in Marxism-Leninism.

Controlling the Media

As in the Soviet Union, the Kremlin has sought to impose its will through rigid control of communications systems and the media. International phone calls, previously routed through Paris, now run through Moscow. Private ownership of cameras, films and recording equipment has been banned to protect 'morality, religion and the traditions of the nation'. In radio and television, the Russians oversee every aspect of programming with the object of projecting the Soviet Union as a victorious and invincible nation supported by a firm tradition of anti-fascism and love of freedom.

Government stations still broadcast highly popular Afghan folksongs which are listened to avidly by much of the population, including resistance fighters. As often as not, transistor radios among the mujahideen are tuned to Radio Kabul for music. Only for news broadcasts do they turn to the BBC, Voice of America and other international shortwave networks, officially prohibited but nevertheless listened to even in the government-occupied areas. As more refugee camps in Pakistan are supplied with electricity and increasing numbers of Afghans obtain TV sets, the Kabul authorities are reportedly in the process of building a transmitter in Jelalabad for broadcasts across the border.

Since the invasion, many favourite Afghan singers and poets have defected. Some have continued performing via tapes broadcast over Radio Free Kabul, the clandestine resistance network, or distributed among the guerrillas, where they are played on portable recorders in resistance-held bazaars or mountain villages. Their works, such as that of the Panjshair poet Shabgir, are highly topical as might be imagined.

Your country calls for liberation.
O! My courageous son. Come and remember me.
For I am being destroyed
By the hands of inhuman men.
O! Man of the Homeland. Come and let me rise.

Other personalities have collaborated with the regime and paid for it with their lives. One of Afghanistan's leading singers, Soi Makbar, was assassinated after resistance warnings not to continue working for the communists.

As part of government policy to re-embrace Islam publicly and appease the population, special efforts have been made to broadcast Koranic readings or the services from the major mosques in Kabul, Herat, Mazar-i-Sharif and other towns. News bulletins, interviews and plays on radio strongly reflect the communist, anti-imperialist line. Constant references are made to the Fatherland Front, with tribal or religious personalities reaffirming their allegiance to the regime.

Soviet influence is more readily evident on television, which is available in Kabul and a few outlying areas. According to Bari Jehani, former vice-president of Kabul TV who defected in early 1982, programme schedules incorporate a mandatory four Russian films a week, usually dealing with Soviet anti-fascist heroism during World War II. Other regular features are Soviet-style programmes geared specifically towards farmers, workers and youth.

Kabulis, however, consider the programming utterly monotonous and often offensive, and they have in many cases abandoned viewing altogether. Nightly entertainment and folksongs have become the target of ridicule. An array of communist and patriotic propaganda, they include concerts by beaming child choirs waving flags of Soviet-Afghan friendship or well-groomed soldiers singing Red Army style about loyalty to the state and homeland.

Attempts to deviate from the menu, maintained Jehani, were cracked down upon by the Ministry of Information on orders from Soviet advisers, who are present at all high-level meetings. For a long time, the only programme that was watched with enthusiasm was the weekend Indian movie. But this also came under the axe when the Soviets ordered the film to be substituted by a Russian one. 'I shall never forget the rage', noted Jehani. 'That night and all through the next day I received hundreds of calls accusing me of all sorts of things and calling me all known bad names.' Indian films were eventually reinstated, notably following improved cultural and development ties with India in 1982.

Discrediting the Resistance: Disinformation and Threats

In true KGB style, the Kabul media serve as a vital disinformation forum. In contrived interviews, mothers of Afghan soldiers, the great majority of them illiterate peasant women, are induced to mouth phrases such as 'patriotic front', 'the Great April Revolution' and its 'irreversible' and 'progressive stages'. Another form of interview is 'the captured rebel'. Normally a party militant posing as a mujahed, the 'rebel' admits to having been trained 'by Americans . . . by Chinese and Pakistani instructors . . . by Israeli experts . . . told to fight against the Fatherland . . . received dollars . . . rupees etc'. Mass pro-government demonstrations are also regularly televised.

Efforts to discredit the resistance as well as the French volunteer doctors were particularly evident during the Soviet Panjshair offensive of May 1982. In a form of psychological warfare now part and parcel of most communist assaults, helicopters dropped flurries of leaflets calling on the people to surrender. If they refused, the government threatened, the planes would continue bombing, and even resort to gas. All invoking 'Allah the Almighty', the leaflets claimed that the 'traitor' Massoud had fled with precious stones from the valley's emerald and lapis lazuli mines. He was also involved, they maintained, with the French volunteer women doctors working in the valley, who were derogatorily referred to as 'whores'.

At the same time, Radio Kabul broadcast similar allegations to the nation but pointedly omitted to mention Soviet participation in the offensive and the heavy bombardments which had already devastated much of the valley. Instead, the radio blithely announced that 'victorious' Afghan troops had 'liberated' the people of the Panjshair from the 'criminal Massoud band'. It insisted that life had returned to normal and that reconstruction of the schools, mosques, hospitals and houses 'destroyed by the counter-revolutionary bandits' would begin immediately. As for Massoud, he has been 'killed' on numerous occasions over the past three years.

Following such offensives, the Afghan authorities have often resorted to well-publicised efforts to impose a political presence in the

Panjshair. On 14 June 1982, for example, the Kabul media gave copious coverage to the departure by bus and truck of some 1,000 party militants, students and militiamen, most of them Khalqis who had been 'recruited' by the Parchami, to help with the valley's 'political re-education'. On the road north, however, partisan groups ambushed the convoy killing or wounding at least 400 government supporters. Despite bitter criticism by the families who lost their sons and daughters, there was no mention of this in the official media. Western diplomats counted no fewer than twenty-three trucks piled high with bodies.

At one gathering in December 1983 outside the US embassy which was elaborately 'guarded' by visored riot police, shouting party militants carried uniformly painted signs (all carefully collected at the end of the demonstration) with anti-American slogans condemning Washinton's 'imperialist occupation' of Grenada. All this was duly reported by Kabul TV and the media in the Eastern bloc. Most of the demonstrators, as it turned out, had been bussed in after having been given the day off from their factories. Although a government interpreter ad-libbed appropriate injections of propaganda in interviews by a visiting French TV crew, few appeared to have anything against the United States, let alone knowing where Grenada was. 'The Americans are at home, and we are here', was the equivocal answer of one man.

Afghan TV has also ensured thorough coverage of 'confessions' by captured Western journalists (three since the invasion) and, in early 1983, a French volunteer doctor. Jean-Paul Silve, a French amateur photographer, who spent nine months in jail after being picked up in 1981 by the security forces, was accused of being a member of the Central Intelligence Agency and forced to appear three times on the air to make self-critical statements, once before his trial, once during it and once after his release. 'This type of self-criticism really demonstrates the absurdity of the communist system in Afghanistan', he said somewhat bitterly after his return to France. 'During the taping, even the Afghan technicians giggled. Only the apparatchiks of the party retained their imbecile seriousness. I could have told them I was a spy from Mars and they would have recorded it in their accusation files.' Another Frenchman, TV reporter Jacques Abouchar, was similarly put on public display after being captured in September 1984, and sentenced to eighteen years imprisonment for 'illegally' entering Afghanistan; he was deported shortly afterwards.

As with the Soviet press, Afghan newspapers such as the *Kabul Times* must be read carefully and between the lines to glean signs of what is going on. 'On the whole, if you relied on the government press', said one student, 'you would never know what was going on'. Apart from the occasional official admission that problems exist in the countryside, only the daily obituaries and reports of government victories over 'bandits' and 'counter-revolutionaries' provide leads on resistance actions.

Guerrilla successes, which are too obvious to hide from the public eye, are often camouflaged as accidents, such as the destruction by the resistance of a major ammunition and petrol depot in Kabul in mid-1982. More recently, the authorities have given certain incidents wide publicity to prove outside involvement in the conflict. Nevertheless, some, such as the Salang Tunnel disaster of October 1982 in which an estimated 700 Soviets and several hundred Afghans died, never emerge in the government press. As far as could be made out from the reports, the victims died from flames and fumes when an oil tanker collided with the lead vehicle of a Soviet convoy in the tunnel. Although obituaries increased drastically for days on end and Afghans were fully informed by the shortwave radio services and underground leaflets known as 'Shabnamah', or 'nightletters', all that the communist press, including *Pravda*, would admit was that a 'serious accident' had taken place.

Soviet Economic Exploitation

Without doubt, strategic reasons featured prominently in the Soviet invasion. But it is also probable that, despite its long-time reputation as a backward and undeveloped country, Afghanistan's substantial natural resources potential was a major consideration in Soviet intelligence assessments.

Although couched in terms of reciprocal trade agreements, it has become steadily apparent that the Soviet Union's colonial-style exploitation of Afghan reserves amounts to nothing less than economic pillage. This ranges from the import of Afghan natural gas at prices well below world prices to the takeover of irrigation water. To a degree, the present military occupation is subsidised by such exploitation and analysts consider Soviet acquisition of resources an important factor in the world mineral situation.

By the time of the 1978 communist takeover, the Soviets had amassed vast amounts of excellent geological information about Afghan mineral resources. These involved no fewer than 70 commercially viable deposits and over 1,400 mineral occurrences. Generally, the Soviets remained secretive about the extent of their findings, even to the Afghans. 'They only told us what they thought we needed to know', said one senior engineer, who joined the resistance at the end of 1981.

'Of course, it is impossible to know all the Soviet motives for controlling what was generally considered to be a rather weak resource base in Afghanistan, but one can speculate on the basis of relatively well known Soviet geology directly north of Afghanistan', maintained John F. Shroder Jr. of the University of Nebraska in a detailed report, *The U.S.S.R. and Afghanistan Mineral Resources.* The geologically similar Ferghana Valley and other nearby regions just north of the border have long been famous for their vast mineral wealth, including rich oil, coal and natural gas reserves. Today, the Soviet Union's most evident economic priority is the exploration and development of Afghanistan's natural gas and oil potential as a possible replacement for its own dwindling Caspian Sea deposits.

In March 1978, less than four weeks before the Saur Revolution, the World Bank produced a confidential two-volume report on the Afghan economy. Based to a great extent on selective information provided by Soviet specialists, the report outlined the prospects for natural gas, oil, copper, coal, iron ore and other mineral deposits as well as hydro-electric power. Pointing out that the country offered considerable potential for future development, it noted that 'a stage has now been reached where intensive studies must be mounted so that decisions can be taken on the selection of projects and their phasing'.

Shortly before Daoud's overthrow, the Afghan President had expressed his intention of opening the hitherto state-controlled mining sector to the public. This greatly worried the Soviets who feared a challenge to their monopoly of exploration in the north. The World Bank report had stressed that, for a country the size of Afghanistan, present oil and natural gas prospecting was totally inadequate. It also noted that foreign interest would be considerably stimulated 'if the government were to introduce legislation offering guarantees and incentives to foreign oil companies to undertake the risks of exploration'. The UN had already begun to advise the Daoud regime on a draft ordinance, while British, American and other European companies were putting out feelers for oil investment possibilities.

The Saur Revolution put an end to all threats of Western interference. At the same time, it opened new avenues for the Kremlin. Under Taraki and Amin, the Kabul government implemented a number of development contracts previously negotiated with the Soviets by the Daoud regime. These included $30 million worth of petroleum equipment and a $50 million rail-cum-road bridge across the Amu Daraya to facilitate industrial expansion. Yet it was only with the invasion that the Soviets were finally able to clinch complete control over the exploitation of Afghanistan's natural wealth.

Through their overseas development company, Technoexport (used both for development and as a front for intelligence operations), the Soviets immediately stepped up mining exploration in the north. According to J.P. Carbonnel, head of the last French scientific mission to Afghanistan, which had to abandon its work in central Hazarajat in 1979 because of the turmoil, the Soviet oil research operation in the Mazar-e-Sharif area alone numbered 2,000 Soviet, East European and Afghan technicians. The Russians were also exploring the possibilities of developing Afghanistan's uranium deposits, which were thought to be much larger than reported in official documents. Afghanistan's inclusion within the Soviet orbit, maintained Carbonnel, 'is good business for the USSR which will seek to exploit (these reserves) and economise on their own resources'.

Economic Incorporation

As before the invasion, Soviet aid to Afghanistan still consists of loans rather than grants. Towards the end of 1980, Radio Kabul announced the signing of five protocols with Moscow which bound Afghanistan even closer to the Soviet Union. These referred to massive new aid projects, notably the training of Afghan technicians in the USSR or other Eastern bloc countries, the supplying of consumer goods for the next threee years, and the provision of chemical fertilisers as well as improved wheat, beetroot and cotton seeds. The radio further noted that the protocols paved the way for an extension of the electricity grid from the Soviet Union to Afghan cities as well as the construction of hydroelectric power stations inside Afghanistan. Considering Afghanistan's substantial hydroelectric potential, critics fear the plan will prove more beneficial to the Soviet than to the Afghan consumer.

The 1978 World Bank report had observed that half of Afghanistan's hydroelectric power potential would depend on harnessing energy from the Amu Daraya (Mother of Rivers), the 'Nile' of Central Asia. Forming a natural barrier between the two countries, the river, 'presumably could be developed only as joint projects' according to the report. If the Soviet Union's one-sided exploitation of the irrigation of water supplies belonging to the two nations is anything to go by, a fair distribution of this vital resource seems highly improbable. For years, the USSR has been using water rightfully belonging to the Afghans for the irrigation of its cotton fields in Central Asia and has shown no indication of altering its dominance in this field. Until recently, the Soviets never allowed the Afghans to undertake any large-scale irrigation projects using water from the Kochka River (situated entirely in Afghan territory) or the Amu Daraya.

Hydroelectric and irrigation schemes are now under construction, albeit severely hampered by guerrilla activity, or have been planned for the Turkestan Basin of northern Afghanistan. So have a cascade of hydroelectric stations on the Kunduz River. Nevertheless, both Western intelligence and Afghan resistance sources indicate that all these projects have been deliberately designed for total integration within the Soviet Central Asian system. As it is, the $1.5 − 2 billion Kara-Kum Canal, which at 1,500 kilometres is the longest in the world and carries water from the Amu Daraya just downstream from Afghanistan, will permit the Soviets to control the entire Amu Daraya watershed.

Oil and Natural Gas: A Major Focus

Another important aspect covered by the Soviet-Afghan protocols was 'assistance' in oil and mineral exploitation. In the year before the invasion, the Soviets committed over $652 million to mineral resource exploration and development, roughly half of all their economic assistance to Afghanistan since 1955. But it was the country's natural gas and oil potential which attracted the major focus of Soviet attention. By early 1982, analysts estimated that over $1 billion had been poured into petrochemical projects alone.

Hardly had the dust settled from the Red Army tanks crossing over into Afghanistan, when Moscow dispatched contingents of technicians with drilling equipment to join geologists already working on the intensive development of petroleum deposits at Dasht-e-Laili, Andkhoi and Sari Pul in the northern and southwestern parts of the country. The fact that the Soviets were already at such an advanced stage of exploration pointed to the intensive homework they had done during the preceding years.

The World Bank had estimated Afghanistan's oil deposits at a paltry 10 million tonnes in 1978. The communist Nifto Promo Export Agency officially upgraded this to 14 million tonnes in 1979. Yet senior Afghan government defectors believe that the country's oil potential could be twice as large because of Soviet tendencies to underestimate reserves publicly for political reasons. Some even argue that Afghanistan possesses reserves equal to those of Bahrain (34 million tonnes). Western oil technicians remain sceptical, often pointing out that, even if reserves are higher than reported, they are not necessarily commercially viable. In 1980, a Soviet embassy news bulletin published in Singapore casually, and surprisingly, noted that Afghanistan had large stocks of oil and that several deposits had been explored already, but it did not identify the fields.

Natural gas exploitation in Afghanistan is certainly one of the most striking examples of economic misappropriation by the Kremlin. Available estimates put the country's reserves at 120 billion cubic metres or more, enough to last 50 years if extracted at the claimed 1982-83 rate of 2.4 billion cubic metres.

The USSR first started importing Afghan gas in 1968 when it signed an 18-year contract at a rate to be specified every year. The question of price, the contract noted, would be negotiated separately. At the start, Moscow paid less than one fifth of the world commercial price, taking advantage of Afghanistan's logistical inability to export it elsewhere. It now imports almost double the 1968 amount but 'pays' roughly half what Western Europeans were paying for their supplies of Soviet gas during the early 1980s. Soviet payment for the product is simply deducted from Afghanistan's massive, and rapidly growing, national debt to the USSR.

All exploitation and prospecting is officially carried out by the Afghan Petrol Company, but it is the Afghan people who must pay for all Russian 'assistance' ranging from geologists to equipment. In 1980, for example, the Kabul regime signed a contract for the purchase of $18.6 million worth of tubing and extraction equipment. There is no way of knowing exactly how much the Russians are extracting as the recording metres (from which Afghans are barred) are situated inside the USSR.

At $100.34 per thousand cubic metres in 1982, virtually all Afghanistan's natural gas is piped into the USSR as a cheap form of energy for the homes and factories in Tadjikistan and Uzbekistan. This permits the Soviets to export Caspian Sea and Siberian Gas to Europe at a much more profitable $180 per thousand cubic metres. 'The Russians take everything they can which Afghanistan possesses and sell it to Europe', said northern resistance commander Habibullah, whose mujahideen have been striking regularly at natural gas facilities around Mazar-e-Sharif. 'The West thus furnishes the Russians with money to fight against the Afghans.'

As for the Afghans, they have to make do with coal and charcoal. Originally, 20 per cent of Afghanistan's natural gas production from 1974 onwards was destined to be used in Afghan fertiliser and thermal plants in the north; the rest was pumped through to the Soviet Union. By the end of 1980, however, not a single cubic metre of gas was being used in Afghanistan itself. There is perhaps some consolation to the Afghans in the fact that they are not the only ones to suffer from such high-handed treatment by the Kremlin. The Soviet Muslims of Central Asia have been dealt with in the same manner. In the bitterly cold winter of 1980-81, when Khomeini halted Iran's natural gas exports to the Soviet Union because of the Kremlin's refusal to pay world commercial rates, the Russians allowed the local population to freeze while they continued to pump Central Asian gas to Europe in return for hard currency.

Hitting the Pipelines

Hardly a day passes without the mujahideen destroying sections of the overland pipelines leading from northern Afghanistan into the USSR. Despite 24-hour military surveillance including armoured ground and helicopter patrols, army engineering crews are constantly seen repairing damage to pumping stations or sections of the pipelines. In one incident in Jouzjan province in June 1982, guerrillas blasted the pipeline causing a fire that lasted for two days despite hectic efforts by Soviet and Afghan troops to put it out. As the technicians and security forces withdrew from the site, the guerrillas destroyed an armoured vehicle and jeep killing over twenty men including a senior Soviet adviser. 'At night, fires of burning gas can be seen and smelled for miles around', said Haji Morad, an Afghan merchant from Mazar. According to diplomatic and resistance sources, gas and oil production has been suspended in many areas because of resistance activities.

If government statistics are a reliable indication, resistance sabotage has inflicted a severe blow on Soviet attempts to pump the gas from the Jarqaduq and Khwaja Gogerdak fields at Shiberghan in the north. Initially, the post-invasion Afghan-Soviet agreements stipulated an annual production of 5 billion cubic metres from 1981 onwards. In September that year, Prime Minister Sultan Ali Keshtmand announced 'economic success' in surpassing the 1980 production of 1.2 billion cubic metres by 0.5 billion, less than a quarter of what the accords had predicted. It was also considerably less than the 2.25 billion cubic metres exported in 1979 when the Afghan resistance was still in its infancy. For 1982, the regime announced a cautious 2.67 billion cubic metres with a similar figure for 1983. For 1984, government officials said they planned to raise production to 2.7 billion and eventually 4.1 billion cubic metres.

Apart from oil and natural gas, numerous other Soviet development projects have been delayed, halted or never begun because of the war. Despite the announcement in June 1983 that construction had started with Soviet assistance on the big copper-mining and smelter project at Ainak south of Kabul (latest copper ore deposits were estimated at 360 million tonnes) reportedly all the country's coal, emerald and salt mines have had to reduce or stop production. Only the Pul-e-Khumri coal mine in the north is said to be still working normally, and this only with the consent of the local mujahideen who exact 'taxes' from trucks transporting the coal to Mazar-e-Sharif and other towns. According to the World Bank, Afghanistan possesses about 100 million tonnes of coal in proven reserves, but it is suggested that as much as 500 million tonnes may exist.

Postponed Economic Schemes

Soviet security efforts have generally failed to stem the country's continued deterioration under the impact of war. It was even decided to channel development funds through the Kabul Ministry of Defence in order to facilitate co-ordination with the armed forces. But by mid-1982, according to one senior government defector, the regime was no longer in a position to initiate new economic schemes. Since then, the authorities, who have blamed the country's 'slow progress' on 'bandit' activities, have resorted to re-opening existing facilities at televised official ceremonies to create the impression of the PDPA's constant involvement in the construction of a new society. In December 1983, for example, the Minister of Health, Mohammed Nabi Kamyar, 'inaugurated' a Kabul hospital which had been built fifteen years earlier under King Zahir Shah. One of the few projects that seems to have been instituted without delay was the marked improvement in air travel facilities between Kabul and the Soviet Union shortly after the invasion.

Moscow's moves to integrate Afghanistan were strategically strengthened in June 1982 with the completion of the 2,674 foot-long Khairaton Bridge across the Amu Daraya linking Termez on the Soviet side with the new terminal of Khairaton in Afghanistan. Started immediately after the invasion in order to ease transportation bottlenecks, it consists of a two-lane roadway embedded with a single railway track. So keen were the Soviets to eliminate the temporary military pontoon bridge and the need to ferry goods by barge across the fast-flowing river with its treacherous shifting sands, that they speeded up the construction and opened it a year ahead of schedule.

As a railway terminal town with a population of 60,000, Termez has become a key military base and depot for the Russian war effort. Although priority equipment is still flown directly to Kabul, Bagram and other airports, the bridge now permits the Soviets to deliver goods directly to the Khairaton terminal by rail, where they are then transferred to lorries. As trade decreases with Pakistan, Iran and other countries, more goods are being brought down from the USSR via this route. In general, the Soviets have reversed the previous closed-border policy by encouraging cross-frontier trade in the northern Afghan provinces. Although worth barely more than $2 million in 1983, this trade is rapidly expanding.

Apart from the bridge's obvious military advantages, if provides more direct access to Afghanistan's natural resources. Afghanistan is one of the few countries in the world without a railway system, resulting from the fact that it was never colonised. Central Asia and India, administered by the Russians and British respectively, both have elaborate railway networks. Iran's proposal to build a $1.2 billion rail link from Kabul to the Gulf would have significantly changed the face of Afghanistan. Moscow is now on the point of fulfilling the old Tsarist dream of building a railway line deep into Afghan territory. Western intelligence reports indicate that a rail link is planned from Khairaton to Kabul and eventually Kandahar. Barely 100 kilometres further east, and the line would reach Pakistan's rail terminal at the Kojak Pass, continuing on to Karachi and the Indian Ocean.

Still on the drawing board because of the fighting is another massive development plan estimated at $1.2 billion closely connected with the Khairaton Bridge: the Hajigak iron-ore deposits in the Koh-i-Baba mountains in northern Afghanistan. Among the world's largest, but also inaccessible, reserves, the deposits total 2.5 billion tonnes of 60 per cent purity. An East European mining consortium believes that the installation of a processing plant could raise purity to 90-95 per cent. The cost of the project would also include the construction of a bucket lift to carry the ore from the mountains to Dushi, where a railway line, still to be built, would transport it to the Khairaton Bridge. With a projected annual production of 20 million tonnes, the consortium reckons it could recoup its investment within three years.

At present, the Soviets are underwriting the PDPA regime with massive economic aid, notably in foodstuffs, consumer goods and industrial equipment. The impact of the war varies from province to province and, despite severe shortages following military operations, the country has remained on the whole relatively self-sufficient. With overcrowding in the cities and guerrilla harassment along the highways, the Kabul regime has become increasingly dependent on the Soviets for wheat, cooking oil and sugar. Sugar exports to Afghanistan have doubled since the invasion, while wheat has more than trebled, with 200,000 tonnes promised in 1984. Moscow can ill afford to deny its own economy such products but considers it necessary to improve the appearance of the Afghan communist regime. The USSR also provides Afghanistan with nearly all its refined petroleum products, ranging from diesel petroleum to aviation fuel.

Nevertheless, such heavy Soviet economic support has failed to halt the deterioration of the Afghan economy. Virtually the entire government expenditure is devoted to salaries. Since the intervention, money in circulation has reportedly increased from 26 million Afghanis to nearly 50 million, resulting in severe inflationary pressures and price rises. According to official Kabul figures, the gross domestic product fell from $2.6 billion in 1978-79 to $2.4 billion in 1981-82. Over the same period, per capita income dropped from $114.60 to $104.60 and was expected to decline even further, making Afghanistan one of the poorest countries in the world.

Paying for the Occupation

As with Russian policy in Eastern Europe, the client state of Afghanistan will be expected to foot the bill for all Soviet activities in the region by forgoing its own valuable natural resources at unfair low rates. The salaries of some 800 Soviet technicians now involved in petrochemical development, for example, are all paid for by the Afghan government. In effect, the Russians have adopted the technique of forcing the invaded country to pay for its own conquest and occupation.

With agriculture, the situation is no different. The northern provinces of Balkh, Samangan and Kunduz, for example, represent one of the best cotton growing regions in the world. Crop yields are estimated at an above-average 1,000-1,200 kilos of cotton seed per hectare. 'The soil is ideal', noted Michel Thiebolt, a former French cotton expert in Afghanistan. 'The cold climate during the winter kills parasites better than chemical products and the presence of the Kochka and Amu Dayara rivers would permit the considerable expansion by irrigation of cultivatable land.'

Since the mid-1930s, the USSR has always bought a major portion of the Afghan crop, but much of it eventually ends up being sold to the West for hard cash at higher prices. Not unlike their natural gas import practices, the Soviets paid two or three times below world prices for the cotton and deducted this from Afghan purchases of imported Soviet machinery and other industrial products. Between 1967 and 1976, the French Textile Fibre Development Company managed to double Afghan cotton production by improved farming methods. In addition, it roughly doubled the amount of cotton cultivation from 55,000 to 112,000 hectares.

The Russians began to worry when the Afghans showed signs of selling their crops at better prices direct to Western Europe, thus breaking Moscow's monopoly. As might be expected, the communist takeover conveniently eased this concern. Since 1978, the Soviets have sought to intensify cotton production in Kunduz to the detriment of wheat production, which forms part of the staple Afghan diet. Forced cultivation of cotton provoked serious disturbances in 1980 among farmers who did not care to be told what to plant.

During the 1920s and early 1930s, the Russians used sheer brute force to impose monoproduction of cotton in the Soviet Central Asian Republics. This led to widespread peasant revolts and severe famine, but it finally gave the Russians what they wanted: complete political leverage over an exhausted and downtrodden people. The similarities with the Kremlin's present policy in northern Afghanistan have led some analysts to believe that it might be preparing the same fate for the Afghans by transforming the entire northern agricultural region into a massive cotton belt.

Overall, Soviet military repression and policies of economic denial have been instrumental in forcing out large segments of the population. Villagers are finding it increasingly difficult, if not impossible, to grow their own food or raise money to purchase it in nearby bazaars. In the end, this aspect of 'migratory genocide' is bound to play a decisive role in draining the countryside of mujahed support. By the same token, however, Moscow might find itself forced to bolster communist-occupied Afghanistan even more with imports from the USSR and Eastern bloc countries, as the guerrillas are unlikely to tolerate government projects unless they serve resistance purposes.

8 THE AFGHAN STRUGGLE: THE PEOPLE'S WAR

'I am unhappy. My heart is in a cage which the birds have left. It is empty. Sad . . . Havoc is everywhere. I don't know how this will ever end. When you walk in the streets all you see are faces hidden behind dusty layers of sadness . . . What am I supposed to do? I want to die. I have lost everything. Everything. I don't know why I live . . . Every day brings bad news . . . I am unable to write any more words which would make you content. I am writing you with tears . . . ' (Letter of schoolgirl to friends in France after losing all the men in her family through imprisonment or death and being expelled from Kabul high school for participating in anti-Soviet demonstrations, February, 1980).

They emerged furtively from house doorways and behind garden walls. Throwing handfuls of dried nuts and boiled sweets, the women and young girls murmured the traditional Afghan greeting: 'Manda nabushi. May you not be tired.' Delicate shafts of evening sunlight oozed like honeyed resin through the leaves of the mulberry and walnut trees, while the earthy smell of wood fires came enticingly from the mud and stone dwellings. Along the narrow dirt lanes, rumbustious village lads wielding long reed switches prodded ambling cows back from the fields.

The passing mujahideen had just spent the afternoon fording the river, brown and heavily swollen with rain from the Hindu Kush. Several miles upstream there was a bridge, but it was controlled by Soviet and Afghan troops. Only slightly to the west lay Bagram airbase, dominated by the perpetual roar of helicopters and jets taking off and landing. Occasional pairs of Mi-24 gunships, delicately pencilled against the sky, passed high overhead emitting wispy traces of dark exhaust. Too close for comfort, we could hardly help but notice the pillars of dust rising in the wake of armoured vehicles as they rumbled among distant villages stretched across the plain.

A contingent of some one hundred men accompanied by forty heavily loaded packhorses, the guerrillas had chosen to cross a wide section of the river where the current seemed least treacherous. It was still strong enough to throw the animals plunging and thrashing into the flow, while the men, water up to their chests, could only traverse in small groups clutching each other by the wrist in a human chain. Men from the nearby villages earned a living guiding merchant and resistance caravans across the river. Sometimes mounted, sometimes struggling in the water beside them, they tugged at the horses' reins and tails as they manoeuvred them to the other side, trying to keep the guns and ammunition dry. One also had to be careful of local wood transports. Cut trees and branches lashed together, the rafts came whipping by at regular intervals ridden by half-clad Afghan Huckleberry Finns whose job it was to release the make-shift rafts whenever they caught on the sandbars.

Leaving the parched, exposed hills on the other side of the river behind, we entered the bucolic tranquillity of the villages on the opposite bank. There, amid the cool of the irrigated fruit orchards and wheat fields, the women's gestures evoked such a touching sense of serenity that we momentarily forgot the war and even our utter weariness. We thanked the women and bent down to pick up their offerings. Normally, the villagers would have offered us tea, but, fearing communist reprisals, they apologetically urged us on our way. Some of the houses already lay in partial or total ruin, while the fields had been churned into deep furrows by the tracks of rampaging tanks. Here and there, the charred and rusted remains of overturned armoured vehicles lay in the steep roadside ditches.

The partisans, rifles slung over their shoulders, seemed uncharacteristically subdued. Apart from the footfall of marching, the only sounds were a smattering of small-talk and the singing of a resistance ballad. For many, their families and homes lay just beyond the mountain ridges. Practically every man had lost at least one relative in the war and no doubt wondered whether he would find his loved ones safe, his home intact.

Nevertheless, trudging beneath a magnificent albeit shrapnel-scarred avenue of trees, the soft beauty of the landscape — the glow of the setting sun, the chorus of frogs in the gurgling irrigation canals and the throaty warbling of mynah birds in the willows — acted like soothing balm. Suddenly, a lone turbaned rider on a snorting gray steed bore down on the group throwing up white clouds of fine dust. Astride an elaborately decorated leather saddle, he gazed intently ahead as he passed. Carefree and yet defiant in the spirit of the Afghan, he was riding for the pure joy of speed. It felt extremely good to be alive.

Without the support of the people, the mujahideen would be nothing. 'Why do you differentiate between fighters and the old men, the women and children?' a village chief once asked me with a benign smile shortly after the invasion. 'If you have courage and treasure freedom, you are a mujahed. We are all mujahideen.'

Afghan opposition to communist rule and the Soviet occupation is above all a 'people's struggle' with the effectiveness of the resistance measured to a great extent by the ability of the guerrilla fronts to remain on good terms with the local population. Furthermore, growing proficiency in modern guerrilla warfare has not sufficed in combating Russian guile. For the Soviets do not represent an irresolute thirteenth century horde of wild horsemen under Genghis Khan massacring, looting and raping as they ride, leaving nothing in their place. Nor are they a nineteenth century British expeditionary force sent out to punish obstinate and scheming Afghan tribesmen. Subtle, calculatingly ruthless and ideologically single-minded, they are a force who cannot be success-fully challenged in the long term by reflex action backed by Enfields and Kalashnikovs.

There seems little question that the Soviets have adopted a grim policy of attrition against the Afghans, particularly the civilian pop-ulation. Regardless of their own losses, they seem prepared to tolerate a low degree of armed opposition lasting years if not decades, but which, they hope, will permit the PDPA regime to lay the foundations of a 'new' Afghanistan, eventually winning over its war-fatigued and dejected inhabitants. Since the winter of 1981-82, they have concen-trated on breaking civilian morale by truculently disrupting social and economic conditions in numerous guerrilla-controlled zones. For an overwhelming number of Afghans, the possibility of eking out a liveli-hood on the land simply no longer exists.

Visions of Emptiness

The cataclysmic impact of such a totally new and horrific style of conflict has wrought a profound and, in many cases, irreversible change on this extremely orthodox Central Asian society. Even if peace were to return overnight, it is certain that Afghanistan will never be the same again. Khalqi excesses followed by the Soviet Union's pitiless application of modern military and psychological anti-insurgency methods have patently shaken the country to its foundations, plunging it into a nightmare of aerial bombardments, armoured ground assaults, brutal reprisals, gas attacks and the ominous knock at the door by the KHAD. Farms, villages and bazaars have been devastated, crops burned and livestock slaughtered, the inhabitants killed or forced to leave.

Often all that remains is emptiness and desolation; dusty, abandoned irrigation canals stringing the mountain slopes, the faded vestiges of once fecund wheat fields in the valleys, cultivated as they were over centuries, the shattered ruins of ghost villages surrounded by bleached and shrivelled fruit orchards creaking in the desert wind. The mere fact that as many as five million Afghans, between a quarter and a third of the population, have been wrenched from their homelands and obliged to seek refuge abroad by the end of 1984 is one of the most tragic manifestations of this terror. So are the huge concentrations of internally displaced persons who, like the two million or more Vietnamese who fled to Saigon during the Indochina war, have flocked to the towns to escape the fighting.

The struggle for survival has forced the Afghans to adapt to new conditions. Many once common traditions such as elaborate wedding festivities have been abandoned in many areas. On the other hand, there is also widespread determination to continue living 'normally', no matter what, even to the extent of playing 'buz-kashi' (a form of mounted polo using a headless goat or calf's torso as a ball) in full view of patrolling Soviet helicopters.

Some Afghans have defiantly stayed behind in regions, such as the eastern provinces, where flight might have seemed the most sensible solution. Caretaker teams of men living with small groups of women and children can still be found among the battered ruins of mountain villages, repairing the canals to irrigate the fields and tending the few goats and cows that have escaped the bombings. Closer to the Pakistani border, most inhabitants have fled, but teams of young men return regularly to cultivate and harvest the crops.

Among those Afghans forced to abandon their homes completely, few have ever had much contact with the outside world. Women, as a rule, rarely left the sanctuary of their mountain communities. Now, in the refugee camps, they must learn to cope with new and sometimes humiliating conditions: cramped quarters with little privacy, charity handouts, poor sanitation. But there are also benefits such as easy access to health care and education.

In the face of such tempestuous upheavals, the durability of the resistance will increasingly depend on whether the fronts can provide inhabitants with the necessary 'public services' — an efficient administrative structure, regular food supplies, health care, schools, shelter and war indemnities — to survive. 'Even in war people must continue living', noted one resistance commander from Kabul, 'If the mujahideen

can offer nothing, there is no doubt that the communists will do everything to fill the gap if they know it will break us. And once they have
done that, they can do what they want.'

By ruthlessly imposing a socio-political revolution from above, the
Soviet-backed communists have inadvertently instigated a vigorous anti-
Marxist people's revolution from below. Nevertheless, in many areas
the guerrilla leadership has failed to exploit this advantage. It has often
been either too preoccupied with the fighting or, lacking initiative, not
interested in providing for civilian needs. Few seem ready to admit this.
'But it is a serious problem', said a former literary student, now a
junior commander from Parwan province. 'The mujahideen know how
to fight, yet have little idea about establishing proper political and
social structures.' As numerous guerilla leaders have discovered elsewhere in the world, it is often easier to wage war than to deal with
what some flippantly regard as the banalities of keeping women,
children and old men alive.

The Makings of a People's Resistance

Each of the heads of the three main fundamentalist parties in Peshawar
began his career in exile during the initial period following Mohammed
Daoud's overthrow of King Zahir Shah in 1973. Apart from forcing the
monarch to leave the country, Daoud had also arrested, executed or
banished numerous conservative and Muslim dissidents. About fifty
fundamentalists fled to Pakistan, where the then Prime Minister
Zulfikar Ali Bhutto used them to his own political advantage by inte-
grating them within a new 'forward policy' against the Kabul regime.
With Daoud back in power, this was designed to counter any attempts
at reviving the Pushtunistan issue.

Between 1973 and 1977, Pakistan trained an estimated 5,000
Afghan dissidents in secret military camps. A substantial number were
Young Muslim dissidents and sympathisers. Founded in 1964-65 by
theologians at Kabul University, who had come under the influence
of the militant international Muslim Brotherhood while studying
abroad, the movement attracted a large following among Islamic
students. Vehemently anti-leftwing, they not only clashed constantly
with the Khalqis and Parchamis, but also accused Daoud of working
with the communists.

In July 1975, Afghan dissidents attacked two police stations in the
Panjshair Valley and succeeded in holding most of the valley for three
days. But before the insurgency could spread, government security
forces put the guerrillas to flight. Daoud immediately accused the

Pakistanis of orchestrating the uprising. This was flatly denied by Islamabad, although several years later senior civilian and military officials with the Bhutto administration privately admitted that they had been responsible for the arms, finance and timing of the incident. The abortive uprising gave the present-day fundamentalist leaders their first taste of armed rebellion. Later, Gulbuddin Hekmatyar of Hezb-i-Islami arrogantly claimed that he was the first to launch the struggle against the communist 'infidels'.

An Opposition-in-Exile

During the Taraki-Amin periods, Afghan dissident groups in Pakistan began to proliferate. By January 1980, well over twenty identifiable parties had established themselves in Peshawar and Quetta. To prevent the situation getting out of hand, the Islamabad government recognised only the six major ones and the remainder, unable to solicit openly for financial or other support from abroad, were forced to merge, close down or operate semi-clandestinely.

Three months before the Soviet invasion, Peshawar exuded the atmosphere of a den of spies. Diplomats, journalists, intelligence agents and mysterious travellers were constantly drifting through this dusty Pathan city, some 35 kilometres from the Khyber Pass, to check on the Afghans, the Pakistani drug smugglers or whatever plots one cared to unearth. With its crowded bazaars and smoke-filled tea shops, Peshawar still retained some of the romantic frontier flavour of Kipling's India. At Dean's Hotel, a run-down but pleasant colonial establishment, the Pakistani secret police made valiant efforts to keep track of all outsiders. While staying at the hotel with several other foreign correspondents, I spotted no fewer than six security men who had settled down in a 'Northwest Frontier Engineering Dept' Land Rover parked just outside our bungalow Doors. Two additional observers lounged on a motorscooter near the main entrance of the courtyard.

At that time, the Afghan political exiles had their party headquarters tucked away in the narrow sidestreets of the bazaars. To meet them, one had to make discreet telephone calls and then slip off for interviews, pointedly not looking at the police as one left. One usually recognised the rebel offices by the crowds of turbaned Afghans outside and the inevitable plainclothes men standing casually a few yards away. Armed Afghan guards would stand in the doorways checking identities and frisking people as they entered. Sometimes the Afghan leaders themselves would come directly to the hotel and then the police would appear at the door under one pretext or another to look inside. It was an absurd little game. For the sake of not further straining relations with the Kabul regime, aggravated enough as they were by cross-border guerrilla activity, the Pakistanis had to give the impression that they were not allowing the insurgents a totally free rein. There was also the fear (later justified) that Kabul would retaliate by stirring up agitation among Pushtun nationalists or Pakistan's own frustrated political opponents.

The Soviet intervention put an end to all this when hundreds of journalists swooped into town, thoroughly overwhelming the Pakistani authorities. The sudden surge of world interest, soon to be followed by a perpetual stream of relief officials, diplomats and foreign dignitaries touring the refugee camps, saved the Khyber Intercontinental Hotel from bankruptcy. Within days, most Afghan political groups had representatives sitting openly in the hotel lobbies or posting press conference notices at the main desk. To get to their headquarters was no longer a furtive operation; one simply asked the cab driver.

The Fundamentalist Parties

Among the fundamentalist parties, Rabbani's Jamiat now appears to have established itself as the most prominent. Since early 1983, it has attracted large numbers of mainly Hezb-i-Islami (Hekmatyar faction) defectors but also mujahideen from other groups. Particularly strong in the northern areas, it is affiliated with a number of highly effective field commanders such as the Panjshair's Massoud and Herat's Ismail Khan.

A Tadjik from Badakshan province where he was born in 1940, Rabbani is a well-travelled, soft-spoken theologian whose boyish face and twinkling eyes stand out incongruously from his sombre beard. Elected chairman of Jamiat in 1972 in Kabul, where he had built up a considerable student base, Professor Rabbani fled from Daoud's political crackdown a year later. With the failure of the 1975 Panjshair uprising, he returned to Peshawar and in 1977 transformed Jamiat into an active resistance party.

The second of the fundamentalists is the Hezb-i-Islami faction led by Maulawi Younis Khales, known as the 'fighting mullah'. Nearly sixty when the Soviets invaded, Khales, a rugged Pushtun from Nangrahar Province, is the only Peshawar-based chief to return regularly to Afghanistan to fight. The other leaders occasionally tour the interior. On 1 September 1982, for example, Khales commanded a guerrilla assault against Jalalabad airport, seriously damaging its installations. A weapons depot was hit, two helicopters destroyed on the ground and an estimated 80 Soviet and Afghan troops killed. Nearly three weeks later, Khales narrowly escaped death when helicopter gunships attacked his mountain stronghold at Tora-Bora killing a number of mujahideen, including three of his best commanders.

A resolute character with an intense hatred of the Russians (his son was executed by the Soviets), he first worked in Saudi Arabia and then returned to Afghanistan where he became a university lecturer and editor of a Kabul newspaper. In the wake of the Panjshair debacle, Khales founded the Hezb with Hekmatyar. But after the Saur Revolution, Hekmatyar closed ranks with Maulawi Mohammedi's Harakat, leaving the Hezb. Later, when Hekmatyar broke with Mohammedi, he established his own organisation and claimed back the Hezb-i-Islami label. Since then, this has confusingly furnished the Afghan resistance with two parties of the same name.

Commanding major support in Nangrahar and other eastern provinces, Khales has never felt comfortable in his role as leader in exile, considering it his duty to be fighting at the side of his men. Despite his efforts to transfer his headquarters to Afghan soil, the Pakistanis, the Gulf countries (who provide much of his finance) and the other fundamentalists have pressured him into staying in Peshawar so as not to break the alliance.

Of all the Peshawar groups, Hekmatyar's Hezb is by far the most controversial and radical. Closely connected with the Muslim Brotherhood, Hekmatyar is reverently referred to as 'Engineer' by his followers, as are many Afghans with any form of technical background. Because of his political activities and a spell in prison, however, he never completed his university studies. A gaunt figure, he is a 'transplanted Pushtun' from Baghlan province, one of the northern and western areas where the Kabul government relocated tribesmen from the east during the nineteenth and early twentieth centuries in a bid to spread Pushtun influence. Considering the Hezb the 'vanguard of the Jihad', he is a fervent admirer of Khomeini's Islamic Revolution (although he appears to have reduced his links with the Tehran regime) and favours a non-aligned Islamic Republic similar to that of Iran but headed by a Sunni caliph.

Now in his mid-thirties, Hekmatyar has been accused of murdering in 1972 a certain Saidal Sokhandan, a supporter of the Maoist Sho'la-yi Jaweid (Eternal Flame) party, while a student and Young Muslim militant in Kabul. He spent more than a year in prison before fleeing to Pakistan where he joined the other anti-leftwing dissidents. Expressing both anti-American and anti-Soviet views, Hekmatyar has constantly espoused pro-Muslim and anti-Israeli causes such as the Pan-Islamism of Colonel Qaddafi of Libya (from whom he has received both money and arms) or the Palestinian struggle. When the Israelis forced the PLO to quit Lebanon in the late summer of 1982, Hekmatyar proposed to send fighters to the Middle East to combat the 'Zionist menace'.

A man of few scruples, Hekmatyar has aroused violent antagonism among his fellow compatriots. He is regarded as ruthless, uncompromising and devious, or as one foreign observer noted 'dictatorship material at its worst', and is often accused of trying to establish his own hegemony at the expense of the Afghan resistance. The Hezb has been associated with the assassination of scores of political adversaries in Pakistan and Afghanistan and is known to operate its own jails, where kidnapped mujahed opponents have been tortured and killed. While the other parties operate detention centres, they are normally reserved for Afghan communist or Soviet prisoners and not guerrilla antagonists.

Above all, many resistance detractors hold Hekmatyar responsible for consistently undermining mujahed groups in the field. Bitter and often bloody clashes have erupted between Hezb and Jamiat followers, the first of which occurred in December 1978 in Parachinar and resulted in the deaths of fourteen Jamiatis. Both outside observers and reliable resistance sources have witnessed armed Hezb assaults against fellow mujahideen, even in the midst of battle with the Soviets. In some reported cases, Hezb groups co-ordinated anti-government operations with other resistance fronts, but then pulled out leaving flanks exposed to the enemy. In June 1982, resistance commanders blatantly charged Hekmatyar with treachery, holding him responsible for the success of certain Soviet anti-insurgent actions against civilians and guerrilla strongholds earlier that year. In one incident that I witnessed, Hezb fighters apprehended four Jamiat guerrillas carrying a severely wounded comrade to the French-run hospital in the Panjshair and, after taking their arms, held them for two days. Because of the delay, the wounded man died. In another, a Hezb group actually kidnapped a French medical team on its way back to Pakistan.

Hekmatyar disclaims all responsibility for such attacks, either disowning them completely or maintaining that his supporters are not involved. His stab-in-the back methods, however, have led many to believe that he is working in tacit co-operation with the Soviets. It is often pointed out that the Kabul authorities constantly brand Hekmatyar as a 'bandit' and an instrument of the CIA. Curiously, he is the only resistance leader to be thus singled out. While the other groups are left to bleed, it is argued, Hekmatyar is being boosted by communist propaganda as the only guerrilla leader of importance, should Moscow ever want to strike a deal.

Most informed observers dismiss any direct Hezb connivance with the Soviets. Nevertheless, Hekmatyar's calculated subversion has played into the hands of the occupation forces. While such policies have damaged the resistance cause, they have rebounded severely on Hekmatyar himself. Hezb mujahideen, disgusted by what they regard as 'un-Islamic' assaults against their fellow Muslims, have been defecting to other groups in growing numbers.

The Moderate Parties

Unlike the fundamentalists, the more moderate and generally less effective nationalist organisations only got going as an active opposition from late 1978 onwards. Many of their backers — former politicians, civil servants, army officers and academics — supported the Zahir Shah and Daoud regimes; some initially hoped that the PDPA meant what it said when it promised reform, democracy and modernisation, but were quickly disillusioned.

Among the three main Peshawar parties, Harakat is reportedly the most influential. At present, it can claim affiliated grass-root fronts operating not only in eastern provinces like Logar, Ghazni, Zabul and Paktya, but also certain areas north of Kabul and even Minruz to the west. Since the beginning of the third year of Soviet occupation, however, it appears to have lost ground to internal fronts with fundamentalist links. In 1983, a sizeable Harakat faction broke away to join the fundamentalist alliance. A similar development has occurred among the Gaylani and Mujadeddi organisations. Some mujahideen have left because of internal disagreements or what they perceive to be a lack of Islamic 'firmness'. But logistical reasons also seem to be a significant factor. Conservative Muslim nations like Saudi Arabia tend to favour the fundamentalists, as do Pakistani officials with Muslim Brotherhood connections, and the moderates generally have fewer funds and weapons to hand out to their supporters.

A gloomy-eyed Ahmadzai Pushtun in his early sixties, Harakat's leader, Maulawi Mohammadi has succeeded in combining both secular and religious sentiments. Not only does he enjoy considerable political backing from traditional mullahs and tribal chiefs, but also urban-based progressives and nationalists. Mohammadi, a theologian and former parliamentarian, is an ardent nationalist who favours government based on the traditional Loya Jirgha (Grand Assembly) system rather than a Western-style legislature.

The second moderate party, Gaylani's National Front, has attained respectable effectiveness thanks to several excellent affiliated commanders like Amin Wardak, who operates in Wardak and Ghazni provinces, and Sayed Nayim from Maidan near Kabul, as well as a number of talented military organisers within the Peshawar structure. As a Sufi pir (the direct descendant of a Muslim saint), Gaylani commands a strong following among Pushtuns in the southern and southeastern tribal areas as well as in Kabul. Gaylani, who is a member of the influential Qadariya section, was dispossessed of his properties shortly after the Saur revolution. In December 1978, he and his family fled to Pakistan to escape Khalqi persecution. Four months later, he founded the National Front and declared Jihad against the regime.

Fiftyish, Gaylani is a quiet man, who prefers to wear European dress, which hardly befits a practising hereditary saint. He has some difficulty in polishing his image of an Afghan religious chief and looks distinctly uncomfortable when wearing tribal robes among his followers. Like his fellow moderate leader Mujaddedi, Gaylani is a monarchist (his wife, Rahila, is the grand-daughter of the ex-King) and basically pro-Western. Both have maintained close links with Zahir Shah in Rome and have been carefully cultivating his nostalgic appeal among the tribes as a symbol of potential unity and stability.

Gaylani often travels abroad in search of diplomatic and financial support, adamantly advocating a democratic constitutional monarchy as the best solution to Afghanistan's religious and ethnic diversity. Also condemning mullah dominance, he appears far more comprehensible to many Westerners, who quite unjustifiably tend to regard Afghanistan's religiously-inspired leaders as 'Muslim fanatics'. Gaylani's pro-Western stance has led many European and American observers to believe that he commands far more respect inside the country than is the case. Concerning the future of the resistance struggle, Gaylani has adopted a remarkably sober approach: 'We cannot defeat the Russians on the battlefield, but we can make it so uncomfortable for them that they will have to sit down and talk out a political settlement. The geopolitical realities dictate a compromise with the Russians.'

The third of the Peshawar moderates, Professor Sibghatullah Mujadeddi, is a pir with family links to the Nagshbandi order and is a nephew of a major Afghan Muslim figure, the Hazrat of Shor Bazaar. A graduate of Al-Azhar University in Cairo and a highly reputed Islamic teacher, Mujadeddi lectured in various Kabul colleges during the 1960s before being imprisoned by Daoud as a religious conservative. He later left for self-imposed exile to become director of the Scandinavian Islamic Institute in Copenhagen.

Mujadeddi is a modest man who strikes one as sensitive and deeply concerned about the plight of his people. A constitutional monarchist to the extent that he uses the Royal emblem for his National Front, he commands substantial support among the Sufi Brotherhood in the North. Some observers argue, however, that he is tainted by the alleged involvement of his forebears in the British-instigated overthrow of King Amanullah, the popular nationalist reformer, in 1929.

Recruitment and Organisation

As exile organisations, the Peshawar parties were well placed to muster grassroots support among the tens of thousands of refugees crossing into Pakistan every month during the first two years of the occupation. The great majority had previously had no contact with the political groups, so party activists based in the frontier villages or refugee processing centres signed them up as they came in. Pointing to the space for political affiliation on the government registration forms, wily militants tried to create the impression, false though it was, that the Pakistanis would only grant them food and shelter if they joined.

Entire families, clans and even tribes were thus enlisted. Unable to read, many refugees had little idea which of the parties they had, in fact, joined. Overzealous recruiters often lied simply to obtain a family head's thumb-mark. There were also numerous cases of new arrivals being registered by two, or even three, parties. While some multi-registrations were part of refugee efforts to obtain more relief rations or an extra gun, the parties profitted by such discrepancies to boost membership, a distinct asset when conducting fund-raising excursions abroad or collecting 'voluntary' contributions among refugees.

On the whole, however, support for the parties has tended to be based on local rather than external factors. In most cases, a mujahed's first loyalty is to his commander, usually a relative. This might be a traditional tribal or religious figure, a regional personality or a partisan commander who has won respect through deeds rather than bloodties. Some of the resistance fronts, mainly Pushtun, consist of refugee recruits with no roots in the region where they are fighting, and they are led, as well as armed, by guerrilla commanders directly responsible to the Peshawar organisations. In contrast to the educated urban elite, few peasant fighters will cite political reasons (being Islamic is a sufficient criterion) for joining a particular organisation. More recently, this has begun to change as the more sophisticated partisan fronts put greater emphasis on ideological indoctrination to counter government propaganda.

For many mujahideen political affiliation has depended therefore on the nature of the relationship between the party and their local or regional commander, a deciding factor being what the exile organisations can offer in return for declared political support. The parties tend to conclude agreements with the internal commanders, promising them funds, weapons, ammunition, medication or even assistance in obtaining the release of an imprisoned comrade from a government jail. Mujahed groups often send delegations to Peshawar to make the rounds of the parties to see who can make the most interesting propositions.

To an extent, this relationship has made life much easier all round. In Pakistan, refugees can channel complaints through party officials or make arrangements for returning to the country to fight. Party affiliation considerably facilitates movement. Mujahideen travelling to and from the battle zones can eat or spend the night in party-run Chaikhanas which often serve as local political headquarters. Or they can pass through unfamiliar regions by showing official letters of recommendation or their party identification cards.

Politics and Propaganda

Perhaps most important, the parties serve as windows to the outside world for the resistance. Generally responsible for receiving and distributing supplies, the parties manipulate this control as a means of political leverage over their compatriots inside. Favouritism and unequal distribution have thus resulted in considerable dissatisfaction, prompting some regional fronts to maintain their own representatives in Peshawar to look after their interests, or even to dispatch emissaries abroad in search of more direct backing.

On the whole, it is the fundamentalists who have faired best both inside and outside Afghanistan. But it has never been easy to determine the exact strength and prominence of each organisation. Prior to the invasion and during the first few months of the occupation, there is little doubt that Hekmatyar's Hezb was the strongest and most disciplined of the groups, thanks in part to his ingenuity and organisational abilities.

As a party, Hezb has attracted militant cadres from a social background strikingly similar to that of the Khalq. Most tend to be in their twenties and early thirties, high-school educated but originally from rural rather than urban areas. They are also distinguished by the same intolerance and inexorable desire to further the aims of the party that characterised the Khalq during the 1978-79 period. Using extremely aggressive tactics, the Hezb gained considerable advantage over the other organisations.

Hekmatyar was the first to understand the importance of operating a well-oiled propaganda apparatus. Although an ad hoc operation when compared to the more experienced liberation movements elsewhere in the world, it did succeed in boosting the party's renown. Well before any other party, the Hezb established its own clandestine radio station inside Afghanistan in 1979. During the first few years of communist rule, many observers, including this writer, came away with the impression that the Hezb was by far the most significant of the guerrilla movements. This was quite possibly the case in the beginning because of the organisation's highly efficient recruiting methods. Party officials regularly asserted that as many as 300,000 mujahideen were actively fighting under the green Hezb banner. The actual number of full-time partisans probably stood at less than one-tenth of that figure by the end of 1980.

The other parties soon caught on. Following the invasion, each group was more than eager to organise lightning press tours into Afghanistan to prove its strength. They loved nothing better than to show off burned out tanks or throngs of tribesmen waving rifles in the air shouting 'Allah o akbar'. Their Peshawar headquarters were plastered with photographs depicting victorious guerrillas standing over the shot-up bodies of Khalqi officials or the shattered remains of a government police station. In constant competition, they ensured that their respective flags or leaders' pictures were in every photograph to prevent rivals from presenting the incident as their own kill.

Some of the groups bold-facedly declared that their mujahideen were killing thousands of Russians every month; as for their own casualties, they shrugged, only a handful of 'martyrs'. It was only when foreign correspondents increasingly questioned such allegations, refusing to report them unless they were substantiated, that the more perceptive party leaders began to issue more credible reports.

Kabul: Nightletters and Demonstrations

The first tentative signs of open opposition to the Soviet invasion in Kabul and other towns came in the form of 'Shabnamah', those crudely printed 'nightletters' which had already made their appearance during the late 1960s to protest against social injustices. Now voicing anti-Soviet declarations or political manifestos, they were distributed in the streets, left in the mosques or pushed into embassy compounds under cover of darkness. At the same time, tape recorders were placed on the rooftops where they blared sonorous 'Allah o akbars' or anti-Marxist slogans into the cold winter night.

The nightletters accused the Soviets of treating the Afghans like 'slaves' and vowed that Muslims 'will not give up fighting or guerrilla attacks until our last breath'. One communiqué referred to Babrak Karmal Babrak as 'Karghal', a play on words meaning 'thief at work' in Farsi. The call of the muezzin, which is customarily heard five times a day, was also regarded as a demonstration of defiance to the new Soviet-backed regime. But Karmal, aware of the mistakes of his anti-Islamic predecessors, took pains to begin his first speech to the country (recorded in the USSR) with the words: 'In the name of Allah, the compassionate and the merciful. . .'

Within weeks of the intervention, leaflets distributed by various underground organisations began to appear in the Afghan capital urging shopkeepers to show their 'unanimous condemnation' of the occupation by rolling down their shutters. On 21 February 1980, commercial life in the capital came to a halt at the start of a week-long strike. Thousands of demonstrators marched through the streets chanting slogans such as 'Russians, Afghanistan is not Czechoslovakia', 'Down with Babrak, puppet of the Russians' and 'Out with the Russians!'. At night, protestors climbed on to the tops of buildings to shout 'Allah o akbar'.

The regime immediately imposed a curfew and sent in the security forces to quell the rioting which had begun to break out in certain parts of the city. Soviet MIGs and helicopter gunships roared demonstratively overhead, while tanks rumbled through the streets or took up positions at street intersections and outside government buildings. Threatened by the spectre of demonstrations spreading to the provincial cities, the authorities closed off the main road links with the rest of the country. By 24 February, with demonstrations in every part of town, as many as several hundred thousand townsfolk had poured on to the streets. five days into the strike, Kabul was virtually paralysed and for the first time since the invasion, *Pravda* reported widespread unrest, blaming foreign-supported 'counter-revolutionaries' for the disturbances.

By now, the authorities were conducting mass arrests in an attempt to suppress the revolt. Tanks and armoured personnel carriers also opened fire against the crowds or buildings suspected of harbouring snipers. 'They first fired in the air', said Mirabudin, a former Lycée Istiqlal pupil who began working with the resistance as a male nurse in the Panjshair. 'But when the crowds did not stop, they fired on the ground and the ricochets hit people.' Several were killed and dozens injured.

The Soviets, who were under orders to stay out of the fray and leave crowd control operations to the PDPA militants and the security forces, found themselves insulted or physically assaulted. Children shouted taunts or threw stones. In some incidents, protesters swarmed on to passing Russian vehicles to drag out their occupants, beating some of them to death. The Soviets retaliated by shooting back.

Sporadic street fighting and protests lingered on until the end of the month, followed by several more outbursts during March. On each occasion, the authorities reacted with heavy-handed security action.

The Children's Revolts

Unusually for such a male-dominated society, hundreds of high school girls, who were quickly joined by the boys as well as university students, held their own anti-government protests on the second anniversary of the Saur revolution. Ever since the communist takeover, Kabul's female high school pupils had acted with aggressive defiance towards the regime. The so-called 'children's revolts' resulted in the killing of some fifty students, thirty of whom were female. Thousands more were arrested and shunted off by the truckload to police stations, army posts and Pul-e-Charkhi. At least six young women from these demonstrations were reportedly still in jail by the end of 1983.

One respected Afghan university professor told Western journalists that he had seen the bodies of several of his students brought back. 'They were riddled with bullets and the marks of torture and traces of cuts on their bodies', he said. For a long time, the schools and colleges were practically deserted. 'No one goes to classes any more except that small group of students favourable to the Karmal government', he added. 'The others are in the streets fighting the Russians.'

One of the chief organisers of the April 1980 demonstrations was the SAMA urban resistance front. Strongly represented among the students and other members of the educated elite, it felt that a renewed series of strikes was vital to follow up the February and March protests. To get the ball rolling, a representative was chosen in each class to maintain contact with the group and to mobilise fellow classmates. As preparations gather momentum, other political organisations joined in.

The launching date was to be 21 April 1980, the date announced by the Babrak regime for hoisting the new national flag using the traditional red, black and green colours to replace the red flag of the Khalqis — another Parcham gesture of public appeasement. The strike began when girls from the Sourya High School began marching on the university. As they advanced, students from other schools and colleges joined them. Once at the university, they tore up paper flags issued by the communist party shouting: 'Neither the red, nor the red, black and green. Only liberty!' SAMA tracts announced that 'the strike today will make the varlets of social-imperialism tremble'.

Government security forces surrounded the university and moved in to disperse the demonstrators without much trouble. On the second day, the high school pupils marched again to the university. But this time armed Parchami militants, many of them students, blocked their path. Crying 'Liberty or Death!' and 'Russians go home', the demonstrators managed to break through and join up with non-communist students on the other side. According to one witness, a Parchami with a megaphone shouted: 'You are being manipulated by the enemies of the revolution. They are the ones who have agitated you.' At that moment, an eleventh grade girl called Nahid from the Rabe-Balkhi High School stepped forward all alone toward the communists. 'You are the ones who have been manipulated by the Russians', she retorted. 'As for us, you know what agitates us? The MIG-21s and Soviet tanks!' Then she added: 'Liberty or Death!'

The communist militants moved in to grab her and fighting broke out. Soviet helicopters hovering overhead started firing into the crowd, killing Nahid and about a dozen other demonstrators. Amid wails of anguish and anti-communist abuse, the protesters were forced to retreat. But female high school pupils were also marching elsewhere in the capital. Passing by armed Afghan soldiers and party militants, they threw their veils over the men's heads shouting: 'Here . . . these veils are for you! You are no men. You, who with your machine guns oppose your sisters armed only with books and crying for liberty.' Some of the girls threw stones at a jeep carrying Russian advisers and their wives, forcing them to stop and take cover behind their vehicle. Firing several bursts of machine gun fire, they killed three of the Afghan girls.

Liberty or Death!

Day after day, the demonstrations continued. The authorities tried to control the exits of all the high schools to prevent the pupils from leaving once they had organised themselves inside. Undaunted, the girls simply escaped into the streets by climbing over the walls. Male pupils from the Habibia High School near the Soviet embassy succeeded in marching almost as far as the embassy itself before being halted by anxious Russian-led troops and police. Unable to proceed further, the pupils screamed: 'Bear! Leave our sacred soil! The Afghan people don't want you!' Again there was firing and six pupils fell dead or dying. One of those shot, a young boy of sixteen, had worn a white funeral shroud to show that he was not afraid of dying. Dozens of others were arrested.

On 28 April, pupils and students held a huge assembly after which they marched for seven miles through the city. Afghan police accompanied them but did not intervene. Throughout the walk, the demonstrators talked with them, telling them that they were only brothers in the same struggle for freedom. 'Don't fight against us, but against the Russians', they argued. When the gendarmes refused to act against the protesters at the behest of a senior PDPA official, armed party militants were brought in. Almost as soon as they arrived on the scene, they began firing on the marchers. Again several students were killed, many were injured and hundreds arrested.

Dispersing in confusion, many students were offered shelter in nearby houses by sympathetic onlookers. 'I was picked up by some Parchami and put into a jeep', recalled one former pupil from the Lycée Istiqlal. 'But a group of passing friends attacked it and released me. A few minutes later, we were all arrested and brought to Pul-e-Charkhi by bus. But we shouted slogans through the windows – ' "Russians, leave our country!" and "Liberty or Death" – all the way to prison.'

Resistance sources maintain that at least some of the detained students were tortured or otherwise brutalised. Nevertheless, despite the gunning down of demonstrators, the Parchami authorities seemed to be making an effort not to act in the same manner as the Khalqis. Party militants tried to discuss with the students, asking them to speak openly and tell them what they wanted. According to the former Istiqlal pupil, when they all shouted: 'Liberty!' one of the Parcham replied: 'But who took your liberty?' 'The Russians through their (Afghan) valets', came the response. 'The Russians have come to help us in the construction of our country', insisted the militant. 'Construction? You call the bombardments of Herat, Baniyan, Dare-Souf, Kunar, Paktya, Nuristan, Panjshair . . . construction?' the students shouted. 'Help? What help? Help to annihilate the Afghans?' Angrily calling the students traitors, the militants left the room. Two weeks later, the

Itiqlal pupil and his 24 comrades were released.. At a teachers' convention in Kabul, only weeks after the 'children's revolts', Babrak admitted that those opposing the regime had succeeded 'to an extent in their provocative activities', but added that thier success was only 'temporary'.

Urban Armed Opposition

By the early summer of 1980, the resistance was making itself increasingly felt in the urban areas, although fighting remained restricted to the outskirts of the capital. 'Residents here regard the nightly gunfire as part of the normal sounds of the city, a sort of "white noise" that generally is ignored until some visitor calls attention to it', wrote *Washington Post* reporter Stuart Auerbach in August 1980, while visiting Kabul on a tourist visa. Pictures of guerrilla leaders, however, were regularly pasted overnight on the walls of buildings, while 'Shabnamah' continued to circulate. Radio Kabul also reported long lists of anti-revolutionary actions. 'These gangsters and murderers', it announced, 'have destroyed hospitals, schools, bridges, warehouses and public buildings and have disrupted roads and communications links. They have captured trucks . . . carrying food supplies to various provinces.'

However mass public demonstrations against the regime came virtually to an end during the second year of the occupation. Heavy-handed security tactics, notably by the KHAD, and government threats to close down any shops or businesses that participated in strikes managed to subdue most public opposition. Day and night, KHAD agents arrested resistance suspects, sometimes beating them up and otherwise humiliating them in front of their families, before hauling them off to their notorious detention centres. Appeals by the resistance to the general population to protest in the streets have since produced few results and indeed it would be a brave man or woman who would face the growing ruthlessness of the government. Yet such measures hardly diminished popular sympathy for the resistance.

Today, schools and colleges still represent a potentially explosive arena; there is constant concern that student unrest could easily erupt again and spread to other sectors. Young men and women in class still dare to break out occasionally into chants of 'Death to the Russians' and 'Death to the Parchami', while several underground newspapers continue to circulate.

For the Saur regime's fourth anniversary in April 1982, the KHAD adroitly removed all known pupil ringleaders and closed down the high schools for several days, now a regular procedure during all important government occasions which might arouse anti-communist fervour. As a result, no anti-government incidents marred the anniversary parade, which in Eastern bloc style included Afghan soldiers, cadets, police and party militants marching past the Afghan tricolour flanked by red flags, while MIGs and helicopters roared overhead. Security was extremely tight and the delegations from the USSR, Cuba, South Yemen, Mongolia and other communist nations were kept well away from the specially convened crowds.

Overcrowding in Kabul

Despite government efforts to portray life in the capital as normal, the shadow of war remains omnipresent. Already before the invasion, the Afghan capital's population had begun to swell with internal refugees in search of shelter, safety and jobs. By the beginning of 1984, the city's population had nearly tripled from 700,000 before the invasion to over two million. Many have flooded in from other provincial towns where fighting has been heavy and food supplies are less reliable.

Guerrilla attacks against supply convoys have provoked constant food or fuel blockades inducing the Soviet authorities to step up imports from the USSR. Food queues were a common sight during the winter of 1981-82, with the prices of potatoes, rice, meat and wood more than doubled. Only wheat, sugar and petrol imported from the Soviet Union remained at respectable rates. By the spring of 1982, large areas of Kabul were suffering regular electricity and water shortages because of internal sabotage or direct guerrilla attacks against power lines or plants. People were resorting to tallow candles and drawing water from old wells. Despite the 10pm curfew, cinemas started their last showings at six o'clock and most taxis were off the streets by eight in the evening. Apart from government patrols or mujahideen, few people ventured out after that.

A significant proportion of the displaced persons are the families of PDPA supporters. But the great majority, even if not actual members of the resistance, display little if any sympathy for the regime. 'The resistance must go on', explained one Kabul-based merchant, who visits his wife and children in a northern guerrilla-held village whenever he can. 'But we must also feed our families. There are no jobs left to speak of in the countryside, so we have no choice but to move to the cities.' Remittances sent back by those working in the capital represent an important source of income not only for dependants but also for the mujahideen. Tragically, many families with sons fighting with the guerrillas have been obliged to accept the recruitment of a son or daughter by the KHAD or the militia in return for financial support.

The population influx has grossly overburdened the existing facilities. With little new construction, this has meant severe housing shortages and property inflation. Most new arrivals live in mud and stone dwellings on the outskirts of the city, while others with more money have crammed two or three families together into single flats. Rents have shot up from 2,000 Afghanis in 1978 to over 10,000 in 1984.

The Red Army may be occupying the country militarily, but the American dollar is just as much part of the local trading currency as the Afghani, with the open market rate nearly twice the official rate. The Russian rouble, however, remains a rare and despised form of exchange. The Soviet High Command has forbidden its troops to use it outside the military precincts. Although Kabul financial rates used to be closely tied with those of Hong Kong, the dollar exchange is now based primarily on consumer goods brought in from Pakistan, Iran and particularly the Gulf countries. As a result, the city bazaars remain well-stocked with goods ranging from American cigarettes to Japanese radio and television sets, and a thriving black market is openly tolerated, if not encouraged, by the authorities.

Nevertheless, such merchandise is only available to those who have the cash. Although the overall annual rate of inflation, officially estimated at 20-25 per cent, is surprisingly low considering war conditions, most Kabul residents find making ends meet extremely difficult, particularly during the winter months when food and fuel are scarce. Acute shortages are usually attributed to slow-downs in Soviet imports, hoarding or fighting in the provinces, but difficulties are also provoked by the refusal of many farmers to sell their products to government officials. The price of meat, whenever it is available, has soared because of the destruction of livestock through bombardments and the migration of refugees with their herds to Pakistan.

Revolution, Resistance and Local Loyalties

In Soviet-occupied Afghanistan words like 'revolution', 'democracy', 'modernisation' and 'progress' are regarded with repugnance by most rural Afghans. Although the last three have been the leitmotivs of Western development programmes since World War II, many already considered these terms distasteful during the 1950s and 1960s because of their left-wing connotations. Since then, the communists have abused their meaning to the point where they are now synonymous with repression.

As a resistance movement, the mujahideen have tended to lack the ideological motivation and discipline of other more sophisticated liberation organisations around the world. The guerrilla fronts, many of which are still dominated by conservative tribal and ethnic considerations, reject the methods by which the Saur revolution governments have sought to modernise feudal Afghanistan. But the average resistance front has introduced few improvements other than basic defence to its wards. Only a handful have established infrastructures comparable to those of UNITA in Angola or the EPLF in Eritrea, by operating their own schools, literacy programmes, medical dispensaries and relief and agricultural facilities.

The government never held much sway over the tribal areas in peacetime; the complete breakdown of authority in the countryside has encouraged communities to fall back on traditional social structures. Decision-making bodies such as village councils headed by clan chiefs or 'maliks' have in many places taken charge of local resistance and contingency organisation, such as rotating local mujahideen to act as lookouts and guard access routes.

Within the Afghan social framework, each man considers himself bound to a 'gawm', a communal body, be it a village, a clan or a tribe, with traditional obligations of honour and blood vengeance often transcending political animosities. Such allegiances have caused a certain ambiguity between the government and the resistance. In one case cited by Olivier Roy, a French Afghan studies specialist who has visited resistance-controlled Afghanistan on a number of occasions since the invasion, mujahed efforts to assassinate a known collaborator in the western province of Ghor were frustrated by local 'gawm' loyalties.

When a resistance group tried to kill him, his 'gawm' made it known that his death in combat would not be considered an offence, but that his execution on his (home) territory would, on the other hand, provoke a duty of vengeance leading to one of those vendettas which the resistance is trying to avoid at all costs. The man is still free.

In many parts, over-reliance on traditional institutions has seriously weakened the resistance. Only gradually are the fronts recognising the importance of evolving beyond mere military organisations by assuming full social, political and economic responsibilities. Many still lack the necessary foresight or organising skills. The feeble response, too, among Western and Muslim countries to providing greater assistance has proved a severe handicap.

Fish in Water

Afghanistan's rising contingent of modernist and Islamic-oriented mujahed commanders like Massoud have been quietly instituting their own 'revolution' among the rural communities, a revolution that has begun to spread to other resistance fronts. The Soviets, for their part, continue to brand such mujahideen as feudal and reactionary, but paradoxically they have abandoned their own efforts to 'bolshevise' the countryside, seeking instead to enlist the backing, or neutrality, of the very elements they condemn — the traditional tribal chiefs, landlords and mullahs.

The more developed fronts (Panjshair, Nimruz, Herat, Mazar, Wardak etc.) have been trying, with mixed success, to mingle the elements of democracy and social reform with local customs. Resistance councils have been established incorporating not only village elders but also mujahed military, political, economic, judicial, social and information representatives. In the Panjshair, where the organisational structure has come to serve as a resistance model throughout northern Afghanistan, political and military council leaders are personally chosen by Massoud on their merits. Each village, on the other hand, elects its own financial and justice delegates. The 'greybeards', the traditional valley fathers, also still have a significant say in the running of affairs, a shrewd manoeuvre by the mujahideen to retain local endorsement. Although it seems more than likely that young bloods such as Massoud will become dominant as the war drags on, they have not made the mistake of dismissing the traditional structures.

Pursuing Mao's 'fish in water' precept, Massoud has endeavoured to prove that the resistance is capable not only of defending the region, but of providing for its well-being and future. Since the early stages of the occupation, the resistance has run the valley along the lines of a semi-autonomous state. Despite the constant upheavals of war, it has its own schools (twenty-eight, taught by one hundred teachers in the main valley and side-valleys), hospital, prison, administrative institutions and representatives in Peshawar to oversee relations with Jamiat and to ensure the co-ordination of supply links. The Panjshairis have also mounted their own relief efforts (including the sending of missions to the Middle East, Europe and the United States) during periods of hardship.

Both Massoud and other perspicacious regional commanders have recognised that their resistance struggle may last for years. Resistance effectiveness in the years ahead will therefore depend, as the 1982 Panjshair communist offensive showed, on the long-term ability of the fronts to assure the survival of local populations during intense periods of conflict and supply them with sufficient food, clothing and medical assistance. The amount of assistance provided by the outside world will prove decisive. But as the Soviets step up their attacks against civilian populations, the guerrillas will find it increasingly difficult to discourage people from fleeing.

Long-term survival also depends on the terrain. While the mountainous regions have poorer agricultural possiblities, they are easier to transform into redoubts with well-hidden food depots. In the resistance-dominated plains around Mazar-i-Sharif, on the other hand, where the Soviets for a long time sought to use the carrot rather than the stick by not destroying the agricultural infrastructure, the land is rich and well-watered but provides few possibilities for defence. In early 1984 a marked rise in Soviet military operations began to force unprecedented numbers of northerners to leave for Pakistan.

Zakat or Protection Money?

Most villagers seem quite content to have the mujahideen defend them and organise their lives. To bring in funds and supplies but also to demonstrate their contempt for the Kabul authorities, numerous fronts have set up their own taxation system, although as more people leave, fewer resources remain available. Depending on their sophistication and organisational abilities, the fronts often raise levies which exceed the financial support they receive from the Peshawar organisations.

Even before the Soviet invasion, certain groups set up control points along the main roads to collect transport tolls or simply confiscate goods from the backs of suspected government-owned trucks. For road controls, groups have printed special tax forms with blank spaces for the driver's name, vehicle registration number and the amount received, usually anywhere between 50 and 100 Afghanis for one right of passage. The Kabul-Jelalabad-Khyber Pass highway is reportedly the most profitable because of the relatively heavy merchant traffic that runs between Peshawar and the Afghan capital.

By the end of 1980 the mujahideen were levying taxes in all the 'liberated' areas. Merchants are all expected to pay between ten and twenty per cent value added tax when transporting or exporting wood, meat, semi-precious stones and other local products. In the Panjshair, the front's financial committee has imposed a five per cent tax on salaries, whether earned in Kabul or in the valley itself, with farmers paying ten per cent on goods sold. While agricultural production has suffered badly from the war, the Panjshairis have managed to continue mining lapis and emerald deposits from the surrounding mountains. Shipped back on return caravans to Pakistan for sale in the bazaars, they provide a regular source of revenue for the resistance.

Some groups, notably those operating in Kabul and other urban areas, charge protection money from government supporters owning property in the guerrilla zones. The guerrillas maintain that Parcham officials as senior as Politburo member Ghulam Dastagir Panjsheri have been reluctant but regular contributors. Certain fronts, notably those in the frontier provinces like Nuristan, have instituted refugee taxes among dependants in refugee camps or charge travellers passing through. This is often in the form of 'Zakat', a voluntary charitable contribution customarily rated at two-and-a-half per cent of annual income. Membership dues from resistance party members are another source of revenue.

As might be expected in any situation of this kind, there has been considerable abuse in fund raising for the resistance. Party members have absconded with group funds; one of them known to this writer is now living in the United States. There has been widespread corruption among the Peshawar organisations, some of the leaders unabashedly feathering their nests with party money or through their positions of influence.

Mujahideen, but also government militiamen or traditional bandits posing as partisans, have robbed refugees fleeing to Pakistan ·by demanding extravagant toll fees to cross the mountain passes. As part of the continuing stife between the various resistance fronts, armed mujahideen crossing the territory of a rival faction are sometimes forced to hand over their guns, ammunition and money. On one trip, a caravan commander asked me to carry the group's financial reserves as we walked through the village of an unfriendly faction. 'Me . . . ', he said in halting French. 'Perhaps some problems. You journalist. You are neutral.'

Typewriters, Tape Recorders and Cameras

Although rural Afghans are often wary of their urban-educated brethren, there is a growing politicisation among resistance communities. Practically every sizeable village or bazaar in the guerrilla-held areas has its own party headquarters. Some even have two or three depending on the strength of each organisation in the region. The spread of government disinformation and KHAD-inspired subversion has persuaded a growing number of fronts of the need to rally public support through their own forms of counter-propaganda. Political sessions held by primarily young and educated mujahed cadres are rapidly becoming part of everyday life among certain fronts. 'We try to teach the people the history behind the rise of communism and the Russian takeover in Afghanistan as well as to explain the concepts of democracy and Islamic revolution', said Massoud's brother Mohammed Yahya, a former veterinary student in charge of the Panjshair's political committee.

Resistance capabilities can be increasingly gauged by the sophistication of information techniques. Progressive fronts will not only boast of their anti-aircraft guns, mortar launchers and Kalashnikovs, but their duplicating machines, typewriters and cameras. Some groups, notably those operating in the western frontier provinces, appear to have easier access to such equipment from Iran. The Nasr and the Afghan version of the Pasdaran Iranian Revolutionary Guards, both trained by Iranians, strongly reflect the propaganda techniques elaborated by the Islamic Revolution, including the mass production of tape recordings for distribution and broadcasting in village bazaars.

Many regions publish their own newspapers and regularly share information with the Peshawar organisations, which in turn put out their own propaganda leaflets or magazines in Farsi, Pashto and English. Furthermore, the mujahideen have elaborated a simple but effective news-cum-postal service involving the carrying by hand of written dispatches from one part of the country to another. Unless secret, they are read aloud at village meetings or chaikhanas along the way. Local commanders then add their own comments and the messenger continues his journey. As with most non-literate societies, oral tradition remains a vibrant means of communication. A people of music and poetry, most Afghans – the Hazaras, the Tadjiks, the Pushtuns – eagerly sing or recite tales of the past and present, resulting in the emergence of a whole new literature about the mujahed experience.

Enforcing group identity, the political parties issue pocket calendars interspersed with Koranic readings, photographs and political essays, while the presence of foreign journalists in Afghanistan has drawn attention to the importance of the visual media in the struggle. In many respects, the mujahideen are like children who have discovered an entirely new world of gadgetry, which, if used intelligently, could drastically alter their lives. It is not unusual to encounter mujahideen carrying their own 35mm and Super-8 cameras. Some Western photo agencies and television companies have even provided them with free film and equipment in the hope of obtaining dramatic war footage.

Jamiat-e-Islami, which runs its own special propaganda and information committee, has its own photographic and film team to accompany mujahideen on missions. In better times, Massoud has illustrated military training sessions with film from the 'front' using a projector powered by a portable generator. A handful of groups in western Afghanistan also have video recorders.

Another form of propaganda, or psychological warfare, is the use of the loudhailer. Any group on operations usually has one or two in its entourage. Apart from unnerving Soviet troops with taunts of 'Allah o Akbar' and other war cries, the partisans use them to establish contact with fellow countrymen on the other side of the wire by bellowing messages across. Lonely government garrisons surrounded by mujahideen are thus constantly inundated by calls to defect: 'Why fight for those infidel Russian dogs?' they shout. 'You are Muslims. Come over to your Muslim brothers where you belong.' For an isolated garrison, hearing these amplified voices echoing across the mountains and valleys is not exactly comforting. In the absence of walkie-talkies, which have been only gradually making an appearance among the mujahideen, megaphones are also used to communicate during battle.

News Over the Airwaves

Afghanistan is still a country where causerie and banter are a major pastime. Throughout the resistance-held areas, the chaikhanas are packed at night with travellers, mujahideen and local peasants to discuss the war situation. Then the group falls silent as one of the men fiddles with the dials of a large Japanese-made shortwave radio set, a constant feature of most chaikhanas and principal village households. The voice of America's (VOA) Dari service introduces the main points of the news, and an excited muttering arises when the speaker, quoting diplomatic sources in Kabul, refers to the latest reports of the fighting in Afghanistan.

Only an hour earlier, Radio Kabul has declared a crushing victory over the 'bandits' in a northern part of the country. But mujahideen passing through the village on their way to Pakistan that afternoon claim that fighting is still heavy and that the communists have suffered major losses. Now the VOA is maintaining that the guerrillas are by no means vanquished. Immediately following the VOA broadcast, the

Afghans twiddle the dial and the BBC's Farsi news programme cites similar reports.

For the foreign observer, the passion with which the Afghans follow events both at home and abroad is indeed striking. Apart from visiting journalists, French doctors and missives from the Peshawar parties, the shortwave radio stations — the VOA, BBC, West Germany's Deutsche-welle and even Radio Moscow — remain their prime link with the outside world. Both the VOA and the BBC have made efforts to improve their services to Afghanistan, such as the introduction of Pashto language broadcasts or more exclusive Afghan news coverage.

Without doubt, the Western shortwave services have their short-comings. Reliable information about events inside Afghanistan is difficult to obtain. Regular briefings by Western embassies in Islamabad and Delhi (based on observations from diplomats in Kabul), although often extremely well informed, can be questionable or sketchy, particularly concerning events outside the Afghan capital where Westerners may not travel. Radio stations regularly broadcast these reports and the Afghans are understandably rattled when they hear that they have just been eradicated by the security forces, when they are in fact drinking tea.

On the other hand, the shortwave networks have furnished a necessary balance by quoting fresh newspaper dispatches from Western journalists or interviews with French doctors and returned travellers. The BBC has on several occasions broadcast excellent reports from commissioned journalists travelling inside, their tapes carried back by hand to Pakistan by couriers in good nineteenth century cleft-stick fahion.

Distant and remote as this geographical backwater may seem to many in the West, what happens elsewhere in the world has become a matter of grave concern to the Afghans thus making news indispensable. The average Afghan has now realised that his country's fate is not being decided solely on the battlefields of Afghanistan, but also in Washington, Moscow, Geneva, Warsaw and Managua. Despite the abundance of communications facilities in the United States, it is ironic that the non-literate Pushtun farmer from Paktya may appear relatively better informed about world events than many an American.

It is not uncommon for outsiders to be probingly questioned by village leaders or mujahideen about international affairs. Once, during the early stages of the war, three Western journalists and I visited the desert camp of a large group of partisans in southern Helmand province where we dined with the local resistance committee, about twenty men in all. For over three hours, the chief and his lieutenants patiently explained their position. Then the Afghan commander turned to us and said: 'Now, you have asked your questions, let me ask mine.' To our surprise, he questioned us in detail about the 1980 US presidential elections. The other men joined in and went through the entire gamut of world events. What were West German-Soviet relations like? Was it true that France had a large communist party? What was the United States doing about Soviet influence in the Horn of Africa? Admittedly, most of the questions dealt with USSR, but we were not let off with short answers. During later trips, I would often have to give my views to ordinary villagers on American involvement in Central America, Britain's relations with Argentina since the Falklands War, the situation in Poland, the NATO alliance and the meaning of Swiss neutrality. Sometimes their interest was naive and patently prejudiced, but at least they were curious about the world outside.

Clandestine Transmitters: Radio Free Kabul

'This is worth more than a thousand Kalashnikovs', commented guerrilla commander Safi when the 40-watt transmitter of Radio Free Kabul (RFK) went on the air for the first time on the night of 24 August 1981 in the Pech Valley of northwest Kunar. This first effort, assisted by European human rights activists and Soviet dissidents in exile, towards the creation of a nationwide clandestine broadcasting network suddenly presented the Afghan resistance with totally new and imaginative possibilities in opposing the occupation. Until then, two or three mujahed transmitters had operated inside Afghanistan but only on a limited scale. 'It is vital to have a means of combatting the radio and television which is in the hands of the occupiers', commented Marparwin Ali, a refugee Afghan university lecturer in Paris.

For some European intellectuals ill at ease about the morality of sending arms without themselves fighting, RFK has provided a means of supporting the resistance constructively. RFK has since been assisted by other organisations like Freedom House in New York and American Aid for Afghans in Portland, Oregon. 'This is perhaps the most extraordinary form of opposition. It is fighting with words and not guns', noted Marek Halter, a Polish-born writer and member of the French Human Rights Committee co-ordinating the network. 'During World War II, it was Radio London which gave the Europeans the true spirit of resistance.'

Compact and easily transportable because of the need for constant location changes to avoid detection, other 4.5 kilogramme transmitters similar to that in Kunar were set up within a 50-mile radius of Kabul. Using their experience in operating FM pirate radio stations in Italy and France, the Europeans helped set up eleven transmitters (ten FM and one shortwave) by the end of 1982 as part of a plan to install thirty-six stations throughout the country at an estimated cost of a quarter of a million dollars. Not only could residents in Kabul receive the FM programmes loud and clear, but one French source reported receiving the shortwave signal along the Soviet frontier in northern Afghanistan.

The stations have worked with varying success, some running into constant technical problems and operating only on an occasional basis, while others, such as the Panjshair's, broadcast for several months until Soviet military activity in the vicinity forced them to go off the air. French volunteer technicians have helped set up transmitters and train producers, but the war has taken its toll. One radio station lost three of its Afghan technicians when two were killed and one captured during Soviet attacks. Some have also simply disappeared or failed to maintain equipment. By the end of 1984 most stations were no longer functioning.

Nevertheless, during its intermittent existence, RFK's broadcasts have met with an overwhelming response among the Afghan public, particularly those living in the Kabul area. When operating properly, RFK opens its nightly transmissions (directly after the BBC and VOA news) with the compelling throbbing of a tabla similar to the haunting 'V for Victory' drums of the wartime BBC. This is accompanied by the announcement in Farsi and Pashto: 'Here is Radio Free Kabul of the Afghan Mujahideen.' Then comes a quotation from the Koran in Arabic followed by its translation. Political analysis, editorial comment, revolutionary songs, poetry and news constitute the bulk of the programme.

One of the most popular sections on the RFK station has been its 'letter box', a fifteen-minute question and answer session with letters from listeners in the capital, the guerrilla-held areas and the refugee camps. The letters themselves are often brought in by visiting friends and relatives. 'Apart from answering their questions, we also try to explain the short and long-term implications of Soviet involvement in Afghanistan and why it is necessary to fight', observed Es-Haq, a former engineering student and information director for the Panjshair.

RFK has also been directing transmissions at the Soviet occupation forces. Pre-recorded tapes by major Soviet dissidents in exile have been broadcast; these include writers Vladimir Bukovsky and Vladimir Maximov, mathematician Leonid Plyioutch and Marshal Grigorenko, once heralded as the 'Hero of Stalingrad'. Using a popular Russian song about World War II to open each broadcast, they seek to compare the war in Afghanistan with that of the Nazi occupation of the western USSR. 'We remind the soldiers that Nazi war criminals were condemned for following orders', explained Bukovsky. The dissidents, however, have been reluctant to call upon Soviet troops to desert until guarantees can be arranged for their safety and asylum abroad.

Claiming that RFK was founded with the assistance of the CIA, the Russians have obviously been disturbed by the presence of Soviet dissidents on the clandestine Afghan airwaves. When a French television news programme featured RFK in one of its reports, the Soviet embassy in Paris lodged a formal protest warning that relations between France and the USSR could suffer.

Apart from government bombardments and heliborne assaults aimed at knocking out the transmitters, the communist press has consistently attacked the mujahed network as an affront to the Soviet Union and the government of Afghanistan. 'The object of this subversive action, of these broadcasts, is to influence the Afghan population ideologically, to consolidate the counter-revolution, to bring into disrepute the political help of the Soviet Union to the Afghan people', commented *Izvestia* in July 1982. According to Halter, the stations are something the Russians cannot understand. 'It is not the BBC or the VOA which they are attacking, but the radio of the Afghan people themselves.'

Political Rivalry and Unity

To a certain extent, the most damaging drawback of the Peshawar parties from the international point of view has been their inability to form any cohesive political unity, let alone a government-in-exile. Unlike the PLO or the South West African People's Organisation, the Afghan resistance does not have the benefit of representation, or even observer status, at the United Nations. One argument often put forward by the West for not granting the Afghans more material support has been this lack of unity.

Bearing in mind Afghanistan's diverse ethnic, tribal and religious background, the notion of rapid political unity is unrealistic. European resistance movements during World War II were hardly any different. In Yugoslavia, clashes between Royalist and Titoist forces often caused greater loss of life than fighting against the Nazis. In France, where rivalry among the 'maquis' was often just as great as it is today in Afghanistan, the United States was still considering even after the

D-day invasion which of the resistance leaders, including Charles De Gaulle, to support. In no occupied European country could the national liberation committees claim more than loose co-operation among the various parties and resistance fronts.

Political sabotage from other quarters has also had much to do with the repeated foundering of attempts at Afghan unity. Infiltration of the refugee community by the Kabul regime has certainly not been without effect. Neither the West nor the Third World, notably the Arabs, have gone out of their way, to push the Afghan issue, other than regularly condemning the Soviet invasion at the UN General Assembly. There has been no official recognition of the resistance.

The Pakistanis, in particular, have never been very keen on a united resistance movement that might prove difficult to control. In general, the Islamabad government has preferred to deal with diplomacy, leaving the fighting to the Afghans. At the UN-sponsored peace talks on Afghanistan, for example, the resistance parties continue to be excluded.

Loya Jirghas, Alliances and Splits

The first concrete attempts at overall unity came during the first few months of the occupation. All the parties, save Hekmatyar's Hezb, agreed to join in a loose 'Islamic Alliance' with Abdul Rasoul Sayyaf as its compromise chairman. A 39-year-old Kabul teacher and lecturer, he had been imprisoned by the Khalqis but was released in January 1980 during the Soviet-Parcham amnesty. This was followed in late spring by the holding of a symbolic Loya Jirgha in Peshawar with the aim of preparing the groundwork for an eventual provisional Afghan government. Presided over by Omar Babrakzai, a forty-year-old high court judge, almost one thousand tribal, nomad and religious leaders, guerrilla commanders, and political and refugee personalities representing all of Afghanistan's provinces converged on the frontier town.

With high hopes that the gathering might lead to genuine unity, the participants elected a 68-man revolutionary council. Within a few weeks the Loya Jirgha had collapsed with a major portion of its membership persuaded to back Gaylani's National Front. The Alliance, lumbered from policy crisis to policy crisis. Constantly arguing, the parties split into separate fundamentalist and moderate factions. In April 1981, this first Alliance was formally dissolved. Two months later, the moderates announced the formation of their own alliance, the 'Islamic Unity of Afghan Mujahideen'.

Later in October, they backed the holding of a second Loya Jirgha, this time in Quetta. Several thousand notables gathered there, but the fundamentalists refused to lend their support and prohibited their members from participating. Nevertheless, a number of Hezb (both factions) and Jamiat mujahed commanders attended, indicating the growing trend among affiliated internal fronts to form alliances contradicting those practised in Peshawar.

Although the Loya Jirgha called for the creation of a Grand Council, it still needed the consensus of its rivals to be successful. But this was not forthcoming. In May 1982, following intense negotiations, this time including Hekmatyar's Hezb, the fundamentalists formed their own Islamic Unity. This they described as the 'total fusion' of their parties, but, in practice, it was run along similar lines to those of the moderate alliance.

Both party leaders and supporters referred to their respective alliances as 'the unity', but it was the moderates who appeared closest to any real democratic fusion. Concerned about being overtaken by the trend toward greater unity among the partisan fronts, both alliances remained receptive to the possibility of a global merger. Nevertheless, the fundamentalists continued to express deep suspicion of monarchist tendencies among their political counterparts; the moderates, in turn, felt that, although they could probably live with Rabbani and Khales, Hekmatyar was not to be trusted.

With the death of President Brezhnev in November 1982, all the party leaders except Hekmatyar announced their readiness to negotiate a peaceful settlement with Moscow if that was what the Soviets wanted. Hekmatyar, however, declared that his party would not betray the interests of Islam and would continue with the Jihad. In August 1983, in another attempt at overall unity, the moderates announced the establishment of the 'United Front for the Liberation of Afghanistan' following consultations with ex-King Zahir Shah.

The Zahir Shah Factor

When the Soviet Union first invaded Afghanistan, few observers believed that Zahir Shah would have more than a remote chance of ever making a political comeback. The ex-monarch's prospects of regaining the throne still remain slight, but his presence, at least temporarily, as the figurehead leader of the resistance could play a significant role in unifying the mujahideen.

Despite considerable opposition to the ex-King, notably among the non-tribal groups who regard the move as an effort to reassert Pushtun dominance, there appears to be increasingly widespread support for his return. In the summer of 1984 a group of Afghan resistance represent-atives arrived in Peshawar to test out the idea. Meeting, sometimes secretly, with numerous commanders from the interior and refugee leaders, they claimed that local reaction was far beyond what they had expected. Frustration with the bickering and incompetence of the political parties had grown so acute that even some fundamentalists said they would be prepared to back the king if his presence could help the resistance struggle.

'The people of Afghanistan need a leader. Everybody wants Zahir Shah because he is all we have. The Peshawar leaders don't think so, but they have failed us', said a Pushtun Hezb-i-Islami (Hekmatyar faction) commander from Nangrahar province. While generally disposed toward Zahir Shah as a temporary figurehead, some Afghans have questioned the ex-King's resistance credentials. 'He has not suffered with us. If he suffered with us, then perhaps I could agree with him', noted another tribal fundamentalist.

Alliances in the Interior

While the Zahir Shah initiative brought a dramatic new development to the question of resistance unity in Peshawar, it has been a different story across the border in Afghanistan. Since 1981, rising impatience with the parties' representation of their interests has led many Afghans to look elsewhere for leadership, notably among the regional com-manders. It is among the internal fronts that a sense of genuine unity has begun to develop.

By the second year of the Soviet occupation, most of the fronts had staked out their territory and were in the process of forging good working relationships with neighbouring groups. In contrast to the political cleavages in Peshawar, it is not unusual to encounter funda-mentalist and moderate affiliated groups fighting alongside each other. The same thing goes for members of the two main fundamentalist rivals, the Jamiat and Hezb (Hekmatyar faction). While travelling through Kunar Province in mid-1984, I met several commanders operating under their respective banners and yet cooperating smoothly with each other as if they were of the same party. 'We are all Muslims', explained one commander.

Elsewhere, joint military co-ordination appears to have spread to most mujahed fronts. But after five years of Soviet occupation, it has remained just that: co-ordination. In the northern provinces, however, co-operation among the different fronts seems to be giving rise to what could soon prove to be a firm, self-sustaining regional alliance.

Since the early days of the war, Massoud has been gradually building up a valuable network of contacts with like-minded guerrilla commanders in other parts of the country. Advocating a regular exchange of ideas, manpower and resources, he has persuaded virtually all the major guerrilla commanders in the north, including Ismail Khan in Herat to the west, to co-operate with his plan. The Panjshairi leader also maintains ties with guerrilla leaders like Amin Wardak to the south and Abdul Haq (Hezb-i-Islami – Khales) in the Kabul region. He has even come to terms with several previously antagonistic Hezb (Hekmatyar) commanders as well as with Sayiid Mansoor, head of the Ismaili sect in Afghanistan, whose followers were in the pay of the Kabul government as a militia force.

While the Pushtuns maintain that they will never serve under Massoud, a number of military commanders have indicated that they would be more than willing to co-operate with him on an equal basis. For the Soviets, it is certain that guerrilla progression towards an overall military alliance, and possibly a fully representative resistance council sponsored by a Loya Jirgha, would bring a totally new dimension to the conflict.

The Hazarajat – A Unique Case

Certainly among the most complex resistance phenomena to develop since the 1978 communist takeover has been that of the Shiite-dominated Hazarajat. Evolving in a totally different manner from the rest of Afghanistan, this central highland region has not only succeeded in isolating itself from the government, but from most other resistance organisations.

For some Hazaras, the Saur revolution heralded the possibility of political and social change in their favour. To their disappointment, however, nothing of the sort occurred. The Khalqis remained a bastion of Pushtun dominance, while the present regime is considered to be unacceptably backed by an 'outside' authority of infidels. With regard to the resistance, certain Hazara fronts such as the Harakat-e-Islami (not be confused with the Sunni Harakat-e-enqelab-e-Islami) co-operate readily with other guerrilla movements.

But most Hazaras have remained wary of working with the Peshawar political parties because of their strong Pushtun influences. Despite considerable internal political problems of their own, the Hazaras feel that, by creating an 'independent' state with its own administration and army, they have succeeded in asserting their national, religious and ethnic identity *vis-à-vis* their traditional oppressors.

The Shura

Already during the initial Hazara revolts against the Khalqis in early 1979, many local communities spontaneously formed their own mujahed committees. Later that summer, the inhabitants of Jaghori, some 135 miles southeast of Kabul, took the initiative in bringing together representatives from all 'liberated' Hazara areas in order to co-ordinate resistance on a regional basis. Thus, in September 1979, some 400 – 500 local leaders, most of them mullahs, mirs (the rough equivalent of landlords), guerrilla commanders and young intellectuals, gathered in the small town of Waras in southwestern Bamiyan province to found the Shura-ye-Enqelabi-ye Ettefag-e Islami-ye Afghanistan, the Revolutionary Islamic Council of the Union of Afghanistan.

Electing Sayed Ali Beheshti as their president and Sayed Mohammad Hussein, otherwise known as 'Jaghlan' (Colonel) and later 'Djendral' (General), as their military commander, the delegates declared that the Shura should become the symbol and base for Shiite unity in Afghanistan against not only Soviet aggression but also Pushtun hegemony. Opting for regional autonomy with equal representation in a future non-communist government rather than outright independence, the Hazaras quickly came to regard Waras as 'Mardaz e Wahdat', the centre of unity. 'Our only enemy is the Soviets', said one Hazara commander. 'We are fighting for the whole world and not just the liberty of our region. . . if we succeed in liberating ourselves, it is not to be dominated by anyone else in the future.'

Creating a civilian administration not unlike that of the Kabul *'ancien régime'*, the Shura divided the region into nine 'Wilayat' (provinces), each governed by an appointed 'wali' (chief administrator), either a Sayed or a mullah, assisted by a security commander. Provinces close to the fighting zones such as Jaghori and Naour come under the direct orders of the military. The Shura also appointed mayors to the small towns, but permitted villages to elect their own councils.

For a long time, the Kabul regime ignored this highland fortress because of its lack of immediate strategic value. Limiting their military actions to aerial bombardments with occasional ground operations into the heartland, the Khalqis preferred to impose an economic blockade inflicting severe food shortages.

Following the invasion, the Soviets made a more determined effort to bring the Hazaras to heel. In the late summer of 1980, they burned the harvests and razed the bazaars of Panjaw, Yakaolang and several other communities on the northern outskirts of the Hazarajat. In mid-December 1980, they carried out further heavy attacks. As one doctor from the Paris-based Médecins sans Frontières (MSF) wrote:

> On my arrival two days after the end of the fighting, numerous villages were still smoking and people were still being injured by boobytraps such as explosive pens left behind by the Soviets. Where-ever I went, the inhabitants accused the Soviet soldiers and the (communist) militia for this terror, while regular Afghan army troops, who had been forced to participate, seemed to be excused.

Barely a month after the Soviet invasion, I met some 150 Hazaras in Peshawar after they had trekked twenty days on foot from their snow-covered mountain hideouts in search of food and weapons for their people. To survive the harsh winter in the mountains, the partisans had taken three months' food supply with them, but it had now nearly run out. 'We are here to seek help', Mohammad Hussein Nasseri, one of the commanders, said as he waited patiently with some of his men in the compound of one of the Peshawar political organisations. 'We want to fight, but we need more guns and food.' Despite attempts by the political parties to claim the Hazaras as their own, Nasseri reiterated the Shura position that they had come to see all the groups concerned and would accept help from anyone who was willing to grant it, but without strings attached. Not surprisingly, little help came from Peshawar.

A Swiss-style Militia

In contrast to many other resistance movements, the Shura instituted a highly unusual and comparatively efficient defence system consisting of some 20,000-30,000 full-time soldiers. All men aged twenty-two are required to undertake one year's resistance service. Similar to the Swiss militia system, those Hazaras unable to do service, notably those working in Iran, are expected to pay a military tax instead. In addition, each group of ten families must pay for the upkeep of one conscript, including wheat rations and a small allowance. Whereas most of the population accept conscription, some observers maintain that the burden of supporting a soldier is not popular.

Military service normally starts with a month's training under the aegis of former Afghan army officers, and includes sports, weapons management and guerrilla tactics. The conscripts are then sent to local resistance fronts known as 'Japhas', usually situated in the mountains overlooking vital access routes to the region. There they live in well-hidden rocky retreats for eleven months conducting operations and undergoing Islamic-cum-political education.

Rare among the resistance fronts, the Hazaras established a regular telephone link between Waras, which serves as the Shura military headquarters, and five other Hazara towns. The Panjshair had an emergency telephone line connected to a hidden mountain retreat, but it was used only on an occasional basis. An open link to which everyone can listen in, the Hazara network adequately fulfills the function of transmitting messages to distant parts of the region and during the heavy fighting of 1980 and 1981 gave the Shura military command an exceptional degree of logistical control. In one incident during the December 1980 Soviet assault around Ghazni, the Hazaras were able to send in reinforcements with astonishing rapidity. Enthusiastic guerrillas spoiling for a fight were still arriving on foot from the more remote parts well after the battle had ended.

Shura mujahideen have generally conducted few operations outside the Hazarajat proper, preferring to concentrate on their own defences. Scattered Hazara fronts, mainly under the control of Harakat but also the pro-Khomeini Nasr or Pasdaran, function in Balkh, Samangan and other northern provinces. During the 1981 and 1982 Soviet offensives against the Panjshair, Harakat fighters co-ordinated attacks with Jamiat-i-Islami Tadjiks.

The fact that the Hazaras have been able to establish a 'liberated' region with its own administration has earned them a new respect among fellow Afghans. Their ability to fight gained them considerable, and sometimes grudging, admiration. While Harakat is the only primarily Shiite front which has opened its ranks to non-Hazaras, Kutchis (Pushtun nomads) normally roaming the mountains and plains of Paktya and Ghazni provinces have often put themselves spontaneously under the Hazaras' commander, an unusual gesture for Pushtuns who have traditionally treated the Hazaras as underdogs.

A 1982 MSF report stated:

> The Hazara people. . . the Afghan Shiites in general. . . have made incredible progress. On the one hand, they have managed to come up from zero in an armed liberation struggle against the Red Army and the communist regime to a point whereby almost the entire region is involved. And on the other hand, they have managed to create a proper political organisation with a relatively democratic

and unitary character . . .

Mirs, Maoists and Khomeinists

Conditions have not been all that rosy, however, inside the Hazarajat. Dominated by a majority of traditionalist clerics and Sayeds with Beheshti at their head, the Shura has had to cope with two diametrically opposed political flanks, causing a substantial disintegration of Shura authority. On the one hand, a lay faction consisting of 'mirs' and left-wing intellectuals, often former Maoists from the Sholay-e-Jaweid; on the other, an exceedingly powerful faction of radical pro-Khomeini 'sheiks' (mullahs trained at the Shiite holy centres of Qom in Iran or Nadjaf in Iraq).

For a long time, the Shura's middle-of-the road leaders were able to play one faction off against the other. But in the summer of 1982, the radically Islamic elements allied themselves with the pro-Iranian Nasr in a takeover bid against Beheshti. Violent outbreaks of fighting followed and a series of truces was able to bring only relative peace back to the region. According to several Western travellers, less than one third of the region remains under direct control of the Shura.

Nevertheless the majority of the population, who remain generally indifferent to Khomeinist attempts to impose their own ideology, still consider themselves part of the Shura. By being initially responsible for institutionalising a sense of regional autonomy and religious identity in the Hazarajat, the Sayed leadership of the Shura has managed to acquire a sense of legitimacy which the other parties have not. For many Hazaras, the presence of an administration and an organised army proudly represents a confirmation of Hazarajat 'statehood'.

Yet the gradual spread of an Iranian-style 'cultural revolution' by the Khomeinists could have a profound impact not only on the future of the Hazarajat but on the whole of Afghanistan. Educated, disciplined and extremely dogmatic, the Khomeinists find no trouble in recruiting supporters among the tens of thousands of young Hazaras living in Iran. Although it remains to be seen whether the Hazara people will accept the new 'revolution', this has not prevented the Khomeinists from establishing schools and libraries and organising political meetings where Western decadence, the United States and the Soviet Union are regularly condemned.

The Hazaras have always looked to Iran for inspiration. Where a decade ago bazaar shops and chaikhanas used to display portraits of the Shah, the stern eyes of Ayatollah Khomeini now hold sway. Apart from its support of Khomeinist groups, however, Iran has been extremely niggardly in its assistance to the Hazaras. Yet, since the emergence of the Pasdaran, its influence has grown. Most of the weaponry and funds for the Hazaras pass through Iran rather than Pakistan. The Nasr, which used to be the dominant Khomeinist group, has lost favour because of its advocacy of a strictly Afghan revolutionary movement. The Pasdaran, who are strictly controlled by Tehran's Revolutionary Guards to the point of calling for incorporation within a greater Iranian state, have steadily developed into the strongest and best organised of the Hazara fronts.

Since installing themselves among the Hazaras, the Khomeinists have concentrated on expanding their own power bases rather than exhorting the people to fight the Russians. For some time now, the only Hazara front to be actively engaged against the Soviet occupation (apart from Sayed Jaghlan) has been Harakat-e-Islami.

Overall, the Iranian factor has remained a side issue in the Afghan equation, with Pakistan's position as a 'frontline' state attracting far greater attention. The Soviets have been content with the relative lack of belligerence among the Hazaras and have done much to encourage it through infiltration by the KHAD and the Tudeh, the Iranian communist party. But the situation could alter drastically. Most informed analysts feel that Iran has no option but to become more involved sooner or later, dependent though this may be on the outcome of the Iran-Iraq war and the uncertain future of a post-Khomeini regime. If the anti-Soviet stance in Iran continues along its present, increasingly aggressive course, this promises to be translated into a more active role by the Khomeinist mujahideen against the Kabul government. If and when Iran does assert itself, it will almost certainly completely overshadow Pakistan's present importance.

9 REFUGEES, DOCTORS AND PRISONERS — A TRICKLE OF HUMANITY

> I don't know what the definition of genocide is, but the way the Russians are forcing out the Afghans by whatever means possible comes awfully close to it. (Father Arne Rudvi, Norwegian Roman Catholic Bishop of Karachi, active in refugee assistance in Pakistan since the autumn of 1979).

Everyday there were hundreds.

Clutching blankets, chickens, kettles and bundles of treasured family belongings, the refugees fled across the snow-clogged mountain pass at Safed Koh along the eastern Afghan frontier with Pakistan. Terror-stricken by Soviet aerial bombardments, the machine-gunning of farmers in their fields or the dropping of anti-personnel mines and boobytraps along trails, they travelled in small groups, families or entire villages. On donkeys, camels or horses, but mostly on foot. While the women and children, some staggering from cold and exhaustion, struggled down the steep winding path towards the distant camps of Parachinar shimmering on the hot plain below, the men scanned the skies for helicopter gunships. For although they had entered a new country, it still did not mean safety from the ravages of war'. (Kurram Tribal Agency, Pakistan — Spring, 1980)

Migratory Genocide: Eliminating the Opposition

Ever since the early days of the invasion, Soviet anti-insurgency methods have led to a deliberate form of 'migratory genocide' as a principal means of eliminating the Afghan opposition. Faced with a repressive policy that offers little choice other than outright submission, five million Afghans or more (the world's largest refugee population) have fled from their homeland to Pakistan, Iran and elsewhere in search of asylum. That is nearly one Afghan in three. As the war drags on, the refugees keep coming, a dramatic bleeding of the country that in the long run can only favour the Soviets.

The first Afghans began fleeing from communist repression within weeks of the 1978 *coup d'état*, the overwhelming majority heading for Pakistan's Northwest Frontier Province. By April 1979 more than

100,000 had crossed the border, creating a problem too large for the Islamabad government to deal with on its own. It therefore asked the United Nations High Commissioner for Refugees (UNHCR) in Geneva to evaluate relief requirements. Immediately granting Pakistan a small amount of emergency aid, the agency drew up a $10.3 million one-year assistance programme, to cover a total of 185,000 refugees until September 1980. Little did anyone dream of what was to follow.

On the eve of the Soviet invasion, the refugee population in Pakistan had grown to over 300,000. Within weeks, the outflow erupted into a veritable flood: by Christmas 1980, there were nearly one and a half million. At the same time, relief estimates provided by the UNHCR, the League of Red Cross Societies and various other international relief agencies had risen to almost $100 million.

During the first eighteen months of the occupation, most refugees lived in crowded tent cities straddling the border areas of the Northwest Frontier and Baluchistan. Unlike earlier asylum seekers, who had dribbled into Pakistan to escape the Khalqi terror under Taraki and Amin, many of the new arrivals were unable to bring anything with them but the barest of personal possessions.

The more fortunate refugees, thirty or forty thousand perhaps at the time, from Afghanistan's eastern frontier provinces found sanctuary in the homes of Pushtun and Baluchi relatives living on the Pakistani side of the border. 'We are of the same blood. It is our duty to help them', explained a Pakistani headman from the Khyber Tribal Agency, who had taken in about a dozen kinsmen from a village only thirty miles inside Afghanistan. For many tribesmen, Pakistani and Afghan alike, the 1893 Durand Line exists only as a wallchart demarcation rather than a respected political boundary.

By now, three million-odd Afghans, half the population of Switzerland, have sought refuge in Pakistan. While some live privately in towns like Peshawar, Islamabad, Quetta and Karachi or with relatives, the great majority have been quartered among the country's more than 380 refugee villages. Women and children, mainly of rural background and illiterate, make up nearly three quarters of their number.

The Pakistani government has allowed the Afghans free movement but only those living in official refugee villages and holding ration cards are entitled to UNHCR assistance. Among the 2.3 million beneficiaries in early 1984, an estimated 70 per cent, most of them Pushtuns from Afghanistan's eastern provinces but also a slowly growing number of Farsi-speaking Tadjiks, Uzbeks and Turkmen from the north, have converged on the Northwest Frontier Province. The remainder (24 per cent), many of whom have fled from Helmand, Kandahar, Ghazni and the Hazarajat, are located in huge windswept camps in the deserts of Baluchistan, bitterly cold during the winter, suffocatingly hot in the summer.

With limited success, the Pakistani government has sought to reduce congestion among the frontier areas by establishing new refugee settlements (2 per cent) in the sweltering plains of Punjab. By the end of 1984, some 100,000 had been housed. But most refugees find the conditions uncomfortable and too far from the Afghan border. The balance of the refugee population are scattered throughout the rest of the country.

A 'Temporary Phenomenon'

Although poor by Western standards, the Afghans are a proud people whose lives are often hard but dignified in their simplicity. Nevertheless, for villagers accustomed to the security of their homes, lands and traditions, conditions in the refugee camps have been psychologically tough.

In the beginning, the Islamabad authorities were determined that the Afghan presence in Pakistan should remain a temporary one. The UNHCR and other international relief agencies initially provided the refugees only with emergency essentials: tents, blankets, quilts, clothes, water, and health facilities as well as basic food items such as wheat, dried skim milk and edible oils. Resolutely, the Pakistani government discouraged anything that tended toward the development of a Palestinian-style situation. Only reluctantly did it permit refugees to construct walls around their tents against the heat, wind, rain or snow.

Progressively, however, Pakistan's refugee camps have become tragically imbued with a spectre of unresolved permanence. Except for new arrivals, the white canvas shelters that used to dot the barren mountainsides and valleys have all but disappeared. In their stead have emerged sprawling suburbs and settlements of 'katchas', dried mud and stone dwellings interspersed with bazaar stalls, storage depots, mosques, schools, health centres, workshops and even gardens behind compound walls. Veterinary facilities have been instituted for local livestock, and Persian flows easily, where only three years earlier Pashto was indisputably the dominant language. 'We no longer discourage them from making "katcha". It only reflects their style of living and does not imply permanent residence', insisted one Pakistani official.

By 1984, the UNHCR estimated annual relief assistance in Pakistan at nearly $500 million, well over $1 million a day. Certainly good news for the refugees but portentous for the future, new humanitarian assistance programmes have sought to consolidate the basic infrastructures of refugee settlements with the construction of utility buildings, access roads, schools and water supply projects. These include the promotion of income-generating projects and vocational training aimed not only at reducing refugee dependence on external assistance but also to help them once they are back in their homelands. The Pakistani Forestry Department, for example, plans to encourage the planting of mulberry trees for the cultivation of silkworms. Many of these improvements have been designed for use by the local Pakistani population, if and when the refugees go home. But the Pakistanis also gloomily recognise that the Afghan problem may be around for years to come.

As one of the largest relief operations since the end of World War II, the Afghan refugee situation in Pakistan appears to be among the best managed. It is certainly the most impressive I have come across since first reporting refugee problems in Africa and Asia in 1980. Considering its size, there have been surprisingly few major problems. On the whole, the international response has been admirably prompt and adequate, while the Pakistani government has set up a comparatively efficient administrative infrastructure (7,000 employees) run on military lines. The World Food Programme, for example, purchases basic foodstuffs locally or from abroad, these are then handed over to the Pakistanis for transportation and distribution. Nevertheless, as with any operation of this magnitude, Pakistani refugee officials are not without their fair share of corruption.

As part of the target food basket designed by the UNHCR for a 'non-productive' refugee population, relief officials aim to provide each Afghan, man, woman or child, with the equivalent of 2,100-2,200 calories a day. This consists of wheat (500 gms), skimmed milk (30 gms), soya bean oil (30 gms), sugar (20 gms) and tea (3 gms). For meat, eggs and other foods, the refugees must rely on their own resources such as home-raised chickens, or the bazaars. Outside supplies are brought up from Karachi by train to Quetta and Peshawar and then dispensed among the camps by a fleet of 450 internationally donated lorries. Although distribution was often severely hampered by poor roads or bad weather conditions during the first two years, the establishment of depots has greatly alleviated the problem.

Apart from the United Nations, twenty-eight international and voluntary agencies are involved in the monumental task of providing the refugees with decent living conditions over a long period. Numerous governments too, ranging from Saudi Arabia to Japan, have granted funds or material assistance for various relief operations. Organisations like Save the Children Fund, the League of Red Cross Societies, Church World Service, Caritas, the Pakistan Red Crescent Society, Aide Internationale Contre la Faim, Austrian Relief Care and the International Rescue Committee have been actively involved in digging wells and installing sanitation facilities, health centres and other aid projects. It is more than astonishing that, despite appalling overcrowding and atrocious hygiene, no serious illnesses have been allowed to develop into epidemics.

Political Mileage, Aid and Tolerance

There is no doubt that President Zia has obtained extensive political mileage out of the Afghan crisis. It is with only a hint of a smile that senior government officials admit that the Soviet invasion put Pakistan back on the map. Yet the refugee overload has created enormous pressures on the local economy and tolerance, which, in the end, may outweigh any political advantage.

Pakistan claims to contribute nearly half the annual relief bill. With only meagre resources of its own, it has reacted far more positively than, say, Thailand to the Indochinese, in playing host to such a mass human influx. Furthermore, many Pakistanis continue to demonstrate an unusual degree of genuine humanitarian and Islamic solidarity with the Afghan plight.

Considering their numbers, the Afghans have managed to live in relative harmony with their Pakistani hosts. Incidents of violence have tended to be few and isolated, usually local resentment at relief assistance for the refugees or reaction over grazing and water rights. In July 1982, four camps were closed in the Northwest Frontier and 35,000 refugees moved to other areas after rampaging Afghans attacked a Pakistani village, burning eight houses and killing one person. Overall, the general Pakistani attitude toward the refugees remains one of hospitality and concern about the war — a state of affairs often commented on by international relief officials when drawing comparisons with situations elsewhere.

Nevertheless, tension has been on the increase. With a $3 billion trade deficit, the Pakistanis are deeply worried about the growing political, economic and social burden as the war continues and the refugees stay on. The overwhelming majority of the Afghans still declare that their sole intention is to return home once the communists have left. But as time elapses, it has become clear that many of these uprooted people will find it increasingly difficult to pick up where they left off.

To the annoyance of many lower- and middle-class Pakistanis, the urban refugees often appear to be far better-off than they are themselves. Some have married locally, while others have bought shops in the bazaars, started their own businesses or simply transferred their trade, be it import-export or precious stones, from Kabul to Pakistan. The refugees have infiltrated two vital areas of the economy in the frontier region — the arms business and the profligate smuggling of consumer goods and drugs. With many Pakistanis complaining about unfair practices, virtually the entire private bus trade in Peshawar has been taken over by Afghans who came over with their vehicles and proceeded to undercut their hosts. Rents, too, have skyrocketed from $500 a month for a respectable villa with garden to over $1,000.

A greater threat to the ordinary Pakistanis, who have found it steadily more difficult to find work abroad because of the tightening Middle East oil market, is job competition from the refugees. In politically sensitive Baluchistan, 'action groups' have been intervening to prevent refugees from working at lower wages than already poorly paid Pakistani labourers. At one stage, police had to be sent in to close numerous small shops set up by enterprising Afghans which were putting the Pakistanis out of business.

A further pressing predicament similar to that in the refugee areas of the Horn of Africa has been the presence of some three million camels, cattle, sheep and goats brought in from Afghanistan. Not only are these animals in competition for fodder with Pakistani-owned animals, but, according to relief officials, they have been 'grazing the pastures into sand'. In addition, the refugees have contributed toward denuding thousands of square miles of land by cutting trees and shrubs for firewood, thus causing severe soil erosion. The international relief agencies have sought to deal with environmental damage through afforestation projects and the implementation of a kerosene distribution system as an alternative fuel for cooking and heating.

Political opponents, too, have seized contentiously on the refugee issue and exploited public discontent to pressure the Zia dictatorship. Baluchi and Pushtun nationalists, a substantial number of them believed to be backed or infiltrated by the KGB and KHAD, have also been using the situation to their advantage. Prohibited from operating their own political parties or free press, many Pakistani opposition members deeply resent the Afghans running exile resistance organisations, publishing newspapers and holding meetings on Pakistani soil.

Officially, the authorities claim that they have only recognised the Afghan mujahed offices as a means of registering refugees and settling disputes. In mid-1984, following a series of bomb incidents involving loss of life outside buildings frequented by refugees, the Pakistanis ordered the Afghan political parties to move their headquarters from Peshawar to outlying areas. While KGB agents or guerrilla rivalry were blamed, Pakistani leftwing dissidents may also have been responsible. Whoever was at fault, the Islamabad government used the bombings as an opportunity to reduce the profile of the parties in exile.

Resettlement or Repatriation?

In contrast to the mass migration of Vietnamese citizens and their later resettlement in third countries, UNHCR policy still regards voluntary reptriation as the most feasible solution to Pakistan's present dilemma. Yet the chances of return without a universally acceptable political solution are slim. Few Afghans have accepted the Kabul regime's offers of amnesty.

A disconcerting number of Afghanistan's educated elite — university professors, doctors, lawyers — have headed for Western Europe and North America, much to the disgust of some of the resistance groups fighting at the front. By 1984, nearly ten thousand had already left with legal visas for the United States. How many will eventually return is another matter. Some mujahed leaders argue that, as long as they do not forget their homeland, they might eventually develop into a lobby strong enough to persuade the West to take more effective action. But the resistance organisations, often because of petty jealousies or resentment, have failed so far to galvanise these overseas citizens into representing the anti-Soviet struggle.

The only Afghans who have been officially resettled in a third country have been over 4,000 Uzbeks, Kirghiz, Turkmen and Kazakhs of Turkish ethnic origin who were flown from Pakistan to Turkey in 1982 and 1983. Perhaps the most intriguing aspect of this airlift was the group transfer of Kirghiz nomads, living in the northeastern panhandle of Afghanistan known as the Pamirs and Wakhan corridor at the time of the Soviet invasion. A 15,000 foot-high plateau of sparse treeless valleys, walled in by towering snow-capped mountains, the territory divides Pakistan and the USSR and touches China at its extreme eastern end. It appears to have been annexed by the Soviet Union with Kabul's consent in June 1980.

Originally, the Mongolian-featured Kirghiz inhabited the inside fringes of the Soviet frontier but fled from Stalinist repression during the 1930s by seeking refuge in China and Afghanistan. They eventually ended up in the Wakhan, where they sought to live in peace with their herds of sheep and yak. Many fled from Afghanistan toward the end of 1978 to escape the Khalqis, but others only left following the arrival of Red Army troops in May 1980. The Soviets immediately established several military bases and set about broadening and resurfacing the road leading from the Qala Panja Pass on the Soviet border into the Wakhan interior. They also sealed off the routes into Pakistan and China with minefields; Soviet patrols can often be seen by observation posts on the Pakistani side of the border.

Although the Kirghiz remained in the mountainous northern areas around Gilgit at 4,800 feet. This was still 10,000 feet lower than they were accustomed to. Within a year 150 of them had died from disease or the unaccustomed heat. About 100 returned to the Wakhan. Because of the scarcity of pastures for grazing, they were forced to sell off most their livestock, mostly sheep, yaks and a few camels. Initially, the Kirghiz tried to emigrate as a group to Alaska because of its similarity with their homeland environment. But this fell through for a variety of reasons, and eventually Turkey agreed to accept them because of their Turkic background.

Refugees in Iran: Only Limited Attention

Less fortunate than the Afghan refugees in Pakistan have been those in Iran, where as many as two million have now fled. In Khorsasan province in Northeastern Iran alone, some 400,000 refugees are believed to have crossed over in 1983. Overall, a significant proportion of these are migrant workers unable to unwilling to return home.

There is little reliable information about their plight. International relief agencies do not have the same access to the refugees as they have in Pakistan. Only in July 1983 was the UNHCR able to visit Meshad for the first time; this was followed by a second mission six months later. In the early summer of 1984 it established a permanent representation in Tehran with the idea of making regular tours of transit centres and camps. The Iranians have also prevented Western journalists from visiting the frontier areas with Afghanistan.

Although the UNHCR has managed to provide assistance toward the financing of certain essentials, notably supplementary foods for vulnerable groups, medical supplies, cooking stoves and the construction of sewage tanks, most sources indicate that living conditions are far less satisfactory than in Pakistan. In general, Afghan refugees are kept only a short time in the transit camps, one or two months perhaps, before being sent to the towns throughout the provinces or to stay with relatives. Many work to support themselves, but jobs are short and considerable auti-refugee discrimination is reported.

Aid to the Interior: The Forgotten People

The most neglected of all, however, are those Afghans trying to survive inside Afghanistan itself. By 1984, according to most reliable estimates, some eight million people were reported to be still living in resistance-held areas and benefitting only from the extremely limited relief assistance provided by a handful of European, American and Muslim groups.

Similarly, many of the hundreds of thousands of 'internal refugees' who have fled to Kabul and other towns are ignored both by the communist government and the UN agencies still in Afghanistan, apart from a few very limited health projects. Although concern has beguan to grow, their plight has failed to kindle humanitarian sympathy in the West like that for Cambodia four or five years earlier.

Some international aid organisations, which have extensive relief activities among the Afghan exiles, are prevented by their mandates from working inside Afghanistan. The UNHCR can only work with victims technically defined as 'refugees', while the World Health Organisation is obliged, by virtue of its charter, to deal at a government level, that is, projects sanctioned by host authorities not necessarily in control of the entire country. Such restrictions reveal a deplorable deficiency in UN responsibility to deal with the plight of human beings – an estimated 40 to 50 million people worldwide – caught between two fronts, be they Kurds in Iran, Eritreans in Ethiopia or Afghans in Afghanistan.

Most of the larger private agencies which are in a position to alleviate the distress of Afghans living in the non-government zones have consciously refrained from doing so. Often for fund-raising reasons, they prefer to restrict their operations to 'official' areas only. As an American CARE official pointed out: 'We are not into clandestine relief'.

Reflecting a certain complacency, if not ignorance of internal conditions, such attitudes underline a major and potentially disastrous imbalance in international aid policies. Like the situations in South East Asia and the Horn of Africa, excessive aid outside, while at the same time turning a blind eye to the interior, has contributed towards attracting more refugees. As numerous cases inside Afghanistan have shown, people often seek to remain in their own regions as long as they have the means to survive, even at the risk of further military repression. 'Help should be directed to where it is needed most, namely at home. By doing this you are at least giving the Afghans a chance to stay on', said Dr Claude Malhuret, executive director of Médecins sans Frontière.

With French agencies paving the way, the number of aid groups from different countries seeking to sensitise public opinion and dispatch relief by caravan to the interior has been growing gradually since 1980. Various resistance fronts have appealed for warm winter clothing, shoes, sleeping bags, portable drills for digging air raid shelters in the mountains, fertilisers, seeds, and school books as well as generators, lamps and medication for underground hospitals. Such items obviously have to be brought in from outside. But as transportation to the interior is costly, dangerous and time-consuming, direct financial assistance is in many cases the most appropriate way of procuring foodstuffs for civilian populations. To carry one kilogramme of wheat or sugar by horse from Pakistan costs $1.85, whereas to transport the same supplies from the bazaars of Kabul and other towns comes to less than thirty cents and is far safer. Ironically, basic commodities such as wheat, rice and sugar may also be cheaper in Afghan bazaars because of Soviet subsidies than in Pakistan.

Funds are also urgently required for long-term humanitarian development in the non-government areas. The EEC and several European governments have been providing funds directly to such inside projects. One Paris group, the International Bureau for Afghanistan, launched a pilot livestock project in Kunar province in the summer of 1984 with EEC backing, while the Swedish Committee for Afghanistan, which regularly sends its own observers to gauge requirements, has established some twenty health clinics and dispensaries in different provinces.

Some Western organisations with backers who are reluctant to support clandestine efforts give donors a choice of designating their contributions to 'internal' or 'external' aid, or both. Others, which do not consider it prudent to send relief personnel, notably Americans, into Afghanistan because of the problems that might arise if one were to be captured, have chosen instead to provide assistance direct to the mujahed fronts or to agencies already working inside. The Afghanistan Relief Committee in New York, for example, has been working in close co-operation with the French medical agencies by providing food and medication. Another group, the Dignity of Man Foundation, organised its own direct aid shipments and provided funds for educational or social projects inside Afghanistan. The Seattle-based Americans for Afghanistan Committee campaigned for the purchase of 2,000 pairs of boots, which were eventually sent to the Panjshair Valley. Private companies, too, have been persuaded to send shipments in kind, such as rucksacks or bicycles suitable for special terrain.

The Afghans: Getting Their Act Together

While the international community needs to be more forthcoming, so must the resistance. Many Afghans have come to regard outside aid as their right and have provided little in return. In some areas, security for voluntary medical teams or relief workers has become slack, supplies are lost or stolen and some groups regularly demand payment for housing or armed guards. According to one British relief coordinator:

> Basically, the Afghans must get their act together and not always think that it is up to the outside world to help them. If they want assistance, they must do something for it. Above all, they must improve their organisation which quite frankly is more often than not disastrous. Sacrifices must be made by both sides to make it work.

This lack of organisation or resolve among certain resistance fronts has led to negligence and even disasters. On numerous occasions, doctors have been obliged to travel for days on end without protection. One medical team nearly ran into a company of eighty Soviet special forces troops in northern Afghanistan because the resistance had failed to furnish them with a guide. On another occasion, a group of French doctors and nurses accompanying a caravan ran into a Soviet ambush because the Afghans did not bother to take precautions.

Outside assistance should also be directed towards providing the training, work facilities and salaries of Afghan personnel to help over-come such deficiencies. This includes relief co-ordinators, teachers, medical staff and technicians. The Afghans could learn a few lessons from such organisations as the Tigré Relief Society in Ethiopia or UNITA in Angola, who have taken detailed stock of their humanitarian requirements in guerrilla-held areas. With the prospect of a long-drawn-out war, basic salaries would enable many educated Afghans to contribute toward internal relief while, at the same time, ensuring that their families are cared for. During my last trip to Afghanistan in 1984, I met a number of competent Afghans on their way to the Gulf countries to seek work — a loss which the resistance can ill afford. Few people have jobs in the rural areas of Afghanistan and only the farmers are able to live off their land. 'Many of our educated people are from the towns who have lost everything', said one commander. 'Food is expensive and if they are not provided with the means to survive, they will leave the country.'

Butterfly Mines, Bombs and Clandestine Health Care

During the early days of the occupation, Soviet helicopters and planes strewed the provinces bordering Pakistan with tens of thousands of plastic 'butterfly mines', coloured green for vegetated areas, beige for deserts. Even more diabolically, they dropped boobytrapped toys, cigarette packs, pens and other objects. Designed to maim rather than kill, these anti-personnel explosives were scattered over mountain passes, caravan routes and fields as a means of terrorising the local population or to discourage the mujahideen from running supplies. With the Afghans forced to transport most of their seriously wounded to Pakistan, the Soviets operated on the premise that an injured person causes more disruption than one killed.

To take the illustration of an incident in Nuristan in August 1981. Leaving the mountainous frontier pass behind, the guerrilla caravan, horses loaded with guns, ammunition, food and medication, descended into the flowered valleys of Nuristan, the 'land of light'. Mottled by the slowly moving specks of grazing herds, the broad alpine pastures provided a lavish contrast to the more desolate upper regions of the Hindu Kush. Long thin waterfalls plunged down narrow gorges, their rising vapours nurturing mini-oases of ferns, mosses and trees, while dozens of streamlets laced their way across verdant slopes. The sun shone warmly and even the beasts of burden appeared content with their miserable existence.

For a moment, the war seemed far away. A three-member French volunteer team of Aide Medicale Internationale (AMI), two young doctors and a nurse, walked dispersed among the men and horses, now straddled over several miles in small groups in case of aerial attack. For all three, this was their first mission in Afghanistan. Two of them, 27-year-old Dr Frederique H., a headstrong country girl from northern France, and the nurse, Evelyn G. also 27, had never worked with victims of war before. On their way to take over a French clinic in the Panjshair Valley, the medical team approached the trek more like a holiday hike in the Swiss Alps than a long walk to the 'front'.

Mines had not occurred to anyone. The caravan was hardly two hours inside Afghanistan when some of the mujahideen up front stopped to make tea. Waiting for the rest to catch up, a young Panjshairi, Shah Mansour, crossed a small stream to hunt for firewood among the bracken and wild rhubarb on the other side. Suddenly, a sharp explosion and his right foot was severed below the ankle, a bloody mess of flesh and bone. A few feet away lay the pathetic remains of his black plastic shoe and the metallic fragments of a booby-trapped watch.

By the side of the stream, the doctors amputated what remained of the young fighter's foot. The horses carrying the surgical equipment were still far behind and would not arrive before it was dark, so they operated using a light anaesthetic, a few basic instruments and a pen-knife. Fortunately, the patient was still in a state of shock. There was also no bleeding, the wound having been cauterised by the explosion. Not far from the Pakistani frontier, several mujahideen carried Shah Mansour the next day in a makeshift litter to Chitral. From there, he was flown to the International Committee of the Red Cross (ICRC) hospital for war victims in Peshawar, where he recovered and was soon walking around with a new artificial foot.

The Afghans have learned, all too often from bitter experience, how to clear the trails of mines. By gingerly picking them up, they can toss them away to explode or they detonate them at a distance with stones. Nevertheless, the Peshawar clinics are filled with pitiful victims, many of them children, their hands and feet blown off.

Only five days after Shan Mansour's accident, the medical team came across another casualty, a small boy whose left hand had been shattered by an explosive object that, according to the child, 'looked like a stone' when he tried to pick it up. The villagers tried to treat the wound by traditional methods, covering it with horse manure and mud. Although the doctors cleaned it and gave the child the necessary anti-biotics, the parents did not take him for further treatment to the Panjshair hospital only three days' horse ride away; the child eventually died.

Livestock too, have suffered badly from the mines. Hobbling cows and goats, often minus a leg or with their limbs in splints, are a common sight. The Soviets later introduced small 'flechette' bombs that spray the surroundings with hundreds of razor-sharp pieces of metal. They have always denied using such weapons.

Many Afghan war casualties are not as lucky as Shah Mansour. It can take days, if not weeks, for them to reach medical care, and gangrene, blood loss and shock all exact a ruthless toll. According to an ICRC official in Peshawar:

Many of the wounded never make it this far. A kind of natural selection takes place during the trip. In general, those who get this far are able to take it, and we manage to save them. The Afghans are a very sturdy people — much more so than Europeans.

Of those who survive long enough, almost all have the beginnings of infection, if not generalised infection, which makes operating more difficult. International relief officials estimate that one out of five victims with thoraco-abdominal injuries die before they reach the clinics. In one incident, a young mujahed commander helped bring in three of his wounded men from the fighting in Nangrahar only to watch two of them die before they reached Peshawar. Roughly 90 per cent of those who are finally admitted to surgery in Pakistan have limb injuries.

Clandestine Health Relief

Many more would die were it not for the courageous work of the French volunteer medical organisations working inside Afghanistan. Since the early summer of 1980, the three groups (AMI, MSF and Médecins du Monde) have dispatched nearly 400 volunteer doctors and nurses, mainly French but also a sprinkling of Belgian, Swiss and other nationalities, to provide basic health care among the civilian population. Working clandestinely, and at great personal risk, they have not only tried to treat some of the country's often horrifying war casualties (85 per cent civilian) but also commonplace maladies such as tuberculosis, parasitosis and whooping cough, normally found in any developing country. Among the consequences of the Soviet destruction of houses, crops and livestock are poor living conditions and food shortages which result in severe epidemics among children.

At any one time, there are twenty to thirty doctors and nurses staying between three and eight months in different regions — some operating on occasion within thirty miles of Kabul, others as far north as Badakshan or Balkh bordering on the Soviet Union. In effect, the French medical agencies are practising a form of humanitarian relief far in advance of the more conventional aid organisations. Operating in war zones such as Afghanistan, Laos, Eritrea, Kurdistan, Angola, Burma but also in Colombia, Haiti and elsewhere, they have recognised the needs of a steadily growing human phenomenon: the world's 'unofficial' populations. Speaking for AMI, Dr Laurence Laumonier commented:

Our view is that humanitarian considerations are far more important than the *'raison d'état'* of a particular country. For the moment, we are working mainly in areas where other agencies do not go. But they too should realise that there are millions of people, far more than the present world refugee population (estimated at 10-12 million), who receive no help whatsoever because their governments do not accept them.

At the time of the Soviet invasion, few Afghan doctors worked in rural areas. By the end of 1980, most of the 1,600 doctors registered in Afghanistan before the Saur Revolution had fled the country, mainly to West Germany, France and North America to 'continue their studies'. Some, no more than one or two hundred, continued to work with the government in Kabul and other towns. Within two or three years, medical care in the capital was mainly provided by Soviet doctors.

Some Afghan doctors have stayed behind in Peshawar to work with the refugees, while others living in Europe or the United States co-operate regularly with Afghan relief organisations. Hardly more than a score of fully-trained doctors have remained to provide their countryfolk in the resistance-held areas with medical care, often without any resources whatsoever. Among the three million Hazaras, for example, there was not a single Afghan doctor during the first year of the occupation. Two or three could be found in Farah province, a similar number in Herat, and the others were scattered around the rest of the country.

Through the Swedish Relief committee, a number of Afghan doctors and medical students have gone back inside to work with the resistance. As more clinics are established, it is hoped more will come. But the great majority appear to have fallen victim to the 'brain-drain' attractions of the West or the oil-rich Gulf countries.

Seen as a whole, this deplorable dearth has meant only one Afghan doctor for every 300,000 inhabitants in the resistance-held areas. Although some areas boast of 'doctors', these are often students with limited experience or charlatans who distribute pills according to colour rather than curative properties, and usually at exorbitant prices. Patients living near the Pakistani border can, of course, travel to Peshawar or Quetta for medical treatment. Many Afghans, even those desperately ill or injured, have been reluctant to seek care in Kabul because of the dangers involved. Young men seeking medical treatment in the towns would immediately be inducted into the army, while those with bullet wounds face arrest. The French medical organisations have tried to help fill this gap.

Medical Care and Conditions

Operating out of improvised hospitals in destroyed villages or in mountain caves, the chief objective of the French missions has been to bring qualified medical personnel to the war-afflicted areas. They have also sought to train Afghans as 'barefoot doctors' and to educate the inhabitants in basic health requirements. The teams have encountered enormous difficulties, occasionally necessitating the abandonment of a particular mission. Local leaders or mullahs, for example, sometimes regard the doctors as a threat to their authority and refuse to co-operate. Or the bombardments have become so bad or the danger of capture so great that they have been forced to flee.

Overall, however, they have managed to adapt themselves to local circumstances. Much of their work is what they describe as 'blow by blow' medicine. This might mean setting up a makeshift hospital in a mountain cave to treat bomb victims or using a lull in the fighting to tour villages for consultations or to carry out mass vaccinations (usually in the winter so as to keep vaccines at chilled temperatures).

Like many developing countries, rural Afghanistan suffers from malaria, bronchitis, diphtheria, tuberculosis, parasitic and intestinal ailments. There is also a 40-50 per cent child mortality rate. Much of this could be reduced through improved diet, hygiene and long-term medical care. Inroads have been made in the treatment of rampant TB and trachoma in the Hazarajat. Anaemia and malnutrition are pronounced among women and children while epidemics of whooping cough and measles have proved particularly catastrophic. In some parts, an unvaried food base of bread, animal fat and tea has led to severe malnutrition. The French teams emphasise that they cannot be truly effective until systematic vaccination programmes, supplementary food distribution and long-term health education are instituted, in other words, the sort of health development normally propagated by the WHO and other 'official' international organisations elsewhere in the world.

Health care has varied from province to province. A major drawback has been the need to find surgeons able to leave their hospitals long enough to travel to and from a region that has been particularly badly hit by the war (several days to three weeks either way), and then spend two or three months working. Most doctors volunteering for Afghanistan have had little experience in operating and must be given creash courses in the basics of war surgery. As it is, most learn soon enough in the field.

One of the first teams to work in Afghanistan consisted of two doctors, a man and a woman, who travelled to Nuristan in the summer of 1980. There they established a dispensary and trained eight male nurses from different backgrounds. Another team, also in Nuristan, trained local nurses while providing basic health care among the villages. One nurse, furthermore, who was a vegetarian, campaigned to introduce wild spinach to the sparse local diet. Because of the heavy fighting, they treated war injured from both sides, mujahideen and Afghan government soldiers.

The first French team arrived in the Panjshair only in early 1981. Until then, the local inhabitants had received virtually no health care whatsoever since the guerrillas first took over two years earlier, apart from the treatment provided by two captured Khalqi doctors. Bringing with them four hundred kilogrammes of surgical instruments and medication ranging from antibiotics to dysentery tablets, the French installed a clinic in the abandoned house of a PDPA member. While AMI's Dr Laumonier, who has since conducted several missions in Afghanistan, dealt primarily with the women and children, Dr Philippe Manière took care of the men. They also trained local students, most of them former high school pupils, who accompanied the doctors on consultations, provided first aid at the 'front', and received theoretical instruction with the help of medical textbooks translated from French into Farsi. During the changeover periods, the students ran the hospital until the replacement doctors arrived.

As with medical missions in other parts of the country, the Panjshair doctors worked on average twelve hours a day, treating as many as 100 patients and encountering a variety of common illnesses, war injuries and psychosomatic problems. Many wounded were carried in from the Kabul 'front' further south; these often involved major operations. 'It was horrible work', said Dr Laumonier. 'We had torn limbs, mutilated faces from explosions and even a case of third degree burns that could only have come from napalm'.

The conservatism of Afghanistan's Islamic society often poses problems in the treatment of women. From the Afghan point of view, the woman is queen within her own domain as delineated by the environs of her village. Here she can move about unveiled. Only in the presence of outsiders, who should respect her anyway, would she turn her head or raise her shawl to her face. But men living away from the hospital are usually reluctant to bring their womenfolk in for treatment, even in the case of serious ailments, for fear of exposing them to the scrutiny of strangers.

For those women inhabiting the village where the hospital is situated, there are few difficulties. The female doctors have even established an intimate sense of solidarity. In the Panjshair, Dr Laumonier started a series of courses for the local women on primary childcare, hygiene and gynaecology. This led to a noticeable improvement in diet and cleanliness. While men will turn up without hestitation at a hospital, the most effective way to encounter sick women is to make village visits and order the hospitalisation of those unable to be treated at home, but male doctors are usually obliged to carry out diagnoses on female patients by asking questions without making a physical examination.

Initially, the Afghans found it awkward to come to grips with the presence of Western female doctors and nurses in their midst. They quickly solved the predicament with almost childlike simplicity by regarding them as 'non-women'. The French doctors and nurses also made it easier for them by emphasising their roles as doctors rather than women. As Dr Laumonier said:

> It is really a matter of accepting and respecting their culture. One must also not judge everything by Western standards. Once one understands this, there are ways of getting round anything.

The doctors have found themselves coping with problems such as depression or severe trauma arising from the constant pressure of war. 'Many men or women just come to the hospital to be reassured', said one doctor. Some patients simply craved attention. Mujahideen encountered while travelling in the mountains would suddenly develop, as if on cue, a host of intriguing pathogenic symptoms. Moaning 'marees, marees' (sick, sick), they would dramatically screw up their faces and, carefully watching the doctor's expression, point to various parts of the body where the pain was supposed to be. Often as not, they were not sick at all.

Bombed Hospitals

The presence of the French teams has meant consistent and embarrassing testimony to the nature of the brutal Soviet anti-insurgent methods. It has also accentuated the urgent need for some form of international protection for humanitarian organisations operating in areas not under the control of an officially recognised government.

During the earlier stages of the war, the Kremlin seemed willing to tolerate the presence of foreign doctors working in resistance-held zones. In return, the French quietly pursued their medical activities, generally keeping a low profile *vis-à-vis* the Western press. But in October and November 1981, the Soviets made a concerted effort to crack down by deliberately bombing three of the French-run hospitals.

The first attack came in late October. Its motor muffled by the mountains, a helicopter gunship suddenly rose up from behind a ridge and bore down directly on the MSF hospital at Jaghori in the Hazarajat. A nearby mujahed heavy machine-gun position immediately opened fire, forcing it to leave. As a precaution, the French evacuated the hospital to another building. Three days later, at 6.30 in the morning, three more helicopters appeared and headed straight for the former location, cannon and rockets blazing. In less than a minute, the hospital was reduced to a pile of burning and smoke-filled rubble. The escape was a narrow one and indicated that the Russians were well-informed about French operations in the region, probably through the KHAD. No other building had been hit and, at the time of the attack, there were a total of eight doctors in the immediate area, some of them passing through to say goodbye before heading back to Pakistan.

At roughly the same period, but 500 kilometres to the north, seven doctors and nurses of AMI were working in the Panjshair Valley. Shortly after midday on 5 November three helicopters descended to attack the valley's main health centre. The rockets caused some damage, but no casualties. The French immediately ordered the removal of all the patients to pre-arranged sanctuaries in the mountains. Less than half an hour later, two MIG jets appeared and razed the building with bombs. Again, the attack was extremely precise, suggesting a thorough knowledge of French whereabouts. A day later, in Nangrahar province, an AMI dispensary was bombarded. Fortunately, the approaching roar of the helicopter gave the medical team just enough warning to run out and hide behind a nearby wall. The building was completely destroyed together with part of the village.

'Over an eight month period we were forced to move the hospital five times because of bombardments or the danger of attack', explained Dr Capucine de Bretagne following a six-month stint in the Panjshair from the autumn of 1981 until the late spring the next year. On one occasion, the hospital was bombed despite a large Red Cross marked distinctly on its roof.

Regarding such attacks as part of a deliberate intimidation strategy, the medical organisations decided to end their relative silence and publicly upbraid the Russians for their 'reign of terror' against the civilian population. 'We feel that it is up to world public opinion to pressure the Russians into stopping such atrocities', said one organisation spokesman. Since then, the Soviets have pulled all stops to capture the doctors. During the May 1982 Panjshair offensive, heli-borne commandos narrowly missed taking Laumonier and de Bretagne, who had fled with their patients, some of them with limbs freshly amputated, into a nearby side valley. As de Bretagne recounted:

> As the Soviets advanced, we moved from one village to another, people carrying the medication and patients behind us. We changed houses every day because of informers. Once we were very badly bombed just as I was leaving our shelter to visit the wounded. It lasted for three quarters of an hour with one bomb dropping near me killing one of our injured.

Several days later, while I was reporting·in the Panjshair region, guer-rillas took me to the exhausted doctors. They had been hidden by the mujahideen in a cave-like shelter in the mountains as planes and heli-copters bombed only two miles away. As it was too dangerous for them to remain, Massoud ordered them to be taken back to Peshawar. In the meantime, however, the Soviets had found their passports and other personal belongings left behind in their haste to leave, and informed diplomatic circles in Kabul that they had captured the doctors plus several journalists known to be in the area. It was only two weeks later in Peshawar that the reports could be proved false.

Capture

On 16 January 1983, the Soviets finally succeeded in capturing a French doctor, promptly turning him into an example of 'counter-revolutionary' propaganda. On mission for AMI in Logar province south of Kabul since September 1982, Dr Philippe Augoyard, a 29-year-old paediatrician from Rouen, was picked up by Soviet troops during a helicopter raid on several villages where he was treating local civilians. Two other doctors, a man and a woman, working in the same region were pursued by the security forces for a week, but managed to escape. According to AMI, the soldiers lined up five old men against the wall, shot them in the legs, and ordered them to reveal the whereabouts of the doctors. They refused. Four of them died, but the fifth was saved by one of the French who later returned to help.

At first, the Soviet troops manhandled Augoyard, but then treated him well, almost with admiration, once it was discovered that he was French. They flew him to Kabul where he spent the first twenty-four hours in a Red Army base. All in all, he was interrogated no more than half an hour by Soviet intelligence officials before being handed over to the KHAD.

From then on, the Afghans conducted all proceedings, with the Soviets remaining out of sight. Three months later, the Afghan government put Augoyard on trial, charging him with illegally entering the country, aiding and abetting the 'counter-revolutionaries' and smuggling out photographs and documents of strategic importance. Threatening him with the death sentence, the authorities pressured him into admitting to the charges at a televised press conference.

Augoyard obediently declared that he had collaborated with the 'counter-revolutionaries' not knowing that they were involved in acts of 'banditry' and 'terrorism'. Asking for clemency, he promised to tell the truth about the 'real situation' in Afghanistan on his return to France and never again to 'act against the Democratic Republic'. He also agreed with suggestions by the public prosecutor that AMI might be involved with foreign intelligence organisations, notably the CIA. Convicted of spying, twice entering Afghanistan illegally and helping the mujahideen, Augoyard was sentenced to eight years imprisonment.

Back in France, the Paris-based medical organisations immediately launched a campaign for his release. Their efforts drew a remarkable degree of public attention (nearly a million postcards) to the Augoyard case and the nature of the medical organisations' humanitarian activities in Afghanistan. The French public was particularly perturbed by the interview of a Paris television news reporter, a member of the French Communist Party, who posed questions with little respect for the doctor's predicament and sounded more like the public prosecutor himself. A more sober approach was taken by a CBS documentary team filming in Kabul at the time, who showed Augoyard testifying to Eastern bloc journalists at a hearing strikingly reminiscent of the 1957 trials in Hungary.

The French Foreign Ministry protested against what it called the 'surprising, even shocking conditions' under which Augoyard's statements were made. The Afghan embassy in Paris countered that 'what is even more shocking is the way (Dr Augyard) entered Afghanistan illegally and associated with a band of murderers'. Nevertheless, increasing media and diplomatic pressure eventually induced the Kabul authorities to release the young doctor.

The French communists, with four ministers in the government, also intervened under pressure from the Elysée Palace. Although embarrassed by the bad publicity, they refused to condemn Augoyard's incarceration and even maintained that he probably was spying. Once safely home, Augoyard immediately recanted his previous statements, claiming that he had been forced to 'perform' in order to gain release.

'It was perhaps cowardly on my part', he said, 'but I had no choice. I was dictated what I should say . . . It is obviously humiliating to say things one does not believe, but it was propaganda, and once the comedy was over, I was sure to be freed.' Despite the persistent dangers and the lack of internationally recognised protection for medical personnel working in war zones, the Augoyard affair has done little to dissuade the French organisations from continuing their work in countries like Afghanistan.

Guerrilla War and Humanitarian Rights

As in most guerrilla conflicts, the present Russo-Afghan war has raised several fundamental problems regarding the humanitarian protection of civilians as well as the status of the resistance fighter as a bona fide belligerent. Although the 1949 Geneva Conventions and their Additional Protocols (1977) take into account the struggles in which people are fighting — against colonial domination, alien occupation and racist regimes — interpretations among the parties concerned do not always coincide. For the Soviet-backed Kabul authorities, the mujahed is nothing but a bandit or counter-revolutionary operating outside the law and disturbing national order and security. The guerrilla, on the other hand, sees himself as a freedom fighter who has taken up arms in a just cause, and since 27 December 1979 against the foreign occupation of his country.

In practice, few governments or outside forces, be they Nazis in Europe, the French in Algeria, the Americans in Vietnam or the Russians in Afghanistan, have shown much humanitarian respect for their partisan opponents. Civilians suspected of collaboration with the insurgents have suffered all kinds of reprisals ranging from mass liquidation to the destruction of property. As for the guerrilla fighter, he can usually expect little more than summary execution if captured, or imprisonment under degrading conditions including torture. At the same time, the insurgents have themselves demonstrated little concern for humanitarian niceties in their treatment of prisoners of war.

Amid all the complexities of guerrilla war, it is the task of the International Committee of the Red Cross (ICRC) in Geneva to encourage the global application of humanitarian law. But the very nature of guerrilla war makes this exceedingly difficult. For one thing, barely more than forty countries have ratified the 1977 Protocols, which stipulate that members of resistance movements in occupied territory who belong to oragnised armed forces are entitled to POW status.

ICRC statutes strictly limit the organisation's humanitarian activities. Only allowed to operate with the permission of the host government, it claims not to be in the position to bring direct medical relief to civilians in the war-zones of Afghanistan. Despite the fact that French volunteer doctors manage to operate there, Red Cross officials argue that the internal situation does not permit the establishment of well-equipped clinics, even, as some observers have suggested, in declared 'neutral zones'.

Nevertheless, the strictness of the ICRC's policy remains ambiguous. Red Cross officials have operated inside guerrilla-controlled areas of Angola and Ethiopia without the 'permission' of the host government. In Afghanistan, the ICRC has opted for the next best thing. It has created two modern, and invaluable, 'war front' surgical units near the Afghan border. Aimed solely at Afghan war victims, the two hospitals have carried out nearly 10,000 operations.

Red Cross Hospitals and War Victims

The first hospital was opened in Peshawar in June 1981, with access to Afghanistan's eastern and northern provinces, and the second in July 1983 in Quetta with access to twelve southern, central and western provinces. Each has a paraplegic centre, a prothesis workshop and rehabilitation programmes; the Peshawar paraplegic centre is certainly among the most modern in Asia. The hospitals offer a form of healthcare for civilians found nowhere in Afghanistan, not even in Kabul. Other medical operations run by independent groups such as the AICF clinic in Quetta also deal with war casualties, but are more geared towards general and preventative health care.

With many Afghans regularly bringing their severely wounded from as far north as Badakshan and Balkh, mobile medical teams run by the Pakistan Red Crescent Society provide emergency care at various points along the frontier. Victims are then taken for further treatment to the nearest ICRC clinic, where rotating Red Cross surgical teams from Switzerland, West Germany, Denmark, Finland, Italy and New Zealand have been operating. Word of mouth travels fast and within days of the opening of the Quetta hospital, Afghans were bringing in their wounded, mainly from the Kandahar 'front'. In a tacit agreement, the French doctors also send their complicated war casualties for further treatment to the ICRC.

The surgical wards painfully reflect the tragic suffering of the people. A young girl without a face, victim of a helicopter bombardment. A woman, whose right leg has been twice amputated following a severe attack against her village. A small boy, his foot blown off by a 'butterfly mine'. Outside, the paraplegics struggle to exercise from their wheel-chairs, while others hobble about on crutches, waiting for a new foot or leg to be made in the special prothesis workship. Most are cared for by their friends and relatives, and most seek to return home once their treatment is complete.

In addition, the ICRC has set up first aid training courses for Afghans. It also seeks to inform them on Red Cross principles and humanitarian law through instruction and booklets published in Farsi and Pashto.

Prisoners of War

The ICRC's other major concern in Afghanistan has been the POW dilemma. For the first time in its history, and in the history of any humanitarian institution, the organisation has been faced with a totally new concept of prisoner responsibility, namely, the proxy internment of conventional (Soviet) POWs captured by (Afghan) guerrillas.

The 1977 Protocols of the Geneva Conventions have taken into consideration certain aspects of the extraordinary evolution of guerrilla war since 1945. But the Soviet-Afghan precedent has lent the possibility of a more humanitarian approach to the fate of prisoners in areas of conflict where one side lacks the facilities or desire to keep captives alive.

Traditionally, the ICRC has assured the proper treatment of POWs according to the Geneva Convention by visiting POW camps, engineering prisoner exchanges and even mediating the release of captured civilians held by guerrillas in rebel-held areas. The freeing of a group of Czech men, women and children kidnapped by UNITA rebels in Angola in the spring of 1983 is but one example.

During the Indochina War, North Vietnamese and Viet Cong prisoners were confined in government-run detention centres, while shot-down American pilots or captured GIs were generally interned in hidden jungle camps or POW prisons in the north. International norms were regularly violated by both sides; atrocities against captured soldiers or guerrillas were commonplace, while 'official' camps were not necessarily open to Red Cross inspection. Nevertheless, both North and South Vietnam had the organisational structures to intern captives, and the ICRC, with representatives in Hanoi and Saigon, could press all parties concerned to respect the Geneva Conventions.

Afghanistan, on the other hand, presents a radically different equation. Prior to the Russian invasion, the fighting bore all the horrors characteristic of an expanding civil war. Captured rebels or 'bandits' were either shot on the spot or thrown into jail. Reciprocally, the mujahideen simply disarmed or turned around most captured conscripts, but the chances of survival of communist supporters or party members were slim. Many were tried by Islamic tribunals and executed.

Organisations like Amnesty International or the ICRC, unable to visit Kabul jails, could only protest about treatment of prisoners by the government or appeal to the partisans on a humanitarian basis. Furthermore, as the 1977 Geneva Protocols do not grant POW status to guerrillas in the case of a purely civil war, international norms did not appear to apply to the Afghan conflict at this point despite its 'internationalisation' through the presence of Soviet advisers.

Whatever the semantics, however, it was evident that sooner or later the problem of POWs would emerge. And indeed, the issue finally came to the fore in the summer of 1981, almost eighteen months after the Soviet invasion, with the capture of Mikhail Semyonovich Gorchniski, a 34-year-old Ukrainian fighter pilot from Kiev whose MIG was shot down over Nangrahar province by Hezb-i-Islami (Khales faction) forces. The incident represented the first documented case of a Soviet prisoner to be taken, and kept alive, by the mujahideen.

An Eye for an Eye . . .

Until then, as far as could be determined, all captured non-Muslim Soviet personnel had been executed on the traditional 'eye for an eye, tooth for a tooth' basis. Apart from having to deal with irate villagers eager for revenge, most Afghan resistance commanders simply did not have the means or the food to intern captives. Not surprisingly, many were ignorant of the Geneva Conventions and few could see the point in keeping the 'Shouravi' alive. After all, this was war and there was no point in being kind to one's enemy. Furthermore, for the mujahed, killing a 'Kafir' means becoming a 'Ghazi', a hero.

Concerned by repeated reports of prisoner executions ranging from captured Soviet soldiers with their throats slit to trussed-up Afghan partisans run over by Russian tanks, ICRC representatives in Peshawar had been negotiating almost from the beginning with various resistance organisations in the hope that some sort of agreement on the treatment of POWs could be reached. Red Cross officials in Geneva and elsewhere also put out feelers to the Soviets. Gorchniski's capture finally prompted the Russians to make a formal request to the ICRC for assistance in recovering captured personnel.

Gorchniski remained only a short time on Afghan territory. The mujahideen smuggled him into Pakistan where he was kept in a clandestine resistance 'safe' house in Peshawar. Aware of the political capital that could be made, Khales had decided to display his man to the international press. Not only would this publicly disprove Moscow's claims that Soviet troops were not actively involved in the fighting, but media exposure would draw attention to the Afghan cause.

For the sensitive Islamabad regime, a Soviet prisoner on Pakistani soil was the last thing it wanted and it pressured the Afghans into handing him over. Discreetly, the Pakistanis in turn passed him over to the Soviet embassy, which promptly bundled him back to the USSR. The mujahideen were furious. The move offered them little incentive to keep their prisoners alive, if they were simply going to be returned to the Russians. Nevertheless, several months later, they had another chance. In a daring daylight raid in Kabul, a team of Hezb-i-Islami (Khales faction again) guerrillas captured a Soviet geologist, Okrimyuk, with the complicity of his Afghan chauffeur. Having learned their lesson, the mujahideen did not take him to Pakistan. Instead, they contacted the ICRC in Peshawar proposing to exchange the hapless geologist for 50 Afghan prisoners, one of whom was Khales' own son.

This posed a serious dilemma for the Soviets. Should they deal with a group of resistance fighters whom they refused to recognise or not? If they failed to negotiate, they ran the risk of demoralising Soviet troops in Afghanistan still further; news would spread that the High Command would not lift a finger for one of its own people. But if they did, the mujahideen would no doubt exploit the case for propaganda purposes. It might set a precedent by encouraging guerrillas to kidnap more Russian personnel, notably civilian advisers.

The ICRC was all for negotiation in order to save Okrimyuk's life, but it was against prisoner exchanges, at least for the moment. With certain justification, Red Cross officials argued that nothing would prevent the Kabul authorities from filling their prisons with people taken off the streets and calling them rebels; thus maintaining a perpetual pool of hostages for exchange purposes. 'Obviously a political matter, this sort of thing could easily snowball out of control', noted one Red Cross official.

In the end, the Soviets adopted the attitude, 'You don't bargain with terrorists'. While on a visit to Moscow in October 1981, ICRC vice-president Richard Pestalozzi sought to re-open the prisoner issue, but the Kremlin stolidly replied that no Soviet troops were fighting in Afghanistan. Moscow's cold shoulder hardly surprised Western and Third World sovietologists. 'Russian military and political tactics are completely based on whether they serve the cause or not', said one European analyst. 'Human life is dispensable.' Just as the Soviet military command will refuse to come to the aid of a besieged unit if it does not suit overall strategy, Okrimyuk had to be sacrificed. To illustrate their intention of never negotiating with the 'bandits', the Soviets shot the 50 Afghan prisoners named by the mujahideen just as the Red Cross had feared. Six months after Okrimyuk's capture, a bitter Khales announced the geologist's execution; other reports, however, maintain that he died of natural causes.

A Red Cross Deal: Prisoner Transfers

Red Cross officials persisted in their attempts to find a solution. One possibility was the transfer of captured Soviet personnel to a neutral country for internment; this would conveniently give the resistance a way of abiding by the Geneva Conventions. In return, the ICRC would have the right to visit mujahed prisoners held by the communists.

The ICRC had initially offered its services to the Babrak regime a few days after the invasion. On 13 January 1980, the Kabul authorities granted it the right to operate in Afghanistan. Over a four-month period, ICRC representatives interviewed 427 political suspects at Pul-e-Charkhi prison according to international requirements (no guard present, etc) and distributed two tons of medication to hospitals and dispensaries in certain parts of the country. But in June, the government ordered the ICRC to leave; as a result, Afghan detention centres were closed to international inspection for the next two years.

Resistance leaders to Peshawar were becoming increasingly favourable to the idea of prisoner transfer to a third country. Made aware by visiting doctors, journalists and human rights activists of its implications, the mujahideen realised that they could only enhance their position abroad by taking prisoners alive. The presence of Soviet POWs under ICRC responsibility would also embarrass the Kremlin by providing a constant reminder to the world at large that there was still a war in Afghanistan.

Pakistan was ruled out as a possible host country, because of the pressures the Kremlin might exert were Soviet POWs interned just across the Afghan border. They would prove too tempting a target to any Soviet heliborne rescue operations. When India was suggested, the mujahideen adamantly refused because of Delhi's pro-Soviet stance.

Switzerland, Liechtenstein or another neutral nation seemed the most acceptable to all parties concerned.

As negotiations continued, so did the fighting, and more and more reports began to circulate of Soviet personnel being held by the mujahideen. In 1981 alone, the SAMA claimed to have taken 85 Soviet soldiers and officers whom it wished to exchange. By the end of 1982, the number of Soviet prisoners or deserters (more than half non-Russians — Lithuanians, Ukranians and Central Asians) in the hands of the resistance had risen to several hundred. Western humanitarian organisations had also compiled a list of at least 50 known prisoners, including their rank and place of origin, some of whom had already been executed.

A few of the more organised guerrilla fronts had established 'prisons' for captured Afghan communists both before and after the invasion. Often these were no more than barricaded holes in the ground with no natural light or fresh air, or they were well-guarded houses. Some maintained reasonably satisfactory jail facilities, such as the Panjshair Valley, where the guerrillas ran a specially constructed stone and cement compound in a hidden side valley. But with Soviet personnel among the ranks of the captives, there was always the danger of attack by the security forces. Through KHAD informers, the security forces have assaulted villages known to be holding prisoners on several occasions, forcing the mujahideen to kill their captives in the face of advancing troops.

In the early summer of 1982, the ICRC finally managed to work out an arrangement for the transfer of Soviet prisoners to Switzerland. The final impetus came with the visit of a group of foreign journalists to the Hezb-i-Islami (Hekmatyar faction) guerrilla camp at Allah Jirgha in Zabul province, twelve miles from the Pakistani frontier. At the desert base, the reporters interviewed two recently captured Soviets, Alexander Petrovitch Sidielniko, a 20-year-old Ukrainian tank captain and Valery Yurkevich Kissilov, a 19-year-old conscript and former technical college student. The reporters saw three other Soviet prisoners, two of whom had been interviewed seven months earlier. Alerted by the media coverage, Amnesty International appealed to the Hezb not to execute them. One of them, Mohammad Yazkouiev Kouli, was a Tadjik from Samarkand and a mechanic by profession, who had apparently embraced Islam and was living in semi-liberty. The others were Sgt. Yuri Grigorievich Povarnytsin, a tractor driver from a collective farm at Sverdlovsk in the Urals, and a Ukrainian conscript, Valery Anatolievitch Didenko.

Strong indications that the communists were beginning to talk business emerged when the resistance and the Babrak regime held a prisoner exchange. On 20 May the guerrillas exchanged Hamesha Gul, the relative of a senior government official and party member, for Amir Mohammad, a captured resistance fighter. A few days later, after twenty-four months of negotiation involving one superpower and fourteen resistance organisations, came the long-awaited Red Cross agreement for Soviet prisoner transfers — the first comprehensive agreement between the ICRC and the Soviet Union since 1945. Although some analysts interpreted Moscow's willingness to allow Geneva to handle the POW issue as a sign of growing confidence in its war against the resistance, others felt it had to react in order to keep up morale among the Soviet occupation troops.

In accordance with the Geneva Conventions, the ICRC assumed full responsibility for the prisoners for the duration of the war, or for two years, whichever was the shorter. They were then to be handed back to the Soviet Union. The Swiss government was to provide internment facilities with Moscow paying all costs. In return, the Red Cross would have access to the Kabul prisons to visit captured mujahideen and other political inmates. Red Cross officials privately hoped that, with such controls on both sides, they would be able to arrange carefully monitored batches of prisoner transfers between the Soviets and the resistance.

The Red Cross Effort Founders

By early 1985, only eleven Soviet POWs had been transferred to Switzerland. One of these Youri Vachentko, escaped to West Germany where he applied for political asylum. Eventually five were repatriated (apparently voluntarily) to an uncertain future in the USSR and two further POWs sought asylum in Switzerland. Three remained in Swiss custody to complete their terms. In contrast to confident earlier predictions of over 100 Soviet POWs in Switzerland by mid-1983, the ICRC transfer effort was foundering, despite the growing backlog of Soviet personnel in guerrilla captivity. This was mainly due to a lack of Afghan confidence in the organisation.

According to various estimates, as many as 300 Soviet POWs were being held alive by different guerrilla organisations in 1984. This did not include a small, but undetermined, number of Soviet deserters, many of Central Asian origin, known to be actively operating with the resistance or living in relative freedom among the Afghans. In August, I met three — an Estonian, a Ukrainian and a Russian — of about a dozen deserters in the Panjshair Valley. A small number of Soviet deserters and prisoners have been taken to Europe and the United States, where they have been granted asylum. In November 1984, however, two former prisoners living in Britain decided to return to the Soviet Union after one of them had received what one Foreign Office representative described as a 'distressing letter' from his family.

Human rights organisations have maintained that, as long as the West is prepared to grant refuge (Canada agreed to take 25), others could be brought out in this manner. Several of these groups are now actively involved in making the necessary arrangements for an 'underground railway'. 'How can we call upon Soviet soldiers to desert if they know that they run the risk of getting killed or never getting out?' said one expatriate Russian.

The ICRC is clearly concerned with finding a solution to its present unenviable predicament. The lives of tens of thousands of imprisoned Afghan civilians, mujahideen, government personnel and Soviets are involved. It is also a predicament which raises both moral and political considerations. From the Red Cross point of view, it would prefer all captured Soviets to be transferred to Switzerland, thus obliging the Kremlin to grant it access to Afghan prisons. In this manner, it might eventually be able to arrange for prisoner exchanges or quietly repatriate the Soviets after each two-year period.

But the war in Afghanistan is no ordinary conflict. While some irate critics maintain that the ICRC has made a secret deal with the USSR, a more realistic appraisal suggests that the organisation's pronounced sense of impartiality has failed to take basic human nature into account. Some observers believe that, in trying not to upset relations with the Russians, the Red Cross has failed to prove to the mujahideen that prisoner transfers are a two-way process. The ICRC is now faced with the task of regaining credibility in the eyes of the mujahideen. The mere fact that the Afghans have been keeping more prisoners alive represents a major step forward. But the guerrillas have been reluctant to hand over more prisoners until the Kremlin makes a gesture by permitting a return of the ICRC to Kabul.

The situation has led to painful uncertainty among the Soviet prisoners. Guerrilla groups, tired of waiting, may start executing some of them. But mujahed obstinacy has also denied the resistance the opportunity fully to exploit the prisoner issue. Each time a POW is scheduled for repatriation, the Soviets can expect a controversial resurgence of public attention to the issue. And by maintaining a steady stream of Soviet prisoners to Switzerland, the guerrillas could draw even more attention to the ugly little war Moscow would like the world to forget.

10 PERSPECTIVES

'A nation is dying. People should know.' (Mohammed Es-Haq, Panjshair resistance).

In the spring of 1984, the Soviet Union launched a series of offensives against prominent resistance strongholds in the Panjshair, Herat, Nangrahar, Kandahar and other regions in Afghanistan. The assaults, among the most punishing of the war, involved an unprecedented number of Red Army and Afghan government troops (over 20,000 in the Panjshair-Shamali-Salang area alone) supported by fast-moving BMP infantry combat vehicles, light tanks, helicopter gunships and fighter bombers. The Soviets demonstrated a striking improvement in counter-insurgency tactics. Instead of deploying a mainly conscript force, they brought in units of highly motivated troops specially trained in mountain guerrilla warfare. For the first time, too, they introduced World War II-style saturation raids by high altitude bombers, notably the Badger TU-16, flying sorties from bases inside the USSR.

The offensives did not represent a dramatic change in overall Red Army strategy. But their vehemence brought the guerrillas under heavy pressure and put a severe strain on their ability to care for the tens of thousands of internal refugees forced to flee from their homes into the mountains or neighbouring regions. Furthermore, each offensive was characterised by a rise in subversive actions. These ranged from the infiltration of assassination hit teams aimed at eradicating key commanders to stepped-up behind-the-line commando operations and ambushes against guerrilla supply routes.

Nevertheless, Soviet intelligence often proved faulty and most of the hit teams failed to get their quarry. Two attempts by KHAD agents to approach Panjshair commander Ahmed Shah Massoud were foiled when one of them, secretly working with the resistance blew the whistle. The communists did eventually succeed in delivering a tragic blow to the movement in mid-December 1984, by engineering the death of Zabiullah, a leading guerrilla commander from Mazar-e-Sharif and a close friend of Massoud. Overall, however, Moscow's onslaughts remained relatively unsuccessful and revealed a certain frustration with its inability to stop the deterioration in security conditions in government-controlled zones.

An Endless Tunnel

A cursory appraisal of the Soviet occupation since December 1979 can only hint at the sheer bleakness and gruesomeness of this still widely ignored conflict. With both sides going hammer and tongs at each other, 1984 witnessed some of the hardest fighting so far, prompting observers to dub it 'The Year of Decision'. From the military point of view, however, the war has come to a gruelling impasse with neither the Red Army nor the guerrillas proving themselves capable of tipping the balance one way or the other.

Bitter fighting raged throughout much of northern and western Afghanistan during the summer. Further combined Soviet-Afghan offensives were also launched in the winter of 1984-85. In some parts, the mujahideen showed striking improvements in combat dexterity and regional co-ordination. Guerrillas from at least six provinces repeatedly ambushed Soviet convoys along the highways leading from Herat to Mazar and the Salang, where Western correspondents travelling with the resistance reported witnessing dozens of vehicles destroyed in a single attack. Periodically, sometimes for days on end, the resistance closed off major portions of the road causing fuel shortages in the towns and forcing the Soviets to fly in supplies. By the middle of 1984, there was an unprecedented escalation in nocturnal guerrilla activity in the Kabul region leading several foreign visitors to describe the capital as a 'city under siege'.

The willingness among many mujahed groups to keep the Soviets occupied on as many fronts as possible was certainly the most notable development in field co-ordination among the resistance in 1984. 'We've got to force the Russians to spread themselves to every part of the country', Massoud explained, when I returned to the region in the summer. 'If they bring in more troops, they will have a bigger war on their hands. A bigger and costlier war. Only then will they consider negotiating.'

For the moment, however, there is nothing to suggest an early end to the war. Nor has the Kremlin seriously contemplated a political compromise. If anything, its attitude has become harder and more brutal.

The Soviet Union's participation, via its Afghan surrogates, in the UN-sponsored peace talks in Geneva is little more than a ploy to soften international criticism while the Red Army gets on with the job of subjugating the country. There is also no reason to expect a significant change during the immediate post-Chernenko period unless the Afghan issue can be worked effectively into a rapprochement of relations between Washington and Moscow, or India, using its influence as a leader of the non-aligned world and its good relations with the USSR, decides to push for a regional settlement acceptable to all parties concerned.

As it stands, Moscow's top priority in Afghanistan is a 'normalisation' of the situation through complete suppression of the 'counter-revolution'. With the escalation of the fighting, its original parallel strategy (war plus persuasion through economic incentives and reform) is being left by the wayside. Some members of the Kabul regime have called for a continuation of social reforms. 'Reality obliges us to seek a higher standard of living for the people', said Prime Minister Sultan Ali Keshtmand. 'We cannot possibly wait with economic construction until we have won this undeclared war.' But the Russians made their position of consolidation by force quite clear to the PDPA Central Committee plenary in September 1984, at the risk of growing dissent and disillusionment among party ranks.

The Soviet refusal to consider a withdrawal so long as the present regime in Kabul cannot survive on its own also spells doom, at least for the time being, for the peace talks. First initiated in early 1982 by the UN Secretary General's special representative, Diego Cordovez, indirect negotiations between Pakistan and Afghanistan (Iran has refused to participate unless the mujahideen are included but remains briefed by the Islamabad government) produced a four-point peace plan: the withdrawal of all foreign groops from Afghanistan; the voluntary repatriation of Afghans; a resumption of relations between Pakistan and Afghanistan on the basis of non-interference and respect for each other's territorial integrity, and finally, adequate international assurances (Soviet, US and Chinese) for the maintenance of Afghanistan's independence and non-aligned status.

Despite over-optimistic assertions by Cordovez in April 1983 that '95 per cent' of an agreement had been reached, negotiations have remained deadlocked. The Pakistanis have been placing greater emphasis on a precise timetable for Soviet withdrawal, which, they insist, should last no longer than three months and should coincide with the return of the Afghan refugees. Moscow, on the other hand, has demanded an 18-month withdrawal period coupled with the proviso that the Red Army could intervene if the mujahideen continued to fight. In other words, Moscow wants a legal guarantee in advance to legitimise its position in Afghanistan.

Cordovez has kept the door open for further talks. The Soviets, who control the Afghan delegation through a senior adviser, are expected to attend if only for the sake of appearances. Most informed observers doubt that anything concrete will result in the months or years ahead, yet diplomatic efforts still offer the only feasible humanitarian solution and should therefore be encouraged.

The Soviet War: A Minor Nuisance?

Like Queen Victoria's 'little wars' during the late nineteenth century, Afghanistan represents a 'little war' for the Soviet Union. Nevertheless, Moscow's military commitment has gone up from the original strength of the invasion force, during the early months of 1980 of 85,000 to roughly 115,000 at present. This does not include the 30,000 to 40,000 troops based inside Soviet Central Asia who are regularly deployed on short-term operations inside Afghanistan.

Some defence analysts question the Kremlin's ability to expand this commitment. Not only is a sizeable expansion politically undesirable (the USSR is thought to be reluctant to risk a further loss of prestige in the Third World), but it is also strategically precarious. The USSR is uneasy about transferring more crack troops from its East European theatre or its frontier areas with China without weakening its overall defences; it is believed to be already deploying one quarter of its available mountain battalions against the mujahideen.

While avoiding a Vietnam-style escalation, the Soviets are still trying to whip the Afghan armed forces into shape. The air force appears to be faring satisfactorily as more (and better paid) cadets complete their training in the USSR. The Afghan army, on the other hand, faces much the same problems as before. Desertion remains high and relations between recruits and their communist officers (and Soviet advisers) have hardly improved. Rivalry between the two communist party factions, too, has not diminished. All this has brought about a changing situation with the Soviets finding themselves faced with a steadily growing commitment, not only in the number of lives lost (between 9,000 and 20,000 by the end of 1984), but also in the economic resources used to prop up the Karmal regime.

Afghan Civilians: a Deteriorating Situation

Another incontrovertible aspect of the occupation is the continued Sovietisation of the occupied areas. There now seems little doubt that Moscow's ultimate goal is to annex Afghanistan, either partially, by leaving a rump state to placate Third World concerns, or totally. More so than before, its application of political, economic and subversive pressures is having an increasingly insidious effect on the ability of the Afghan people to survive.

Although the Soviets are stepping up military repression as a principal means of crushing the resistance, they still seek to maintain the myth of an independent Afghanistan and are persisting in their efforts to indoctrinate the young. Even if it takes a generation or two, they hope to replace the present administration with appropriately groomed pro-Moscow cadres. Already, some 50,000 young Afghans have been dispatched to the USSR or Eastern Europe for education. Many of these are mere boys and girls who are sent abroad for short periods, usually three to six months; one reason for such brief sojourns is that those who stay longer are less influenced by Marxist-Leninist thinking because of the intense resentment and outright racism they experience in the USSR.

For the guerrillas, it is on the civilian front that they are in danger of losing the struggle. As a liberation movement, the Afghan resistance still lacks the resources and organisation to provide for those populations wishing to remain inside the country. Since late 1983, guerrilla leaders and Western observers have warned that, unless drastic action is taken, effective resistance in many regions could be crippled in as little as two or three years.

Aware of the resistance's inability to provide succour, the Kremlin has accentuated its disruptive acts of 'migratory genocide'. 'In many places, the Soviets have dropped all pretence of trying to win over the people with a hearts-and-minds programme. All that Moscow is offering is a stark take-it-or-leave alternative', noted one West European diplomat in Pakistan. In early 1984, large numbers of Afghans from the northern provinces bordering the USSR began fleeing the consequences of war and, increasingly, famine for the first time. By 1985, nearly five million Afghans, one quarter to one third of the pre-war population, had left the country. Countless others have sought refuge in the mountains or in the overcrowded communist-occupied cities.

Increasingly numerous, too, have been the incidents of the Soviet Union's systematic reign of terror. Only recently, however, have regular accounts reached the outside of deliberate assaults against would-be refugees. In August 1984, I witnessed a raid by MIG-27 ground attack aircraft against columns of hapless civilians fleeing to Pakistan. By the time the planes left, at least forty refugees lay dead. More were to die later of their wounds. In a dispatch to *The Christian Science Monitor*, I wrote:

The signs of carnage . . . lent only partial testimony as to the ruthlessness of the onslaught. Dozens of mutilated animal cadavers, twisted metal pots, scorched clothing, torn saddles, and a tattered boy's slingshot littered the ground, itself churned by shrapnel or ripped in long furrows by machine gun bullets. With the little they had, the (nearby) Panjshairis helped treat the victims. Later, they buried the dead in a yawning bomb crater, covering the bodies with a tarpaulin and then piling stones on top in the Muslim manner. A single prayer flag, a piece of green, pink and orange cloth hanging from a wooden tent pole, and an inscription headed by a quotation from the Koran recorded the massacre.

In December 1984, the Helsinki Watch Group in New York issued the most detailed report to date on human rights violations in Afghanistan. A compilation of accounts by Afghan victims and witnesses, French doctors, foreign relief workers, Western journalists and other outside observers, the document lists an array of atrocities by Soviet forces and their Afghan surrogates. It refers to mass executions of villagers, prisoners crushed by tanks, the mutilation of children by plastic 'butterfly' mines, and the burning alive of resistance sympathisers.

'The crimes of indiscriminate warfare are combined with the worst excesses of unbridled state-sanctioned violence against civilians', commented researchers Jeri Laber and Barnett Rubin. As before, the Soviet Union continues to deny, or simply ignores, such allegations. Still barring internationally recognised humanitarian missions (the Red Cross, Amnesty International etc.) from visiting the country, it has refused to co-operate with the Special Rapporteur on Afghanistan appointed by the UN Human Rights' Commission.

Western Interest in the War

The Soviet occupation of Afghanistan is far from being a negligible or isolated affair but it is undoubtedly one of the most under-reported strategic wars today. Even after five years of World War II-style repression and atrocities, Afghanistan's predicament in the mid-1980s has failed to arouse the righteous indignation, or imagination, of the international community as did Vietnam, Biafra, Bangladesh, Chile, Cambodia or Poland let alone the present situation in the Middle-East or Central America. No mass rallies, candle-lit marches or rock concerts lamenting the murder of innocent civilians; only small scattered demonstrations outside Soviet embassies or Aeroflot offices.

Despite initial outrage at the invasion and routine condemnations by the UN General Assembly, both Western and Third World opinion has failed to acknowledge the implications of a war in which a primarily peasant resistance movement with limited resources has succeeded in pinning down a major expeditionary force representing the world's largest standing army. Indeed, Soviet calculation has banked on world opinion gradually forgetting the war. Already, the Kremlin has obtained resigned acceptance in many quarters of its tutelage over Afghanistan, just as some consider Grenada or El Salvador within America's sphere of influence.

But legal condonation of the occupation continues to evade Moscow's grasp. Since early 1983, there has been growing concern in North America, Western Europe, Japan and other democracies, not only because of a more acute perception of the region's strategic import-ance, but also because the aspirations of this independent-minded people are being considered worthy of approval and support. Further-more, without presaging an immediate break-up of the Soviet empire, it is felt that continued fighting in Afghanistan could one day precip-itate ethnic and political upheaval within the USSR, notably among Muslim and other minorities.

Ever since the invasion, Afghanistan has engendered far more interest in Europe than in the United States. For many Americans, it is simply too remote and unknown to inspire curiosity, an attitude strengthened by a mainly crisis-oriented press which tends to regard 'an Afghanistan' as a euphemism for any news story too boring to print. To a considerable extent, it is the failure of the American press to report more fully on the war that has led to this lack of public aware-ness.

Newspaper and magazine reporting has been good but patchy. Amer-ican television coverage, on the other hand, has been very poor. While the European networks, particularly the French and the British, have produced some fine documentaries over the years, the Americans have made little effort to provide more consistent in-depth reporting. Although some producers and journalists have pushed hard for greater commitment by the major networks, news programmes have concen-trated on 'bang-bang' footage depicting 'rag-tag' mujahideen rocketing government installations or Soviet Mi-24 helicopter gunships bombing their mountain positions. Only recently, notably in the months leading up to the fifth anniversary of the invasion, have the American media adopted a broader, and more interpretative, approach.

During the early 1980s, the search for a peaceful solution in the Middle East, US involvement in Central America, the Libyan intervention in Chad and even the invasion of Grenada tended to dominate America's outlook in the world. As a nation of immigrants, it also has the habit of responding to foreign policy along the lines of ethnic identities, be they Irish, Jewish or Polish. 'As we have no sizeable Afghan minority', noted Thomas Payne, a professor of political science at the University of Montana, 'there is no important group to articulate a concern for Afghanistan'. Thus, for a long time, the only basis for any generally expressed concern in the United States was the fact that Moscow represents its principal adversary in international affairs.

Providing Effective Aid

Towards the end of 1984, the US Central Intelligence Agency began taking the necessary steps to provide more effective aid to the resistance. Until then, much of the $325 million of military support destined for the mujahideen is believed never to have reached the interior. At the behest of Congress, the CIA reportedly earmarked $250 million for fiscal year 1985. The move, which represents America's largest such covert commitment since the Vietnam War, also signalled an expanding role for Afghanistan within US foreign policy considerations.

Among the many questions now being raised is what the implementation of such a massive aid programme will mean for the resistance. Furnishing outside aid should not be a matter of throwing money at the problem, but rather of dispersing it effectively, intelligently and, dare one say it, morally. It also requires a deeper understanding of Afghan requirements and the nature of the war the resistance is fighting. Certain political circles in Washington, for example, would like to see the CIA programme used as a means of giving Russia its Vietnam. Some critics, however, warned against an escalation of the war or overtechnologising a 'primitive people'. Others maintain that it is pointless to support a resistance which has no hope of winning.

None of these arguments take into account the Afghans themselves. The mujahideen have no desire to be manipulated as an instrument of American retribution. Nor is supplying weapons going to purchase pro-Americanism. Traditionally, Afghans have sought to maintain their independence by forging temporary alliances only if they are to their advantage. The present struggle is not aimed at 'defeating' the Russians, but rather at making continued occupation so costly that they will leave, or at least negotiate. Many Afghans also recognise that, even if and when the Soviets withdraw, their nation will be forced to live in the shadow of the USSR. Neutrality towards the superpowers could prove once again to be their best course.

To be effective, outside aid, whether military or humanitarian, should be highly selective and should concentrate on quality rather than quantity. It should also respond to the Kremlin's own strategy of attrition by including weapons better suited to present war conditions (portable easy-to-use missiles, more lethal anti-aircraft guns, long-range mortars etc.) as well as military training, education and basic humanitarian relief. The Afghans must be encouraged to help themselves. For, in the end, persuading the Soviets to leave their country will be up to them.

The Resistance: Still Far to Go

Despite growing co-ordination among the internal fronts, division among the parties in Peshawar has continued to prevent the creation of a liberation government or a government-in-exile. A distinct sense of war fatigue and frustration has crept in, underlining an urgent need for greater national co-operation if the resistance is to survive.

By the end of December 1984, a glimmer of hope appeared on the horizon. A loose centrist alliance had formed. Consisting of two 'fundamentalist' parties, Rabbani's Jamiat and Khales' Hezb, a 'moderate', Mohammedi's Harakat, and, for the first time, a Shiite, Sheikh Asaf Mohseni, who was formerly based in Iran, their combined strength represented the bulk of military effectiveness and popular support inside Afghanistan and among the refugees. Were this new coalition to develop into a serious working body and attract further consensus among other fronts, it could eventually carry enough conviction to act as an alternative government.

A more balanced distribution of aid has long been an indispensable prerequisite if resistance capabilities are to be improved. For the moment, the bulk of Arab support continues to be channelled toward the old 'fundamentalist' alliance. More Western aid would greatly strengthen a centrist alliance and release Rabbani and other more moderate fundamentalists from having to pander to Arab desires for a rigid, wholly artificial form of Islam that has little respect for the Afghan character and culture.

Better Weapons But Also Food and Money

As other resistance movements elsewhere have discovered, successful modern guerrilla warfare requires well-trained fighters as well as qualified teachers, doctors, organisers and even office workers. As a result, both the resistance and various Afghan support groups in Europe and North America have proposed a number of initiatives aimed at improving mujahed capabilities. These include the creation of a Free Afghan University based in Pakistan and the setting up of literacy programmes, schools and more health centres inside the country as well as backing for better organised resistance offices both at home and abroad to coordinate relief programmes and information.

Afghanistan, which was badly hit by famine in 1970-71, is once again facing similar conditions in a dozen provinces. Large-scale starvation could be a reality by the end of 1985. While the last famine was caused mainly by drought, the present food shortages have been exacerbated by war. Some areas of the country remain virtually untouched by the fighting (the central Hazarajat highlands, parts of Nuristan etc.), yet almost everyone is vulnerable to attack or other forms of Soviet pressure. Ground and air operations have prevented many farmers from cultivating their land. The continuing exodus of people from the countryside has also severely impaired food production. The abandonment of entire villages leaving no one to cultivate the fields or to maintain fragile irrigation systems has caused a steady deterioration of agricultural infrastructures that may take years to rectify.

Inside humanitarian assistance has remained a trickle. But there is far more of it since late 1983 when the governments of Britain, France, Sweden, the United States (which officially acknowledged its support in January 1985) and other Western countries began taking more constructive steps toward alleviating the distress of Afghans living in resistance-dominated regions. For diplomatic reasons, they still prefer to channel this help through voluntary agencies; in December 1984, these launched a large-scale emergency relief operation to bring food, boots, clothing, medication, seeds and money to the most critically affected zones.

The Logistics of Aid

Foremost among the difficulties in helping the mujahideen are the political implications of actually passing aid through a second or third country before it reaches Afghanistan. Pakistan represents the main conduit of foreign support. Iran still plays a relatively minor role, but has the potential of becoming a major supplier. The participation of a Shiite leader in a centrist alliance could be the first step towards a more universal form of backing for the resistance.

For Western democracies, putting all one's eggs into the basket of a military dictatorship poses certain risks. For the time being, however,

Pakistan remains the only feasible option. As a 'frontline' state, it has regulated the flow of arms into Afghanistan at a level calculated not to provoke the Soviet Union. This has not prevented the communists from putting the regime of Zia ul-Haq under heavy pressure for allowing supply caravans, Western relief workers and journalists to slip into Afghanistan. In 1984, Soviet and Afghan aircraft stepped up their attacks against frontier towns and refugee camps, killing over one hundred people. Red Army troops are steadily being stationed closer to the border. And although the Soviets have been laying the foundations for widespread subversion by supporting Baluchi and Pushtun nationalists in western Pakistan, it is among the anti-Zia (mainly left-wing) political opposition that they can give the regime its worst headaches. In the view of some analysts, it is only a question of time before such destabilisation tactics provoke a change in attitude toward Afghanistan, even without major upheavals in Islamabad.

Despite its $3.2 billion military and economic aid package to Pakistan, the United States has refused to agree to automatic intervention in the event of a Soviet attack. Improved support for the resistance is therefore dependent on Pakistan's willingness to permit a direct distribution of aid by the West. If Pakistan is reluctant to do this, it should at least guarantee a halt to present discrimination between the Afghan fundamentalists and moderates.

Most observers agree that the resistance would best be served by channelling most outside assistance through the Peshawar parties. Despite charges of corruption and inefficiency, the exile organisations still function as a vital window to the outside world. Yet some aid should be dispersed direct to the more capable internal guerrilla commanders, permitting them to develop according to their own abilities.

As Afghans are coming to realise, modern guerrilla wars are not won solely on the battlefield, but through more adroit political organisation and lobbying in the corridors of the United Nations or on television. Improved public relations can often speak more loudly than the burning of Soviet convoys along the Salang or the blowing up of electricity pylons outside Kabul. Political offices abroad would enable the resistance to tap the expertise of thousands of Afghan doctors, lawyers, teachers and former administrators in exile, many of whom would like to lend their support but who have been unable to find a constructive niche within the movement.

In mid-1984, educated Afghans in Europe and the United States with close ties to the resistance began to take steps towards forming a representative body abroad to lobby for their country's cause. This included preparations to contest the right of the Kabul regime to hold the UN General Assembly seat, a move which would bring the Afghan issue out into the open and prove exceedingly embarrassing to the Soviets.

There is also room for the participation at the international level of former King Mohammed Zahir Shah. Though a controversial issue, the return of the Pushtun ex-monarch as a temporary figurehead might be one way of providing the resistance with a rallying point. He still commands considerable respect among many Afghans and his support among the refugee communities and inside the country appears to be growing. Much of this declared backing is less than enthusiastic, however, and is more a case of frustration at the lack of any other leader.

Russia: Bringing the News Home

Without doubt, there are growing similarities between Soviet involvement in Afghanistan and America's involvement in Vietnam. But the differences that remain are still considerable; however, the most striking being that Afghanistan is not a media war.

From 1965 onwards, news coverage of Indochina became more critical of the American presence, pointedly questioning the feasibility of continued involvement. By 1968, it had begun to play a prominently disruptive role in the administration's efforts to prosecute a war which few Americans wanted. Writing in *Newsweek* in 1968, columnist Kenneth Crawford pointed out that Vietnam was 'the first war in America's history where the media were more friendly to America's enemies that its allies'. American and other foreign correspondents could report on virtually every angle, making it the best covered war in history.

Unlike their American counterparts, Soviet citizens do not have the full horrors of war thrust into their faces. Soviet and other Eastern bloc journalists report the government side, but the Soviet role is portrayed as a heroic commitment against 'bands of terrorists' supported by the United States, China and other 'reactionary powers'. Recently Moscow also claims to be protecting its own borders against outside aggression in view of the reported increase in CIA assistance.

The result is that the Soviet public has learned little about the realities of the situation in Afghanistan from official sources. Even during the invasion itself, it took nearly a week for the Soviet press to notify the nation that it was providing 'military aid' under a 1978 bilateral Friendship Treaty. Until then, all that had appeared were two brief announcements referring to Babrak Karmal's request for assistance against his country's 'external enemies', and the formation of a new government in Kabul.

During the early stages of the occupation, the Soviet media were careful to show only positive aspects. Life in Kabul was always portrayed as normal. Only eight months after the invasion did Soviet TV broadcast an hour-long documentary giving the official version of the situation. The film used extensive footage of Soviet tanks patrolling the streets of Kabul and earnest-looking soldiers administering first aid to injured Afghan civilians allegedly wounded in 'bandit attacks'. The commentator explained that it had been necessary to provide military assistance to the Afghans at this 'critical stage' of their Marxist Revolution.

By September 1980, the Soviet press began to admit the existence of widespread fighting but this was couched more in terms of a condemnation of guerrilla activities than of difficulties facing Russian soldiers. Somewhat stifling previous optimism about peace and reconstruction, the authoritative Moscow weekly, *New Times*, maintained that anti-government insurgents were spreading death and destruction throughout Afghanistan. Citing a report from the Soviet news agency TASS, it said that scores of small shops had been reduced to smouldering ruins by the 'bandits' in Herat while elsewhere they had blown up bridges, trampled crops, destroyed power lines and mutilated the bodies of old men, women and children.

Protests and Criticism: for Democracies Only

Another obvious discrepancy is that the Soviet Union does not have to worry unduly about public reaction back home. In a totalitarian state, there is no chance of Afghanistan developing into an election issue.

Open criticism of the war hardly exists; the KGB and government censorship have seen to that. Only a handful of dissidents like the Sakharovs have dared to speak out.

Moreover, the Kremlin has gone to extraordinary lengths to conceal the extent of its involvement. Injured and disfigued soldiers have been sent to clinics in East Germany or to sanitoria on the Black Sea where they are kept well away from public view. Initially, too, bodies were returned in closed, zinc-lined coffins with strict instructions that they should not be opened. Returning veterans are under orders not to talk about their experiences. 'The majority of soldiers fighting in Afghanistan have been drawn from the 'deaf place' of provincial Russia, where there are no foreigners, no dissidents, no uncensored books', observed

David Satter, a former *Financial Times* correspondent in Moscow. In addition, the authorities regularly jam BBC, VOA and other shortwave broadcasts reporting the war.

The truth, however, still seeps through. According to *Ausra* (Dawn), a Lithuanian 'Zamizdat' (underground newsletter), some mothers who succeeded in prising open the coffins found only a soldier's cap and some sand. In one case, reported the journal, a Lithuanian family discovered an Asian corpse. By the second year of the occupation, the Soviets were burying some of their dead in military cemetaries, specially guarded to prevent desecration, in Afghanistan itself. The relatives were informed simply that Cpl. Igor X. or Pvt. Misha Z. had died in an accident while 'on manoeuvres'. When the number of 'accidents' became absurdly high, the line was changed to a more candid 'fell in active service' or even 'inscribed for eternity in the roll of honour of the company (battalion, regiment etc.)'.

As with any war, it is the assortment of personal effects – identification cards, letters, diaries and photographs – taken from the bodies of Soviet soliders killed in Afghanistan and spread out on the floor of a guerrilla hideout that tragically humanise the 'other side'. For me, another pathetic, if not painful, image is that of young Russian, Ukrainian or Baltic prisoners and deserters in the hands of the mujahideen, some of them living under atrocious conditions. Eighteen, nineteen, perhaps twenty years old, rarely more, they look miserably out of place as they sip tea, guardedly answering the questions of visiting correspondents. For them it is a matter of survival hidden among these distant mountains and deserts among a people whom they fear, hate or know nothing about.

There is little doubt that the Soviet death toll is beginning to have its effect. It is also evident that Afghanistan returnees (over half a million by early 1985) will confide in their close friends and relatives. Public resentment, however, exists primarily in the form of subdued murmurings or 'zamizdat'. In the unofficial Soviet Peace Movement, Afghanistan accounts for little more than a seed of discontent. The dangers of nuclear war between the two superpowers preoccupy the young far more than the dirty little war south of the border. Few, if any, are burning their draft cards.

At the same time, few are enamoured with the idea of risking their necks to 'save' Afghanistan. For many Soviet youths faced with military service, being sent to Afghanistan is equivalent to being sentenced to death. Those with connections, normally the sons of party cadres, will go to great lengths to be deployed elsewhere. 'Lines at recruiting stations are notable for their absence — about the only place in Russia where they are', drily commented one Western diplomat in Moscow. Afghans who have studied in the USSR have recounted incidents of being bitterly accused of living in comfort while Soviet soldiers die in the mountains of Afghanistan.

If there is any questioning, it is usually by members of the older generation who remember what war is all about. The questions are variations of one theme: how much longer is the fighting going to last? The responses are generally unambiguous. The leadership admits that the struggle for victory may take time but the blame for the continuation of the war lies with the help the counter-revolutionaries are getting from the outside. Comrades, the party line goes, the fighting may last, ten, twenty or thirty years, but we shall persevere. As long as is necessary to support the revolution. The armies of socialism march in only one direction.

It is this aspect of time which is perhaps the greatest threat to the resistance. It is also one which Soviet propaganda feels obliged to justify. As part of a carefully orchestrated strategy to prepare for what could be a long and tedious war, the Kremlin is gradually confronting the Soviet people with a picture somewhat closer to reality.

While saying nothing about low morale or drug addiction among the troops, more stories are appearing on stark conditions at the front. Already in the autumn of 1981, *Komoskaya Pravda*, the leading Soviet youth daily, reviewed a 63-page pamphlet written by *Pravda's* military correspondent, Victor Verstakov. Rhetorically asking 'Why are our boys from Ryazan, Khabarovsk and Uzbekistan carrying out their military service in the environs of Kabul?', Verstakov examined the 'uneasy days' and the internationalist and patriotic duty of the Soviet soldier and admitted that life in Afghanistan was hard. Troops had to use coal dust for fuel and were forced to slog through the mud, but the Afghan army was taking the brunt of the fighting.

At about the same time, *Krasnaya Zvezda* made the first reference to the death of one of its soldiers, a young lieutenant whom it described as an 'unsung hero'. Since then, reports have appeared with increasing regularity detailing the dangers of serving in Afghanistan: a day-in-the-life of a helicopter pilot struggling to save his shot-down comrades or the brutal killing of an APC crew member, shot in the head as he peered out of his vehicle. Systematically, the dispatches emphasise the heroism of men willing to risk their lives in the line of duty and in defence of the revolution. By early 1985, the Soviet press had officially reported the deaths of fifteen soldiers and officers. A paltry number indeed when compared to the thousands known to have died, but Soviet deaths in Afghanistan are no longer the result of accidents or the odd assassination by a terrorist, but of war.

The Future: More International Focus

Writing as a journalist, I have no doubt that the war in Afghanistan is one which deserves far more international attention. To be sure, there are dangers in covering this war. At least two reporters are known to have lost their lives through Soviet military action, while another died in an accident. Others have been injured and some captured. In the summer of 1984, French TV reporter Jacques Abouchar was apprehended by communist troops, largely according to his companions, due to his own lack of precautions. He was later tried, sentenced to 18 years imprisonment and then released, prompting Moscow to deliver a dire warning to the press. In Islamabad, the Soviet ambassador coldly remarked that from now on, any reporters caught with the guerrillas would be 'eliminated'. When I asked an official at the Soviet embassy in Washington several weeks later whether this now constituted Soviet policy, he responded that anyone 'violating the territorial integrity of Afghanistan would have to face the consequences'.

For reasons such as these, many editors consider the Russo-Afghan conflict too dangerous, too remote and too costly to merit dispatching a correspondent on a regular basis. But there has never been a shortage of journalists and photographers willing to report a war, as Vietnam or Beirut have demonstrated; it is more a matter of sufficient editorial interest, or the lack of it.

Restrained coverage by the Western and Third World media suits the Soviets, who would like nothing better than to contain all 'unofficial' access to the country as the effects of migratory genocide become more apparent. The suppression of news and the constant rewriting of history have always been a classic weapon of organised totalitarian regimes, be they Nazi Germany or the Marxist Soviet Union. 'Ideally', noted one West European diplomat, 'they would like to get on with their war without the outside world knowing'. However, now that the United States and other Western countries appear to be expanding their commitment to the resistance, the need for greater public scrutiny might stimulate better and more consistent reporting.

As for the years ahead, the ability of the Afghan resistance to withstand Moscow's war of attrition will depend largely on whether it can adequately develop its organisational capabilities on the military, humanitarian and political fronts. Ultimately, however, a peaceful solution to the conflict must be a diplomatic one. In the meantime, it is still too soon to determine whether this formerly non-aligned and independent nation will fall as yet another victim of Soviet expansionism, or whether the resilience of its proud and obstinate inhabitants will one day prove too strong for the Soviets to break.

ABOUT THE AUTHOR

Edward R. Girardet was born on 24 March 1951, in White Plains, New York, but was educated in America, the Bahamas, Canada, West Germany and Britain. He completed his schooling at Clifton College, Bristol, took a year off to work and hitch-hike to India, and then went to the University of Nottingham, England, where he received a BA degree in German Studies. He also did a semester at the Free University in West Berlin.

On completing university in 1973, Girardet went to Paris where he taught English before joining United Press International, first in Brussels and then back in France. He then became a reporter for NBC Radio at the UN in Geneva, but soon returned to Paris to cover European issues for various British and American newspapers as a free-lance journalist. In 1977, Girardet received a 'Journalists in Europe' fellowship.

In the autumn of 1979, Girardet travelled to Pakistan and Afghanistan on a six-week assignment for CBC radio, *The International Herald Tribune* and others. Shortly afterwards, he was taken on by *The Christian Science Monitor* and ABC News as a Paris-based special correspondent. Following the Soviet invasion of Afghanistan in December 1979, he was sent back to the region to report the war. Since then, he has made numerous visits to the Indian subcontinent including six major trips into Afghanistan — once with an official visa and five times clandestinely with the resistance.

As a correspondent for *The Christian Science Monitor*, Girardet has travelled widely throughout Africa and Asia. He has written mainly on refugees, politics, development and guerrilla movements, but has also collaborated on documentary films/news shows for European and American television on Angola, Ethiopia, the Iran-Iraq war, Afghanistan and other issues. Girardet has written for U.S. News and World Report, *The Economist, New Republic* and has broadcast on the BBC, VOA and National Public Radio. He has reported on a number of occasions for the Public Broadcasting Service's McNeil-Lehrer News Hour in New York. He won the 1980 Sygma Delta Chi aware for distinguished foreign reporting.

250

INDEX

Voice of America (VOA) 81, 148,
    188, 189, 246
volunteer agencies 7, 10, 205-6, 242

Wakhan corridor 208-9
'Waltan Palanzai' 148
war: Indochina 225; Indo-Pakistan
    100; Iraq-Iran 29, 201; World
    II 90
Wardak province 55, 172, 184
Wardak, Col Abdul Rahim 65
Wardak, Mohammad Amin 55, 172,
    196
water, irrigation 152, 154-5
Waziristan, Northern 39
Western interest 238-41
wheat 160
Wikh-e-Zalmaiyan (Enlightened
    Youth) 91, 92, 98
withdrawal, Soviet 6, 40, 235, 240
women 164, 218-19; Democratic –
    Organisation of A. 140; education
    of 115; rights of 106
World Bank 153-5 *passim*, 158
World Food Programme 205
World Health Organization 146, 210,
    217
Writers and Poets, Union of 140

Yemen, South 27, 120
Yepishev, Gen. Alexei 22
'Young Afghans' 90, 91, 99
Young Muslims 166
youth 147-8, 237; *see also* students;
    Democratic Organisation of A.
    Youth 140
Yugoslavia 192

Zabiullah (mujahed commander)
    54, 55, 233
Zabul province 171, 229
Zahir Shah, King 90-1, 95, 100, 158,
    166, 172, 194-5, 244
zakat 185-6
Zalmai (nephew of Amin) 14
Zariffar, Ahmed Kasim 147
Zia, Ahmad (Massoud's brother) 78
Zia ul-Haq, President, 36, 206